TO
BRING
GOOD
NEWS

Books by the Author

Authored Books

The Psychoanalysis of Symptoms

Dictionary of Psychopathology

Group Psychotherapy and Personality: Intersecting Structures
(reissued with the subtitle *A Theoretical Model*)

Sleep Disorders: Insomnia and Narcolepsy

Curing Psychological Symptoms
(translated into Romanian, Japanese, and Bulgarian; originally published as *The 4 Steps to Peace of Mind: The Simple Effective Way to Cure Our Emotional Symptoms*)

Love Is Not Enough: What It Takes to Make It Work

Greedy, Cowardly, and Weak: Hollywood's Jewish Stereotypes

Hollywood Movies on the Couch: A Psychoanalyst Examines 15 Famous Films

Haggadah: A Passover Seder for the Rest of Us

Personality: How It Forms (translated into Korean)

The Discovery of God: A Psychoevolutionary Perspective

A Consilience of Natural and Social Sciences: A Memoir of Original Contributions

Anatomy of Delusion

Psychoanalysis of Evil: Perspectives on Destructive Behavior

There's No Handle on My Door: Stories of Patients in Mental Hospitals

Psychotherapeutic Traction: Uncovering the Patient's Power-Theme and Basic-Wish

On the Nature of Nature

The Origin of Language

The Unconscious Domain

The 7 Keys to: Your Unconscious Mind

Injustice of the Predatory World: A Book of Essays

Covid—A Love Story: On the Psychology of the Virus

Acting-Out and Sin: Psychoanalytic and Theological Perspectives

The Psychoanalytic Codes: Encryption and Decryption

The Psychology of Diagnosis: What Your Diagnosis Is Saying to You

To Bring Good News: A Memoir

The Ghost Trilogy

The Making of Ghosts: A Novel

Ghosts of Dreams: A Novel

The Ghost: A Novel

Coauthored Books
(with Anthony Burry, Ph.D.)

Psychopathology and Differential Diagnosis: A Primer
Vol. 1. *History of Psychopathology*
Vol. 2. *Diagnostic Primer*

Handbook of Psychodiagnostic Testing:
Analysis of Personality in the Psychological Report
(reissued in 2nd, 3rd, and 4th editions; translated into Japanese)

(with Raphael Osheroff, M.D.)

Shackled, Beaten, and Starved:
The Untold Story of One of the Most Shameful Scandals in
American Psychiatric History (The Raphael Osheroff Story)

Edited Books

Group Cohesion: Theoretical and Clinical Perspectives

The Nightmare: Psychological and Biological Foundations

Coedited Books
(with Robert Plutchik, Ph.D.)

Emotion: Theory, Research, and Experience
Vol. 1. Theories of Emotion
Vol. 2. Emotions in Early Development
Vol. 3. Biological Foundations of Emotion
Vol. 4. The Measurement of Emotion
Vol. 5. Emotion, Psychopathology, and Psychotherapy

The Emotions Profile Index: Manual and Test

TO BRING GOOD NEWS

a memoir

HENRY KELLERMAN

Copyright © 2025 by Henry Kellerman

ISBN: 9798316510207

To
the memory of my loving parents

Samuel (Sol)
and
Esther Kellerman

Contents

Acknowledgments   xv
Preface   xix

PART 1
A RETROSPECTIVE MONTAGE
Historical Context

1. Beginnings   3
   On the Left   3
   A Little Political History   3
   My Political and Philosophical Influences   9

2. To Contribute   15
   Tikkun Olam (To Repair the World)   15
   My Other Part   18
   The Three Themes   19
      1. The Importance of *Home*   19
      2. The Importance of *Anonymity*   20
      3. The Importance of *Contribution*   20
   The Power-Theme and Basic-Wish   22

3. Home, Culture, Ideology   29
   Yaruga, Ukraine; and the Bronx, New York   29
   The Atom   32

4. Yiddish and Kamen   39
   My Twelve-Volume Performance Archive   39

5. Never Say Never   55
   Dancing Away   55
   Taking a Breath   64

6. Girls and Women — 69
Promiscuity? — 69
One of the Greatest and Most Memorable Events of My Life — 80

7. College — 83
Saved by the Bell — 83

8. Marriage — 97
Linda, Me—All of Us — 97
Musings — 103

9. Friends and Dance Halls — 113
Close Friends — 113

10. Different Worlds — 125
Important Venues, Important People — 125
Professional Job and Sudden Affluence — 131

11. Precursor Career — 135
My Psychotherapy Compass — 135
The Family Psychodynamic — 138

12. A Seven-Year-Old Psychotherapist — 145
Mr. Jaskowitz — 148
Bubba — 149
Simon — 154

13. Professional Career — 157
The Promised Land — 157
Staff Positions at Three Hospitals — 164

14. Assignments and Experiences — 171
Treatment and Teaching — 171
1. The Grand Rounds — 172
2. My Car with Leaves — 173
3. "I'm Goin'!" — 174
4. Breasts — 176
5. Bottles Under the Bed — 179
6. He Wouldn't Unlock the Door — 181

15. My Personality, Psychoanalytic Treatment, and Yiddish — 183
Intersecting Structures — 183
The Shoes Are Strong — 190

16. Sons and Books — 193
Max, Sam, Harry, Jack — 193
Let's Go to Maryland — 199

17. Fight Back — 207
Helplessness Is Not an Option — 207
A Disappearance — 213

18. Mitch, Lenny, Ray, Sam — 221
Mitch and Lenny — 221
Ray — 224
Sam — 231
Looking for Sam — 232

PART 2
INFRASTRUCTURE
Home, Anonymity, Contribution

19. Power-Themes — 239
Introduction — 239
  1. The Theme of *Home* — 241
Pogroms in Yaruga — 244
  2. The Theme of *Anonymity* — 248
Is the Past Really Past? — 250

20. The Power-Theme of *Contribution* — 253
Introduction — 253
  3. The Theme of *Contribution* — 254
"Seek and Ye Shall Find" — 261

21. Original Professional Contributions — 267
In the Natural and Social Sciences — 267
  1. A Theory of Basic Nightmare Themes:
    Its Relation to the Structure of Personality — 268

2. A Theory of the Basic Small-Group Structure as a Parallel to a Proposed Shape of the Physical Universe 269
3. Remembering My Hospital Work 270
4. The Basic Emotions Inherent in DNA Structure 272
5. The Code to Unravel Psychological Symptoms 273
6. Penetrating a Dilemma of Parkinson's Disease 274
7. Dolphins 277
8. Is Language Innate? 280
9. *Covid—A Love Story: On the Psychology of the Virus* 280

Epilogue 283

Afterword I: The Bringer of Good News 297

Afterword II: Original Preface (First Draft) 299

A Note About the Text 305

Yiddish Literary Material by Poets and Authors Included in the Memoir 307

Yiddish Writers and Poets Represented in the Memoir 309

Bibliography 311
   Books, Clinical and Scientific Papers, and Films Referred to in the Memoir 311
   Other Papers I've Published 317
   Presentations I've Made at Professional Conferences 318
   List of My Books 321
   List of Publishers 323
   List of My Twelve-Volume Yiddish Performance Archive 323

Photos for the Memoir 325

To Dear Friends Not Yet Referenced 327

References to Mentors 329

Acknowledgments

There have been several people over the years who have suggested, encouraged, and persevered in lobbying for me to write a memoir. Those who in the immediate past who have done so include my loving cousins Sandra and Leonard Kassan, both in the field of education: Sandi as administrator of educational process, and Lenny as principal of a school and consultant to school administrators.

The other couple who has made it impossible to refute their claim that for me to write a memoir is almost required are my dear friends Dr. Jeanne Safer, noted psychologist, psychoanalyst, and author, and Mr. Richard Brookhiser, noted historian, political journalist, and author. I think of Jeanne as the shrink who makes psychological principles accessible to the world (Safer, 2002); and I consider Rick to be the keeper on the one hand of the wondrous flame lit by America's founding fathers (Brookhiser, 2006), and on the other, of an America sans the sins of these fathers: a racist infusion regarding African slaves as well as the genocide against Native Americans—in which both victims of these genocidal nightmares were rendered first helpless, then of course entirely vulnerable, and therefore finally merciless at the hands of their tormentors, or as I see it, their Anglo-American profiteers.

As an aside here, Brookhiser (p. 7) says, "Our founders are close by and they cast long shadows." His statement begs the question: Are we pleased with the shadows they cast? In view of the history of my family, from Ukraine to America (with a side trip to pogroms and the Holocaust), of course in my opinion sometimes the question of being happy with such long shadows is answered with a resounding yes, and sometimes with a reverberating no—meaning that shadows, especially when they're long, can, and usually do, have an up/down personality; in certain ways they're successful, in other ways not.

Much of this Brookhiser issue regarding casted shadows in this world will be featured herein as an important underpinning to this memoir.

I would like to thank both couples for their emotional support and persistent urging for me to do this stuff of a memoir; and yet I'm a bit chagrined, vexed, aggrieved, even irate at my personal high-index suggestibility in the face of really needing a break from writing, editing, and therefore from my output after writing and editing forty-three books (including this memoir) over a span of fifty years. So that now, look at me: rather than lying on a beach somewhere experiencing my stream of consciousness while feeling the embrace of the sun, here I am, attempting to write a memoir!?

Nevertheless, thank you sincerely, Sandi, Lenny, Jeanne, and Rick for insinuating me into this new universe.

—Henry Kellerman
New York City
October 16, 2019

P.S.

Then again, it's occurred to me that perhaps this memoir universe may not be such a "new universe" to me at all. In thinking about the entire domain of memoir, I neglected to consider that in all the years of my professional life I've been actually and continuously involved with every nook and cranny of memoir.

What I mean is that in my entire professional career of dealing with personality, the mind, the psyche, pathological issues, and the emotional makeup of individuals, I've actually been organizing and synthesizing what any person's personality looks like—of what it consists—its mechanics, its psychological and emotional engineering, its feelings and its side effects. In addition, I've been writing books on psychotherapy, psychopathology, and psychoanalysis—all embraced by my full six-decade career of seeing individual patients as well as patients in therapy groups, both in private practice as well as in mental hospitals.

And to my surprise, I now have the thought that in all of my professional career (which began in July of 1958 when I was a staff member of Pilgrim State Hospital in Brentwood, New York), I was also therefore always and consistently occupied in a sense, and in one way or another, in what perhaps could be considered the formulation of memoirs of the people I've seen. This included the several years of hospital work as well as all the years of my private practice, as well as my experience over this entire time in psychological assessment of individuals (by virtue of understanding responses given on psychological tests so that I could see an x-ray of the personality), so that all of it was an ever-present analysis with respect to those specific issues of the personality—the issues that reflected that person's world, inner and otherwise.

Essentially, therefore, I was always trying to identify the smallest number of crucial variables of the person's life that became the longitude and latitude of that life—that which accounted for most of what the person thought, felt, and did. I guess I was really reaching into that individual's life in order to excavate what might be considered a basic philosophy of that life.

Now, it occurs to me that herein I'll try to further excavate more of what I did in my own psychoanalysis when I was in postdoctoral psychoanalytic training—the same excavating and discovery of *my* life (that which makes *me* tick)—in this, my own memoir, titled *To Bring Good News*.

Date of this P.S., November 17, 2019

Preface

When my son Harry read the first draft of this memoir, he said it needed to start with something more dramatic. He then suggested I start it with a story I had told him about concerning what I was thinking once when I was a kid, while sitting one spring day on the stoop of my apartment building in the Bronx, New York.

I sat there thinking: If or when the Nazis attacked, it would come from the Crotona Park side. I'd need to run up to our apartment (one flight up), get my mother, father, and bubba (Yiddish for grandmother) down into the basement, which would take us through the building's subterranean catacombs and into the backyard. There we would climb up to the back door of the Fenway movie house which would take us out on Washington Avenue, around the corner from Claremont Parkway (where we lived). From there we'd run one block north and another short block west to Park Avenue, where the trains from Grand Central Station in Manhattan would streak each day all the way up the Northeast Corridor to Canada.

So, no, I was not sitting on some stoop in Germany or somewhere else in Europe. I was actually safely ensconced in the good ole US of A. My only problem was in climbing the fence to get down to the station in order for the four of us to catch that train. I knew my father and I could do it, and that we probably could get my mother over the fence as well. My bubba would be the problem. She was about four foot ten, and squat. Geometrically, it always looked to me as though she was only a touch more rectangular than square. She was also close to eighty. I knew for sure we wouldn't be able to get her over the fence. It was then that my fantasy would fade.

In any event, that's essentially what Harry's sense of the beginning should be.

And here's the true backstory to this little fantasy of mine. It was 1948, three years after World War II. My Italian Catholic blood brother/best friend, Richard Grillo (Richie), was sitting with me on that stoop at 493 Claremont Parkway in the nexus of Southeast and Central Bronx, New York. We were both ten years old. 493 Claremont was sandwiched between two parks—Crotona Park to the east and Claremont Park to the west. The streets were paved with an ever-so-slight, barely discernible slope going from east to west (at least that's how I saw it). It was then, as I visualized this slight decline of the streets from park to park, that this escape fantasy popped into my head.

As I was seeing this scenario, imagining it, I never mentioned it to Richie because his was a very nice Italian Catholic family and I would never seek to get them involved in anything that might be dangerous. The point was that if the Nazis came, it wouldn't necessarily be dangerous to Richie's family, but it would be dangerous to our family—our Jewish family.

In our four-story apartment building (which was a notch above a tenement building), all the residents were foreign-born. My family was Jewish from Ukraine, and Yiddish was the language of the home. Richie's parents were from Italy, and of course in his apartment Italian was spoken. We had a Czechoslovakian lady in the building, a Greek lady, a German lady, three other Jewish residents, and a sprinkling of other ethnicities, all living in this four-story building of three apartments on each floor plus a sole apartment on the street walk-in floor. That one was the super's apartment. She was a German American lady who lived there with her boyfriend and her dog (whose name Richie and I never knew).

I was an only child and Richie was one of seven. He and I are still blood brothers, by virtue of having cut our arms a bit and mixing blood. We did this cutting and mixing when we were about eleven or twelve years old, and to this day, from the day we first met in 1942 (when we both were four years old), we're always still in touch—these eighty-one years later.

The other thing that Richie and I hadn't ever discussed was my participation as a leader in the cultural life of the Yiddish-speaking left-wing world. In this respect, from the age of seven—in my role as a young performer of Yiddish poetry and prose in venues all across the city—I was the child who was anointed as the one to confirm for progressive, left-leaning, Yiddish-speaking immigrants the hope that continuity in America, as the place where the Yiddish language could survive and thrive, could be achieved, especially in a socialized equanimity.

In this sense, the review of this memoir both by Richard Brookhiser (the noted historian and author) and wife Jeanne Safer (noted psychoanalyst and author) pointed out that I needed to refocus the entire memoir on the meaning of my contribution to this left-leaning, progressive, Yiddish-speaking Jewish audience (approaching in the U.S. more or less about a million people), and then to try to relate what my role and contribution to this group was, and what it ultimately meant to them and, of course, to me.

And by the way, I never actually discussed this with Richie because it was so far afield from who we were on Claremont (along with all of our friends) that the idea of explaining it all seemed like taking on too much of a complex issue.

Richie and I were defined as first-generation Americans, and we played punch-ball, running bases, off the point, asses up, ring-a-levio, marbles, slug, and skully, as well as any of the street games that were played in the New York City boroughs. Rich and I were part of a five-guy group. There was Frankie Carbone, Willy Travalli, and Richie (Italian Catholics), Joey Eskenazie (a Turkish Jew), and me (an Ashkenazi Jew). Frankie, Willy, and Joey were two years older than Richie and me. All of our parents were foreign-born.

Therefore, this second draft of the memoir will focus on the important suggestions by Rick Brookhiser and Jeanne Safer regarding the very special story of how I became a relevant voice to this particular immigrant Jewish population who worked toward having Yiddish as a daily language in America—especially in an imagined progressive, left-leaning America. (This is the second draft of this preface. The first draft of the preface is included in Afterword II on page 299.)

Yet, as it pertains to my personal story, there is another part to me that is equally occupied solely with personal inclinations, my sense of freedom, and my dancing soul. And this too will share space with my cultural contribution to the hope of the palpable progressive, Yiddish-speaking world of the 1940s through the end of the twentieth century.

I should note that, with respect to motivation as it relates to preparedness, industriousness, and willingness to take on and even suffer through major projects, I identify with both of my parents, because they were similar regarding these specific qualities. It is in this sense that I began to see that luck favors preparation (or is it the other way around?).

In trying to reach a more central relevance (also based upon my having for many years been the instructor at the Postgraduate Center for Mental Health's Psychoanalytic Institute's seminar on dreamwork and dream interpretation), I have known that in any dream, the dreamer is actually spelling out his own cast of characters based on various facets of his own personality. In my case, in the rare instance that my mother appears in my dreams, I instantly know she is representing something in me: either an emotion, or a motivation, or a solution to a problem.

Thus, through it all, even though my mother was obviously and unquestionably the most important person in my formative years—especially as it related to my anointed role in which I performed high-level Yiddish literature to this massive Yiddish contingent—it was nevertheless my father who was my strength.

Therefore, I begin this memoir with my father.

PART 1
A RETROSPECTIVE MONTAGE
Historical Context

1
Beginnings

On the Left

My father was a Marxist. Ergo, I was born into a family with a strong socially conscious worldview. My mother was also implicitly a Marxist, although it was not particularly a pragmatic ideology for her. More to the point, she simply dished out good deeds for individual people rather than spending her sacrifice or preoccupations on humanity generally. Underneath it all she was, indeed, a true humanist. Personality-wise, she was on fire. She could sing beautifully (with that smoky alto) and did so in several languages. She was also quite beautiful and had great virtuosity in any number of ways—as, for example, a great dancer. She said my father was the only man she ever loved. They were married for fifty-six years.

A Little Political History

Why was my father a Marxist? It's because he hated the idea of people living in poverty or in some other sort of oppressive condition, which he personally experienced because he was born in Tzarist Russia in 1902. Parenthetically, what unites progressive people of all ideological stripes is the fight against oppression of any subjugated group. And it was that that defined the essence of my father's take on his ideological position. Although he was a strong man, he was nevertheless also risk averse and therefore an example of the classic non-entrepreneur.

As a child growing up in a little hamlet (a shtetl) in a Jewish ghetto of western

Ukraine (bordering Romania), at about ten years of age, my father witnessed his first pogrom (an organized massacre of a particular ethnic or racial group—in this case against Jews). By the way, pogroms were incursions on Jewish ghettoed areas for the purpose of looting and killing Jews—no other way to put it. If you look it up in the dictionary it will spell out that "pogrom" is a Russian word meaning "to wreak havoc" or "to demolish violently"—which was done. "Pogrom" is also, and for all intents and purposes, a synonym for "genocide." And so here I'm going to go off preaching and spilling my guts: It was the Protestant Reformation, with Martin Luther raving his rabid dialogue regarding how Jews should be punished, and punished sadistically (Luther, 1533), along with poison against Jews propagated and disseminated by the Vatican, plus the assist given by the Russian Orthodox Jew-hating church, as well as Spain's Iberian Peninsula Inquisition—all of it prepared the groundwork of hate. Therefore, to sum it all up, these Christian "pogromshchiks" felt thus justified in killing Jews.

Of course the pogrom was a cover for their under-the-radar motive—stealing and looting. The conscious rationale for all this killing, stealing, and looting was ostensibly blaming Jews for the death of Jesus (known as the "guilt of deicide"), as well as accusing these penniless Jews of controlling the world—as attested to by that manufactured *Protocols of the Elders of Zion* (1903); that is, the blasphemous manufactured screed that was secretly written by a group of vitriolic Jew-hating Russians and published in 1903. It then was disseminated globally in the twentieth century. Our own Henry Ford was the point man in America, printing fifty thousand of these so-called *Protocols* and having them distributed.

I'm telling you all this because my instinctive reaction to it was what laid the groundwork for my motive to do whatever I could to help Jews (and anyone else who was being made helpless). In my case, what I could do—and especially on a grand scale—was to deliver the message of rescue: to Yiddish, to my parents, and to the overall population of American Jewish immigrants who were hoping for a safer world, one in which a small segment of the politically left-leaning contingent of Jews felt that a socialist America would be a safe place for Yiddish-speaking Jews, as well as for everyone else.

Whenever any rationale for incursions against Jews occurred, the *Protocols* as well as church sermons were utilized as a perfectly good and correct justification to kill Jews. Even during the Spanish Inquisition of the fifteenth century, Jews were hounded, killed, and exiled, and whatever valuables they had were distributed among church higher-ups (liars, who typically, and of course falsely, accused Jews of this or that) and the loot was also distributed to noblemen. It was an ongoing heist of the first order.

These sorts of so-called data (like the *Protocols*) always justified pogroms or even large-scale genocides. Example of such genocides are numerous, as in the one considered the first of the twentieth century, in 1904, the German Empire waged a genocide against the Herero and Nama people in Namibia, Africa (which was then German South West Africa). Then, from 1915 to 1924, Turkish society perpetrated a genocide against their Armenian citizens, with 1.5 million or more Armenian people destroyed; in this case it was the Armenian Christians who were murdered—and by the way, the Armenians were the first Christians.

Then again, during World War II, the German/Nazi genocide against the Jews was the one that murdered more than six million Jewish men and women, along with a million and a half children or more—which became the boundless genocide of the twentieth century—and again, by the way, that six-million figure might be greatly underestimated. The truth is that the Nazi killing machine eviscerated a multiplicity of Jewish ghettos in small Eastern European villages (by firing squads) and in such cases these killers were not interested in recording data. Where data was recorded was in the camps. My estimate of this ethnic-cleansing annihilation of just about all of the shtetls of Eastern Europe was probably another million or so—all told, probably more than seven million Jews annihilated—way more than one-third, but not quite half, the Jewish population of the world.

And by the way, here I go: Who, we may ask, were these Nazis? Sorry to say, but it needs to be said—they were all Christians who went to church on Sundays and heard these ignorant brain-dead priests, hypnotizing these persuadable innocents who believed in all this supernatural hocus-pocus—which reminds me of what my father once said to me.

It was when I was in second grade. I came home from school one day and I told him the teacher talked about God and religion and praying. I told my father that I didn't believe in any of that, and asked, What did he think? He immediately told me that he too didn't believe in any of that, and that the teacher was wrong to talk to the children about it. He said, "It's all a lot of bunk." And he said it with an exclamation point. I remember thinking, *Right*—that my father was way smarter than that teacher. Therefore, my paternal grandfather, Meyer, my father, Samuel (nicknamed Sol), and I were all stone-cold Jewish atheists. One thing is for sure: there was no Jewish God protecting Jews. That was for sure. Does anyone really think there's a God (any God—even a Jewish one) protecting Jews?

In any event, I never believed the story of Moses receiving the Commandments on Mount Sinai. However, a Yiddish writer, Moishe Shulshtayn, actually did see a mountain. He claimed that the mountain he saw was higher than Mont Blanc (of the European Alps)—and here's the kicker: Shulshtayn said that this mountain that was higher than the Alps was even more sacred than Mount Sinai. When I came across what Shulshtayn said about this mountain, it was not its height that interested me. Rather, I really wanted to know, in what way was this mountain more sacred than Mount Sinai?

In a Yiddish poem Shulshtayn wrote, titled "Ikh Hub Gezen a Barg" (I Saw a Mountain), he starts with:

Ikh hub gezen a barg (*I saw a mountain*)
Iz er geven hekher foon Mt. Blanc, (*So it was higher than Mont Blanc,*)
Oon haylicker foon Barg Sinai (*And more sacred than Mount Sinai*)

More about that later.

So who were these Germans who fell for what the Church taught, what they heard at home, and fell correspondingly in love with Hitler and Nazism? How do we explain that as regards "good Christian people"? And I'm not through yet. How about: Who's responsible for America's original sin? Who built the ships and controlled the slave trade in America? And who hanged these Black people? Along with this: Who owned the plantations? Who were the ones who tortured, murdered, and raped Black slaves? And, further, who decimated the Native Americans? That's right, you guessed it! It was the Christians who went to church on Sunday, said grace before meals, and heard in church and at home vitriolic hatred toward Black people, or, at the least, heard godly justification for the validity of the role of African Black people—as slaves. And even ostensibly good people like Thomas Jefferson and Alexander Hamilton (no less George Washington) could be slave owners because getting rich most often puts an anesthesia over one's humanity. It's a matter of affluence satisfying the deep wish for the promise of survival (and the Darwinian survival of the fittest). Emotionally, getting rich often sets one apart in the sense of feeling superior. Reparations for African Americans? Absolutely!

In the same sense, scapegoating Jews became extraordinarily handy. And yes, the Church, over centuries, is to be blamed for infecting the families of their congregants with this infamia—the homicidal hatred of Jews.

These priests and ministers of the Church did it! The Vatican is at the very least implicated in this infamia, directed by the Austrian Bishop Alois Hudal, who was located at the Vatican. And further, it was this Bishop Hudal who masterminded the escape of thousands of Nazi criminals to South America and to the Middle East. And his escape plan was also assisted by—are you ready for this?—the International Red Cross!

Therefore, am I angry at the Church? You bet I am. And with respect to this issue, I will not be finding my Jesus moment anytime soon because I will not forgive. Not that my possible forgiveness means a hill of beans.

Nevertheless, in my own family, the first time I ever saw my father cry was in 1946 when he received a letter from an eyewitness who reported that my grandmother Miriam (my father's mother), his sister Rokhl (Ruth), his sister's husband, and their two children, ages fourteen and sixteen, were all shot and killed at a place called the Yevpeteria ditch in Crimea, where they were among twelve thousand massacred Jews.

In my not-so-humble opinion, the Church has lost any smidgeon of justification to exist. And by the way, to repeat, that psychotic leader of the Protestants whose name adorns its own church sect is Martin Luther (the Lutheran Church), who in the mid-sixteenth century published that vicious screed against Jews which was used by the Nazis as evidence and justification for genocide against Jews. I invite and challenge all Christians to read Luther's vicious screed—it's called *On the Jews and Their Lies*. And this motherfucker, Martin Luther, is venerated by the Church. And in 1880, the Vatican organ, *Civilta Cattolica*, spewed the same poison.

In fact, the great writer Thomas Mann made a speech at the Library of Congress (1945) pointing out that Nazi ideological roots led directly back to the fifteenth century, to Martin Luther's proclamations promulgating hatred of Jews.

Well, perhaps I should take it back and not have used the noun "motherfucker." Rather than referring to Luther as a motherfucker, perhaps I should have said: "This poor excuse for a Christian!"

On the other side of it, I do recognize that many Christians grow up in church communities and *in community*, and take away from it strong ethical and moral values and actually lead honest lives in a loving Christian spirit. In this respect, my bitterness toward the Church is mollified, insofar as with that kind of kindness of spirit of such churchgoers and church-givers, I have absolutely no argument.

Now, what do I think this all means? It means that I'm walking around like a time bomb. That's what it means. I think it also means that this world is still in a very primitive state and that I believe that most people operate, at best, on a C-minus level. At best! One of the only hopes that the growing-edge Church has is to practice generosity and charity for all people and to be socially conscious about the issue of oppression toward any group. And for me to say that any religious organization actually can be socially conscious is a big step in my thinking, because I really feel that what religion has done to humanity is nothing less than tragic. In my opinion, the Nobelian (Nobel Prize winner in physics) Steven Weinberg of Big Bang fame said it best (1999)—namely: "Good people can behave well and bad people can do evil; but for good people to do evil—that takes religion." Is *that* ever true! As an addendum, I would also add that certain political ideological positions can have the same pernicious effect.

Therefore, in my review of my father's formative years, in my revulsion of oppressive behavior of governments (and individuals) toward targeted people, and in my understanding of what's horrifically happened to Jews and others throughout history, along with my direct challenge to typical Christian Church history (which is actually anti-Christian and replete with disgusting hypocrisy), as well as with my sense of always wanting to rescue my parents, I believe all of it forms the understanding of how I naturally was swept up into the role of being the young voice reaching just under a million people with the Yiddish spoken message that touched every fiber of the wishes of such people regarding their hope for a better world.

And with this little intro, the next couple of lines in Shulshtayn's poem about the mountain he saw, "Ikh Hub Gezen a Barg," are:

Nisht it troim (*Not in a dream*)
Oif der vour (*Rather, in reality*)
Oif der erd iz er geshtanen (*This mountain stood on solid ground*)
Azah barg, azah barg hub ikh gezen (*Such a mountain, such a mountain I saw*)
Foon Eedisheh sheekh (*Of the shoes of Jews*)
In Mydonik (*In Majdanek extermination camp*)

Now we know why this mountain was more sacred that Mount Sinai! And I agree. This particular mountain was really the sacred one. Again, later for more of the poem.

My Political and Philosophical Influences

The people I was reaching in my role as the anointed one *to bring good news* were Jewish left-leaning individuals (liberals, socialists, and communists) as well as those Zionist Jews who were also immigrants with the sole goal of supporting the making of the State of Israel. My relationship with such Zionist Jews was one that arrived at my doorstep, when gradually these Zionist Jews (before Hebrew became the operant language supplanting Yiddish) began hearing about this vunderkind who was in the process of rescuing Yiddish. These Zionists were also immigrant Jews who fervently wanted a State of Israel to exist and whose everyday language was Yiddish (along with a Yiddish-accented English).

Having given you, the reader, a thumbnail sketch of how I was introduced to all of this—what I refer to as the atom of my life—I feel that my contribution to these Yiddish-speaking humanists, and my agreement with their life-affirming goals (both toward Yiddish as well as for a progressive American soul), is likely the most influential part of my early life. I will now first kind of quickly sum up some personal reflections of my family, and later describe how I became the young voice of this Yiddish-speaking immigrant population who hoped for a better world.

Again, about my father. Samuel Kellerman (nicknamed Sol by my mother), was not formally educated, but was a stellar autodidact and inhaled books. Where they both came from in Ukraine, there was no such thing as grammar school leading to middle school leading to high school, then to college, then to graduate school, then to a postdoctoral institute. In that little hamlet, regularly attending some school was iffy, though a little school for Jewish children did exist. It was called a little cheder (pronounced with a throat-clearing sound).

The teacher was somehow and somewhat educated, and several little boys would comprise the class. I knew this teacher here in America and, believe it or not, he was in fact educated. His pen name was Ber Green (from Itsik Greenberg), and he had become an editor at the *Morgen Freiheit* (a Yiddish communist daily newspaper, the name of which means *Freedom of Tomorrow*). How it happened that this man was able to educate himself as well as to learn Mandarin was and remains beyond my comprehension—given that he grew up in Ukraine, in that little hamlet, Yaruga, on the Dniestr River, bordering Romania.

My father said that they studied the Cyrillic alphabet, did some reading and whatever else, and he was one of those types who could learn any language and in no time flat. He was attracted to literature and learning generally. He could converse in a half dozen of these languages, including of course in Slavic languages, as well as in Romance languages like Romanian (he lived in Romania for a few years), but also in Indo-European languages such as English, and Yiddish, and could get along in Hebrew as well—a Semitic language.

My parents arrived in the good ole USA separately, at the end of the second decade of the twentieth century—about 1919 plus or minus a year or two—each not knowing a word of English, and stone-cold broke. They were both from that same little shtetl, Yaruga.

In the Bronx, New York City, we lived in an old, beat-up building—a notch above a tenement-like building—with my bubba, Pessie Pellis. She was born in 1864 (Civil War time in America), and died in 1958 when I was twenty. She spoke only Yiddish, Russian, and Ukrainian—not a word of English. So my first language as a first-generation American was Yiddish, which was mostly spoken at home. I learned English on the streets of the Bronx.

My father's little sister, Bella, was my mother's best friend more or less since they were born. So my parents knew one another all of their lives. In fact, my father was targeting New York City as his destination because he knew Esther was there. He was also looking for the best possible escape from the pogroms against Jews of his Eastern European homeland. Not only was he successful in finding that lamp beside the golden door, but he also found her—Esther Pellis.

My father had witnessed pogroms that occurred in Yaruga; one in which his brother, Zonia (as well as another resistance leader), killed one of the attackers, and another in which my father witnessed the murder of an elderly man. I've always thought that my father's risk-averse personality was based on these experiences. As mentioned, he was classically risk averse but was very bright, with an incisive, dry, sardonic sense of humor. My mother loved his humor, and anyone could see that he was the template of Earth's honest person. He could not tolerate unfairness—which he saw as injustice. Therefore, he was destined to be frequently disappointed because, as we all know, *life does not cooperate* and cares not a damn about fairness.

To reinforce this notion of the indifference of life to individuals, I usually say that the state of evolution is still, and at best, in its infancy, and in this sense life can be rated C minus! And I say this because I, as an optimist, give it that sort of exaggerated grade. The question is: Can one simultaneously be optimistic as well as cynical? Yes, I think that's who I am!

Later on, in 1956, when I was eighteen years old, and when Khruschev made

Mom and Dad—Esther and Samuel (Sol) Kellerman. In the exuberant generational dedication of my first book, I wrote:

> *To my beautiful parents, Esther Kellerman, my mother, who is the personification of talent and, like sunshine, is the embodiment of color and warmth; and my father, Samuel Kellerman, a rare example of a person of pure authenticity and conviction. These are the central, caring, loving, and guiding figures of my life who share an irrepressible zest for life and are ultimately responsible for any capacity I have to work meaningfully, to acquire wisdom, and also to be loving; I embrace you and additionally dedicate this book to your 50th anniversary in 1980.*

The photo is circa 1967. My father was born in 1902, my mother in 1904.

his twentieth Congress speech revealing to the world the horrendous genocide that Stalin had commanded, it was then that such news confirmed for me what I personally had been sensing all along: that is, that no totalitarian state could be trusted to value the community, much less the individual. I discussed this with my father (who was in his mid-fifties at the time), and his lifelong belief in the progress of society based on a concern with the idea of the value of a shared community (in the Marxist sense) was somewhat stilled. My sense of it all was that although communists generally claimed to love humanity, nevertheless it seemed to me that, instead, they hated people. That may not be true of the rank and file, but it seems historically to be quite true of most of the communist rulers over the world.

That absolute power corrupts absolutely is not to be taken lightly, especially when Cambodia's Killing Fields occurrence of 1975–1979 was engineered by those *genius* communist rulers who tortured and killed at will in their ridiculous, undereducated, and maximally stupid and arbitrary deindustrialization policy of bringing the economy of Cambodia to, as they said, "year zero." And that's where these communist leaders were living—in a zero mentality.

As a matter of fact, I was always suspicious of, and kept my distance from, anything regarding the Rosenberg spy case. It always bothered me that the Rosenbergs and their lawyers refused to make a deal with the government (without the proviso of naming names); at least by making the deal they could perhaps have saved Ethel Rosenberg so that the children wouldn't be left as orphans. What the government did with the death penalty in that case was atrocious, but what Julius and Ethel Rosenberg did by trading their children for Stalin was worse! Yes, I said worse! No doubt. And that's the way I've always felt about it. This was my opinion during the time of the trial, and it remains my opinion today.

In addition, many years later when I read Whittaker Chambers's book *Witness* (1952), it had for me the unmistakable ring of truth. Of course Chambers was torched with withering criticism from those on the extreme left because he named names for the House Un-American Activities Committee—especially the name of Alger Hiss. Those on the radical left took up the gavel—the cause of supporting the presumed innocence of Alger Hiss. In my opinion and again with no doubt as with respect to Hiss, they were wrong, dead wrong, and Chambers was right, absolutely right. People may not like what Chambers did by essentially besmirching Hiss and naming names, but that does not mean, with respect to truth, that Chambers was wrong. I don't like the idea of naming names, but truth is something else. The book by Sam Tanenhaus titled *Whittaker Chambers* (1997) impressed me with Tanenhaus's research and conclusions. Yes, Chambers was a person in turmoil, but perhaps he wasn't wrong in what he claimed.

So, at the time, as a child growing into a young adult, my character as a good boy gradually became more or less the good boy in the embrace of a more cynical view of the state of the world—even of the state of evolution—which I began to consider, as I've noted, as still quite primitive. And as far as political views were concerned, I loved the land that gave my parents a chance. Therefore, in my mature years, my politics are a bit neocon in foreign affairs. I see myself as a hawk. I happen to like John Bolton's position when he confronted the United Nations' policy of including some tyrannical, murderous leaders of various countries who had gained power positions on the United Nations Human Rights Commission, but I'm quite on the left with regard to domestic affairs (including on the issue of immigration). I should note that my father was originally an illegal alien.

And further, with respect to political advocacy, I am a staunch supporter of the State of Israel despite conflicts that, at times, they (it) as a government may even exacerbate. But is that true only of the Jewish state—that they're not perfect? Yes, I said "the Jewish state." In reading Professor Eugene Goodheart's memoir, *Confessions of a Secular Jew* (2001), I immediately recognized parallels with my life, especially in the political sense. Gene and I were friends. He had also matured into more of a liberal or perhaps liberal centrist on any number of political issues, and eventually eschewed any kind of totalitarian system—as did I. Goodheart was one of America's leading literary critics. He died in 2020.

Later on, I crystallized and coined what I considered to be the best, and most telling, oxymoron yet invented: "modern man." The point of course in my sense of it all (meaning that the state of evolution in so-called modernity was, as stated, quite primitive) is that most people are actually operating at that C-minus level (at best), and governed by an underlying devotion to materialism and to an extremis of self-preservation even in the context of a liberal education—or no education—and more certainly also in the absence of any serious cultural exposure. In fact, many college students graduate without having understood the context and meaning of a bona fide education. I think I felt the only *exception* to this focus on the nature of the modern overall solipsistic self existed primarily among the left-wing Yiddish-speaking immigrant population of the early to mid-twentieth century (the soil in which I grew).

It's also pretty clear to me that I was an American who lived essentially in separate worlds. First was my American neighborhood assimilated self who loved Frank Sinatra, the New York Yankees, and Fred Astaire—also with a special nod to Brando. Second, I equally lived in the progressive non-assimilated Yiddish world of literature and performance as an actor in the Yiddish theater, as well as a contributor to such audiences of the poetry and prose of Yiddish writers. Third was my social life, with an accent on playing ball with my neighborhood friends (especially with Richie), and very much including my very active encounters with girls and women—and of course, in my world of social dancing.

Thus, in this memoir, although my distinctive participation in a particular part of the Yiddish world in America is a major focus of this rendition of my life, nevertheless, any such life must include other compartments of overall experience, as it is a rendition of the life of a person with a personality, points of view, needs, and feelings. Along with the worlds in which I lived, which included grammar school, high school, college, graduate school, and postdoctoral education. It all coalesced with my profession as a psychologist/psychoanalyst/author in the private practice of psychotherapy, and of course in the creation of my family, composed of me; my wife, Linda; and our four sons—Max, Sam, Harry, Jack. Oh, those boys—the fabulous four.

It has occurred to me that my role in the progressive Yiddish world, as actor and recitationist, seems to be the standard by which I assess my presence in any of my other worlds as to whether here and now, or there and then, these venues—or even any aspect of such venues—do or don't feel like "home." I believe that wherever I am, I measure whether I feel at home by the way I felt in my Yiddish world. This central position of my Yiddish contribution to this particular progressive Jewish population (as the seven-year-old whose voice promised continuity of a progressive Yiddish life in America) constitutes the most important and central position—certainly of my formative years.

2

To Contribute

Tikkun Olam (To Repair the World)

However, it was not solely about achievement—academic or otherwise. This special underpinned ingredient of this left-wing Yiddish-speaking Jewish culture could be expressed as the most important value of the Jewish people generally. It is a value that perhaps, in a complex way, worked its meaning into the general Jewish collective unconscious—actually probably meaning, in essence, what in psychoanalytic lingo is known as an *unthought-known* (Bolas, 1987): that is, something that was known in the absence of any literal specific thought; an unthought-known can be even inferred as an intuition. It was a feeling that was actually sitting there, although not quite crystallized as a thought and therefore without ever actually being verbally stated (for example, as by parents to children)—yet still necessarily being understood as the persuasive force that needed to be heeded. This force and value in Jewish culture that needed to be heeded could be stated as:

> *You must make a* contribution—*you must make a contribution to the greater good, and therefore be involved in things that are greater than the self.*

I believe this idea of *contribution* became, at an early age, the signal message of my life, which I expressed as the definition of my role: the "tip of the spear" of the left-wing Yiddish cultural life (at that time in the 1940s through the 1960s). It was then that actually most of these culturally oriented Yiddish-speaking immigrants (left-wing or not) considered or hoped that their children (who were first-generation Americans) would be interested in developing continuity in America with respect to their Yiddish-speaking cultural heritage—in this new world—in the new world of Emma Lazarus's "The New Colossus"—her *golden door*. And on the left, I was the child at the age of seven who would carry the torch. But I think I was chosen to carry the torch because of what I naturally understood; that is, as Joshua Bennett writes in *Spoken Word: A Cultural History*: "What you say, and how you say it, means everything. Truth is embedded in the telling." Tas Tobey, in his review in *The New York Times Book Review* (April 16, 2023, p. 13), adds that "it is in the telling that the true magic of [spoken word] comes alive." It was in this sense, and as the great muckraker Lincoln Steffens (1931) stated in his autobiography, that I also say, "I was born a remarkable child." Of course, to normalize this quote as it applies to my personal development, I need to explain how it is that I come to write about myself in this way. And the "telling" of the word is a key to my stature as the tip of the spear.

I had a feeling of being powerful, which had been continuously validated by what had been consistently happening to me. As it turned out, I had several careers in which I excelled. I was good in school, I was good athletically, I had rhythm and was a dancer (who could pick up any dance just by observing it done once or even never seeing how it was done; instead by feeling the rhythm of the music and understanding how it all fits the "cool" culture of America). Over the years, I had entered many dance contests—fourteen in all—and, with a number of partners, won them all. And by the way, "cool" in American lingo simply and usually means "great."

In fourth grade, it was difficult for me not to somehow wonder about my influence on others when our teacher decisively stated that I could no longer be president of the class. She came to this conclusion because during the punchball game in

Myself at age three, circa 1941.

the schoolyard (while she was acting as umpire on the first base side), she incorrectly called a ball foul that grazed fair territory by about an inch on the third base line. I was umpiring that third base line, standing only a hair off that line. I shouted to her across the infield that it was for sure a fair ball. That did it. On the spot she decided I could no longer be president of the class. The outcome was that when she called for a new election—are you ready for this?—this class of nine-year-olds refused to vote! Lincoln Steffens, hello. I was president of my classes all through grammar school and junior high. In high school I was nominated again, but this time I declined this so-called opportunity.

In my adult years I became a psychologist/psychoanalyst/author, achieving a high level of recognition in my field. I had a master of arts degree with a major in general/experimental psychology, and a master of science degree and Ph.D. (doctoral degree) in clinical psychology. Finally, I successfully achieved postdoctoral certificates in psychoanalysis as well. I'm also the author and editor of forty-three books (including this memoir). I've done this publishing of books in a forty-nine-to-fifty-year span. I feel it's a privilege to be able to write books. In my case, my ability to synthesize ideas in order to unearth something new is extremely exciting. I've also had four years working professionally in mental hospitals as well as teaching at several universities, and then also conducting a private practice in psychotherapy and psychoanalysis (at this count, fifty-eight years) at my private office at a Gramercy Park address in New York City. There I hold a ninety-seven-year lease with an option to renew for ninety-seven years. I guess the landlord felt optimistic about me!

As adjunct professor in the graduate schools at New York University, the City University of New York, and the New School, my relationship with the students in class reminded me quite easily of how I felt comfortable with audiences in my Yiddish performing world. In these positions, I would get positive feedback. In fact, I was once invited to lecture at a Yiddish function regarding Yiddish poetry and how it's best conveyed to audiences. The students then petitioned the director of the institute to have me teach another full course.

But none of these achievements had quite the effect on me that my tip-of-the-spear career had; that is, I actually became the prototype of carrying on all that encompassed my Yiddish-speaking left-wing political message in this, the new world. Thus, I became the example of what this representation could all mean; representing and reflecting the hopes of immigrants for their children. This tip-of-the-spear role was my *contribution* as this voice of hope of such Yiddish continuity in America. But I was lucky. Why? Because a ready-made context was awaiting a seven-year-old child to be the atom in the center of a burgeoning aim—providing this populace with an example of how such a Yiddish progressivistic context could work in America.

In this sense, in 1945, when I was seven years old (and because I was fluent in Yiddish with a prosody of Yiddish that was indistinguishable from those born and raised on the other side), I began to perform poetry and prose, both as an individual performer and as an actor in Yiddish theater, which at that time was in a tremendous ferment in our overall American Jewish Yiddish subculture. The more general point here is that all the other Yiddish-speaking Jewish organizations (no matter their political leanings) also had strong cultural venues. Thus, this contributory part to my life more or less constitutes the most important part of my development.

And then Shulshtayn again enters my domain—the part of my development that says: *Stand up and march toward justice.* Nothing less! So his "sacred mountain" poem continues:

Oon plootzlikh vee s'volt vee voonder geshen
    (*And suddenly as though by a miracle*)
Khub derzen (*I saw*)
Vee er reert zeekh foonem ort
    (*That the mountain of shoes begins to move*)
Oon dee toizenter sheekh (*And the thousands of shoes*)
Shteln ois zeekh alaine (*Arrange themselves*)
Tzoo der moss, tzoo der pore (*To size and pair and*)
Oon in ryan—oon gayen. (*In rows—ahead they move [march].*)

To whom these shoes belonged and the destination toward which they now march will continue to be told as we proceed through this memoir.

My Other Part

In my original preface to this memoir (see Afterword II), I set forth what I determined was the essence of memoir reportage—an ostensible template of what comprises a memoir.

In my case, I felt that there were three issues of my life that governed what I did and where I went. These issues of my personal reflections emerged as my focus on what *home* meant to me; and further, the theme of *anonymity* seemed to be exceedingly relevant to me.

When I read *The Day of the Jackal* by Frederick Forsyth, published in 1971, it was one of the two best books I had ever read (the other was *The Double Helix* by James Watson), primarily because the central theme of the *Jackal* book was underpinned by the aggregate of at least two of these three, what I considered crucial, themes: namely that of *home* (the assassin was consistently without a home), and *anonymity* (even when he was killed he still couldn't be identified). My third theme, the issue of *contribution*, was also included, but this so-called contribution was a contaminated one in Forsyth's book due to a sole focus on assassination for fee.

Therefore, the three identified themes of my life, that moved me in the direction of how these themes informed my life, led me to a realization that a memoir of my life might be interesting to contemplate, then to understand, and finally to be based on these thematic issues as though it were a map indicating a three-dimensional longitude and latitude of my life.

It was in this sense that I felt that casting a light on the vicissitudes of my life would be more clearly surfaced, and more profoundly understood (especially by me), with the focus based upon these three themes—*home, anonymity, contribution*.

And by the way, in reading *The Day of the Jackal*, I couldn't be oblivious to the fact that assassination was not always necessarily a bad thing. In that sense, I had the thought that I could have been the one to pull the trigger in a successful assassination project—the objective, of course, being that of assassinating Hitler. Yes, I had those thoughts. And I also had the thought that those shoes in Majdanek belonged to my paternal grandmother, my aunt, her husband, and their two children—those murdered by the Nazis.

The Three Themes

1. The Importance of *Home*

This is the question I began asking my patients as to what experiences of their lives led them to identify such experiences as revealing to them a sense of *home*.

In turn, this led me to consider this idea of "home" as something quite personal to me as well—although perhaps in an idiosyncratic way; that is, in a way about which I was homesick for a place I'd perhaps never been! And I'll explain this as we proceed.

2. The Importance of *Anonymity*

The need I had to be unseen was also impossible for me to ignore, and so I was actually able to see that I had such a need for *anonymity*. This need for anonymity kept insinuating itself into my compelling need to not deny what it was that I was generally sensing and that I continued to sense in my thinking and feelings—actually up to that point, and then throughout my formative years. This need for anonymity contrasted dramatically with the reality that even at that early age of seven, I was already experiencing a certain celebrity.

Thus, my second critical issue of *anonymity* reflected what I began to notice about myself. This meant that over many years, gaining a condition of *anonymity* was important to me, and that without any conscious intent, nevertheless I was in many ways already implementing it. I could tell that this need was more a need to perhaps escape my sense of responsibility (or even my sense of the imperative of making a contribution to the greater good)—which in my case meant my responsibility to being the tip of the spear of the Yiddish progressive movement, insofar as this responsibility meant that I was the chosen one deemed to validate all the hopes and dreams of such people of this ethno-socio-political cultural movement.

A crucial issue reflected my third theme: that of making a contribution.

3. The Importance of *Contribution*

I believe this value of *contribution* is one that fundamentally resonated throughout my early formative years and was most driven by my stage performances in this socially conscious Yiddish-speaking subcultural environment in which I found myself, and where I was performing the literature of those individuals who were concerned with the hope of a world of fairness and especially along with the absence of oppression of any people; an equitable world that actually might be able to be forged.

Thus, it became just about crystal clear to me that this memoir would only be true to itself if these three themes were synthesized as the critical issues of my life—*home, anonymity, contribution*. Of course, the issue of *contribution* became the essence of what, to me, necessitated a monumental commitment.

It became an assumed definition for me that to be able to contribute implied the corresponding characteristic for me of being relentlessly productive. This considerable bandwidth to be able to do it all was a sense of it that I continuously felt—meaning living and bringing to life the tribulations of innocent people, and the optimistic implications of being able to manage tragedy through productive struggle. I considered it all as the importance and excitement of participating in all of these miraculous moments. In this sense, for example, I performed the poetry of Itsik Feffer, who was the best-known of all the Soviet Yiddish writers and who, along with other Yiddish writers, was murdered by Stalin. With respect to one's struggle to gain some ascendancy, Feffer's poem lit me up—especially in his last stanza:

Oon oif tsepikenish dee sunim vus graytn khvorim shoin far meer Veln meer
    (*And in spite of our enemies who prepare a deadly fate for me*)
Oonter aygeneh foonen nokh hubn nakhess un a sheer.
    (*Will we under our own flag have unending pride.*)
Khvel mine vinegartn farflantzn oon foon mine goirl zine der shmeed,
    (*I will yet plant my vineyards—*)
Oif Hitler's Kayver vel ikh tantzn— (*From out of the flames I will come through!*)
I'kh bin ah Eed! (*On Hitler's grave I will dance, I am a Jew!*)

In the sense of feeling as one with such struggle, I believe I absorbed all the horrors of oppression-led miseries, which irrevocably also generated in me the need for retribution. I'm also certain that this sort of socially conscious material that was uppermost in my mind contributed, of course, and necessarily, to my interior life. This inner life of mine ultimately also gave me a more powerful conceptualization regarding what was necessary for me to learn; that is, to become even more introspective—ultimately as an adult, as it turned out, defined as learning the material of the psychoanalytic domain when I became a psychologist and psychoanalyst.

Also, it is probably not an accident that I had built a hierarchy in which my tip-of-the-spear activity ascended in importance over my American life. The point here is that neither of my parents ever attended an open-school week, nor ever spoke to one of my teachers. I kind of knew that they depended on me to deal with all of that. To this point, it has also occurred to me that perhaps I was unconsciously, and in one way or another, really living in Yaruga!

The Power-Theme and Basic-Wish

First, several friends, a colleague or two, as well as relatives, have over the years strongly (and with passion) suggested I write a memoir (see the acknowledgments section)—essentially to explain what my son Harry said to me. Harry once said, "Dad, you have a very wide bandwidth." He meant that I have varied interests that required me to actively participate in each one, and to attend to the specificity of details corresponding to each. In addition to Harry's comment, my son Sam once said, "You know, Dad, you have this wisdom and insight that is rare, but it's only visible in your office and to us here in the family. So you're always kind of hidden." Without knowing it, both of them hit upon my instinct to be simultaneously both a psychotherapist *and* to be anonymous. My other sons, Max and Jack, as well as Harry and Sam, have also referred to me as having "a whammy." I'm embarrassed to say they first heard the phrase from me. This "whammy" reference is the one I gave to myself because of certain occurrences that kept recurring throughout my life. It is the phenomenon of understanding what the other person thinks and/or feels. It is this thing usually defined as "empathy" which for me is the key to deep insight (despite that empathy also has an up/down personality), and yet is perhaps the door to the interior of "mind."

I've also had several other successful so-called virtuoso careers and believe (with empirical data supporting this contention) that I've gained such virtuosity—as defined in what might be considered important contributions in at least some of these careers.

Thus, several years ago I figured I'd better jump to it and jot down in black and white all of this seemingly diversified contributory life. This life of mine has never been chaotic; rather, it was diversified and exuberant, and as stated, I thought that before it's too late, I'd better memorialize as much of it as I could. The "jump" and "jot" I'll make will be to start at age seven, with the event that I consider to be the *most* important one of my formative years. I think of this event as the atom. Therefore, barring getting married and the birth of my children, I understand this event to be *the* most important one because I believe it illustrates the genesis, the jumping-off point, or perhaps the pivotal one that reveals the *power-theme* and *basic-wish* of my life.

My sons, Max, Sam, Harry, and Jack, at various ages. (*Top*) When they were young, circa 1983. Left to right: Jack, age four; Harry, age six; Sam, age eight; Max, age ten. (*Bottom*) Studying at YIVO's Yiddish language program in Oxford, England, summer 1998. Left to right: Sam, age twenty-three; Jack, age nineteen; Max, age twenty-four; Harry, age twenty-one.

I also dedicated more than one book to the four of them. In my first published volume, in which I had included dedications to generations of my family, the last was to my sons in 1979, immediately after Jack, our youngest, was born. I wrote:

> *To the new generation: To my loving, joyous, and beautiful children—Max Kellerman, Sam Kellerman, Harry Kellerman, and Jack Kellerman. May you sing and dance, draw lots of pictures, study hard, and express all the qualities inherent in your generational heritage, in a peaceful and just world that is free from want.*

As a psychologist/psychoanalyst/author, as well as a faculty member of curricula in the broad field of psychology, psychopathology, and psychoanalysis, I maintain, or actually more to the point, I proclaim, that each person in this world has a power-theme and basic-wish. To express what a basic-wish is, I'll illustrate it with what I've discovered by thinking it through over many years and for digging and probing into my putative introspective self—in order to try to crystallize and correspondingly then to identify, and finally even label, what this basic-wish of mine is. I've gotten to it by creating a phrase that, to me, resonates in a real way. This single-fold way of my basic-wish is cited as the title of this memoir: *To Bring Good News*.

Yes, at an early age I decided I was going to bring good news to people—although at that point it was only a vague intuitive feeling, in contrast to something crystallized or planned. Of course, this idea of bringing good news to people has as its more basic reference that of bringing good news to my parents. Basically, I think specifically it meant I needed to rescue them. I believe this rescue issue is the one that identifies the *detail* of my basic-wish of bringing good news. And details are very important. Of course, "specificity" and "details" sound redundant. Yet these are not redundant, because of what is in the detail. It is the devil that is in the detail, and this devil needs to be identified.

I'm not unaware that in the devout Christian world (among clergy), letters to one another are almost always signed by phrases referring to the *good news* that "Jesus is here." I refute any claim that in this sense I would be referring to myself by using the same phrase as a *bringer of good news*. So, yes, my basic-wish is *to bring good news*, but the *detail* in it all means that I always felt I needed to *rescue* my parents.

For me, the good news was that my parents were hardworking people, and even at a very early age I could see the enormous effort they expended to keep us going. Their consistent and irrepressible effort was what nourished my own effort gene. So although they worked very hard and through long hours in that little hole-in-the-wall luncheonette they built, nevertheless they were also an optimistic, effervescent, and exuberant couple; my mother was blessed with multiple talents. She was highly intuitive and full of the color of life. As noted earlier, she was on fire.

My father, also as stated, was strong and handsome. He had this wicked dry sense of humor. I always wanted to be like him, and even developed my gait and physical stance in a way that imitated his. Despite my motive to be like him, as it turned out and in certain undeniable ways, I was more like her. I could never say that he was intuitive. With respect to how he saw the world, it seemed to me that he was inherently pessimistic, and certainly, again, as I've said, characteristically risk averse. But definitely he was never afraid of physical threat.

He was loving and respectful, along with being dedicated to a sense of fairness. Along with all of this, he was quite social and gregarious. Yet if he was treated unfairly, look out—because, for example, if physically threatened, anyone could see he was unafraid.

My father was never discernibly depressed; anxious, yes, but if ever depressed, he apparently hid it well. It was clear to me that my parents were a so-called power couple. Although people were generally attracted to them, more specifically the evidence solely with respect to gender was that men were attracted to her and women to him.

With respect to the role I gave myself, an early memory is telling. At the age of about two and a half or perhaps close to three, I remember a certain summer vacation in Sharon Springs, New York. We were registered at a hotel that could be characterized as one of shabby gentility. On Saturday evenings the hotel would sponsor a dance, with a live dance band leading the festivities. Almost all at once, the hall would be crowded with people dancing to ballroom music.

On one weekend, my father needed to be in the city for something regarding the store (luncheonette), so that my mother and I remained in Sharon Springs, and there we were at the dance. My mother could never resist live music, and among her many talents was her dancing art. So here we were sitting on a bench in the back of the hall with the music starting to swing. I was sitting next to her, and as far as I could tell, I was the only child at the dance. I remember while sitting on that bench and looking at my feet that they seemed miles away from the floor—not even bent at the knee, so that they were not at all dangling off the bench.

I spotted a man approaching us, trying to navigate his way around others who were already dancing. He walked up to my mother and asked her to dance. She looked at me and said, "Henry, I'm going to dance right here, so that you can always see me." Of course, she was implying that I shouldn't worry about being abandoned. My response was to just look at her as she got up and began walking a few steps toward this man. I was not at all frightened. As they were about to dance, I wouldn't have any of it. I instantly turned, acrobatically slid off the bench, and did what I needed to do. I approached her and pulled her back by the only method available to me. I pulled on her dress from the back. She turned and looked down at me. Soberly looking up at her and with a rising lilt in my voice, I said: "You've got a husband?!" She immediately excused herself to this man, and we both then sat back down on the bench.

I could tell, even then, of the supreme sacrifice she made at that moment, because to dance was in her blood (as it is in mine). My father arrived the next day, and when she told my father what I had done, I distinctly remember them both laughing—I believed laughing with a certain satisfaction; that is, feeling that a child as young as I could and would do such a thing. However, I knew, I could feel that I could do such a thing because it's what imitated the kind of assertion my father had when he felt something was awry.

So here was an early memory of how I saw myself—as someone who was in charge when my father wasn't there—even though I was still at the end of my toddler stage. Thus, I must have known that this family of mine (emphasis on *mine*) was not to be tampered with in any way, and as far as I was concerned, no interloper was going to interfere with that arrangement. Thus it was clear to me that when my father was absent, I would take over (I'd be in charge as a self-appointed manager taking care of my mother) and would make sure that all was, and most importantly would remain, kosher.

This was an early indication of what my power-theme in life would be. The power-theme is that which touches every fiber of one's feeling, thinking, saying, and, of course, which influences one's doing—and the atom within this power-theme is that of the person's *wish*.

Thus, gratification of one's basic-wish (without fail) generates the feeling of empowerment. However, it is also a universal truth that a person will always be angry when disempowered. Why? The answer is because anger is always a re-empowerment (Kellerman, 2005b). To illustrate how the connection of basic-wish and power-theme represent each side of one coin, I would consider that my basic-wish was one of wanting *to bring good news*. Thus, my personal power-theme has apparently always been fueled by what I feel, what I think, and ultimately what I say (or don't say), and what I do (or don't do), which will be ultimately and always in the interest of satisfying my basic-wish, which is *to bring good news*. And this wish was obviously initially fueled by its specific source wish, which was to bring good news to my parents—also representing the template for how I felt and responded toward others generally.

My mother, Esther Kellerman, father, Samuel Kellerman, and me, circa 1950 when I was twelve years old. My mother was the one to teach me how to interpret and perform Yiddish literature. My father was always my strength. I tried to imitate him in any way I could. I remember even trying to imitate his gait and stride.

In this early experience of getting my mother back to the bench, the good news was that I was protecting the integrity of my family by keeping my mother safe and my father from being bested—and of course, and most importantly, not losing what I considered to be the fusion of my parents, which at that time of my life, of course, was the single most important key to my life.

Of course, my mother dancing with a strange man must have been a vague yet strong hovering danger I felt, and so I went into action—at the age of perhaps about a touch under three. However, a note of caution here is that one must be careful for the other kind of danger that could always be lurking. That is, feeling, thinking, saying, and doing something to only bring good news (especially to oneself) is when one needs to be more tentative. In this sense, the good news that one brings to the self should be to eschew undue self-interest at the expense of others; should not be something sickly competitive, assiduously greedy, or unethical/immoral. Good news means just that—good! And in the highest order of things, one's basic-wish and power-theme perhaps needs essentially to serve something, of course, greater than the self.

Having said all that, it's now time for me to get down to the practical brass tacks of my life; that which I call the "atom" or very first important step. And it had nothing to do with the denotation of dancing, even though in my deepest unconscious I'm sure that all of my self-defined talents are expressions of the same thing—rhythm—for me the optimistic beat of life.

3

Home, Culture, Ideology

Yaruga, Ukraine; and the Bronx, New York

As mentioned, my parents were from the town Yaruga, on the Dniestr River, in Ukraine, bordering Romania. In contrast, we lived in the Bronx, in a tenement-like building with my bubba, Pessie Pellis. My neighborhood was a blue-collar Southeast Bronx neighborhood. The entire neighborhood comprised a little United Nations of cultures, ethnicities, and races. It was populated mostly by Italian, Irish, Jewish, African American (known then as colored and Negro), and Puerto Rican families, and of course that particular arrangement of integration was the composition of my grammar school class, reflecting the nature of the neighborhood surrounding our school, P.S. 42 on the southwest corner of Claremont Parkway and Washington Avenue.

We, all people in the neighborhood, lived in four-story buildings each a notch above tenement housing. None of us even knew about private school education, which was a fixture in Manhattan and where tuition was required. None of us ever heard the word "tuition." Other than the African American population, all other recent immigrants were for the most part from Italy, Ireland, Poland, Puerto Rico, Russia, and Ukraine, as well as their origins sprinkled here and there from other mostly European countries like Greece and Turkey.

These were all immigrant families arriving here in the USA in the early twentieth century. Therefore, I and almost all my friends were first-generation Americans, while our parents emigrated here from all over the world. As far as I remember, there were no families in our neighborhood from any of the Asian countries. Some of the Black families were Caribbean, and their children were also first-generation

Americans. Their parents spoke with a Caribbean accent, while the children spoke quite well, including with a tinge of Black American English. Of course, the Black families were descendants from Africa and from the horrors of the slave trade.

Almost all commercial stores in the neighborhood were little family businesses owned and run, by and large, by Jewish families—none of whom lived in our neighborhood. On our block alone there were three apartment houses. My friend Willy lived in the first house, then my blood brother Richie and I lived in the middle house, and our friend Frankie lived in the third house.

Directly around the corner, on Claremont and Washington, lived my friend Joey. From Joey's building to Willy's building to my building to Frankie's building was one continuous concatenation of rooftops, with one gap that all the guys except Richie and me would jump. On Willy's roof was a pigeon coop. Frankie, Joey, and Willy were two years older than Richie and me. Frankie, Willy, and Richie were

(*Left*) My boyhood neighborhood five, circa 1951, when I was thirteen years old. From the left: Frankie, me, Willy, Joey. They were on skates and I happened to walk by so they pulled me into the shot. Richard Grillo (Richie) wasn't there at that moment, so I felt that in all justice and even in the face of the so-called irrevocable "past," I wouldn't stand for Richie's omission. Therefore, I photoshopped Richie standing between Willy and Joey. It's an example of how I will not tolerate unfairness, and at times disregard or ignore the past—and even alter it. (*Right*) We're both ten years old in the photo in front of the movie poster, circa 1948. The book I dedicated to Richie is titled: *Love Is Not Enough: What It Takes to Make It Work*. My dedication reads: "For Richard Grillo, lifelong blood brother. Love you, Rich."

Italian Catholics; Joey was a Turkish Sephardic Jew; and I, an Ashkenazi Ukrainian Jew. The five of us were all first-generation Americans.

Richie and I played ball in the schoolyard of our school, P.S. 42, as well as throwing and catching in front of our building—the middle building on the block: 493 Claremont Parkway. The truth is that playing ball for us meant living! We simply loved it, and part of loving it was that we were both good at it.

This playing-ball thing was my *first career* starting about at age four or five, of course in concert, always, with Richie. My implicit first career was making sure that my immediate family stayed intact—retaining its integrity. Richie and I played throwing and catching to one another for years and years and must have thrown that "Spaldeen" a billion times. As I'm suggesting, we both became virtuoso throwing-and-catching athletes—he ultimately throwing faster (almost beyond belief), although I could also throw quite fast. However, my catching was something professional. I could catch that ball with either hand and with grace—also behind my back also with either hand, and in every and any other which way.

One of my neighborhood friends actually stated that he really noticed and liked the way I handled catching the ball, and he said, "You also look cool walking." Given the kinds of things we talked about in the street, and the language we used, his comment seemed like an out-of-the-box non-sequitur, because it was taken for granted that we all threw and caught very well and that we were all pretty cool. But from time to time, others would also tell me that my catching the ball was something special. I immodestly could feel it as art, and that comment about my walking cool has also been said to me by others. I think it means walking in a way that perhaps could be called "conscious-cool," although in the absence of self-consciousness—but meaning in a way that almost felt like a cool rhythmic beat.

If I hadn't been such a skinny-malink kid, but rather ahead of my years as an early developer, and in addition muscular, and therefore if my bat would have been as good as my catch (my fielding), I believe I would have had the tools to become a professional baseball player. But at that point in my life, I qualified as a great fielder (catching), hitting but not with power, very good in throwing, and only about average in speed.

Richie and I would usually play in the lower schoolyard of P.S. 42, throwing and catching the ball the length of the schoolyard while shouting compliments to one another on great catches. We would deliberately throw the ball in a way that forced the other to try making great leaping or otherwise miraculous catches. And by the way, in an insightful flash, it has occurred to me that playing ball actually felt like "home"; that is, playing in the schoolyard was a pleasure also because there was no clutter whatsoever in sight, and therefore the arena of the schoolyard had something I had always dreamed about. It was having a home which was decorated sans clutter and aesthetically with simplicity and artfulness. In the schoolyard there was no clutter, and it was Richie and I that brought the artfulness in throwing and catching.

But, as I've said, for more than one reason, my ball-playing career was not going to be my direction in life, because I think I knew (although I was never directly told) that Jewish boys were going to go to college and then even further. Therefore, at the same time that I was hanging out in the street with my neighborhood friends and playing our usual street games (ring-a-levio, asses up, off the point, skully, running bases, marbles, and slug—along with throwing and catching with Richie), at the age of seven my mother sent me into a mutational spin. And here comes arguably the most important experience of my life (barring my marriage and birth of my children).

The Atom

One day about two weeks before my seventh birthday, I was playing with my friends in the street around the corner on Washington Avenue. We were playing immies, or marbles. In those days we had a category-one marble, which was single colored or striped or blotchy colored. A second-category marble was a smaller steel one, which we called a "steelie." Finally, a third-category marble was what we called a "jalopy." This jalopy was the largest of all the marbles.

I should detour for a moment and say that nevertheless, despite the fact that all of us kids played ball together and went to school together, and the neighborhood was at first glance seemingly integrated, the essential truth is that except for the integrated school classes, the neighborhood was a segregated one. From Claremont Parkway south (especially from Third Avenue, Washington Avenue, Park Avenue, Brook Avenue, and Webster Avenue), the population and residents of the buildings were Black. Starting in the mid-1950s, some were also Puerto Rican. In contrast, from Claremont Parkway along those streets that went north (with the exception of Brook Avenue that started south from Claremont), it was all white. Along Claremont from Fulton to Washington was all white, and along Claremont from Washington to Webster was also all white (1940s), with an influx of Puerto Rican families in the 1950s.

I grew up in the house with my mother and father and, as I've noted, with my maternal grandmother, who spoke no English. The language of the house was Yiddish, so that my first language was Yiddish. But this was no different with respect to the myriad of foreign languages spoken as the language of the house in all the homes of all my friends. For example, in Richie's house, his parents spoke Italian. In my friend Junior's house, the language spoken was Spanish.

As I've noted, my parents, Esther and Samuel (Sol) Kellerman, were from this little shtetl (a hamlet), Yaruga, in Ukraine, directly on the Dniestr River bordering Romania. I notice that I very much like to repeat this geography because it seems that I'm really seeing Yaruga, as I've noted above, as *my actual home*, despite the fact that it wasn't.

My father was not formally educated; that is, he never went to a regular school with a prepared curriculum. Yet, as I've said, he was a highly intelligent person who was a savant linguist insofar as he spoke these several languages—Ukrainian, Russian, Romanian, Yiddish, some Hebrew, English, some Albanian, and a smattering of the other Romance languages like Italian and Spanish. Had he been born in the good ole US of A, he would surely have been a scholar of languages. He was a voracious reader who, as I've also said, practically inhaled books, and essentially he became an autodidact.

My father was born in 1902, my mother in 1904. Both families grew up in that little shtetl with those Chagall thatched-roofed little cabinlike houses. Again, my mother was talent personified. She could cook up a storm, design and sew any type of clothing, and sing in several languages. Her smoky alto had a beautiful arresting quality and exemplified all that is important in the prosody of language and song,

My mother's house in that hamlet of Yaruga, Ukraine. My parents visited this little hometown of theirs in 1967. They hadn't been there for about forty-five years.

and to repeat, she was also really a great dancer. In addition, she spoke Russian, Ukrainian, and Yiddish beautifully, and was a gifted actress. She was the one who coached me when I joined the Yiddish theater as an actor as well as performer of Yiddish poetry and prose recitations.

And here is where the atom of my life was gestated, developed, and surely thrived. Thus, as I was playing marbles with my friends in the street, I felt a tug at my sleeve. Well, let me detour again and get back to the tug on my sleeve in a moment or two.

In order to set the stage to how I became transformed into the tip of the spear representing and reflecting the particular Jewish culture in which I was raised, I need to describe the political/social climate and the overall cultural climate of the time, and of course the specific cultural landscape of the Jewish immigrant experience to and of America from the last part of the nineteenth century to the early part of the twentieth century—roughly from 1880 to 1930.

In those fifty years, Jewish immigration to the United States totaled about two million people.

These two million people kind of organized themselves according to their political and social inclinations—conscious or not. There were the majority who read the *Daily Forward* (in Yiddish called *Der Forverts*). This was a democratic-socialist-oriented group, but stood far away from any communist ideological position. In fact, during the Vietnam War in the 1960s, the editorial position of *Der Forverts* supported the war—even in the face of a more or less widespread progressive and popular opposition to the war.

There was another more centrist and relatively nonideological group, and they read the Yiddish newspaper called *The Day* (in Yiddish, *Der Tug*). The third and more problematic group was the leftist group that more or less supported the Soviet Union because they thought that socialism and communism preached equitable distribution of wealth and were concerned with civil rights—especially in America, with our terrible racist behavior toward colored people.

These colored people later became Negro people, and still later became Black people, and also still later reinvented or rediscovered themselves as African Americans. Therefore, African American people were like anyone else insofar as they were trying to locate and recognize themselves with a true identity—one that faithfully reflected who they were.

The progressive leftists therefore felt that such people should be protected and supported in their fight for equality, and on all levels of society. This group of progressive Jewish individuals of the far left read the *Morgen Freiheit* (in Yiddish, literally *The Morning Freedom*, or figuratively meaning "the freedom of tomorrow"). As a postscript, before the *Freiheit* finally ended its publication, I was gifted their remaining Yiddish typewriter—which I still possess.

Yes, ideologically they supported the Soviet Union in the sense of cherishing a more ideal world, but they were not in the category of saboteurs or spies. They were people who believed that workers of the world should unite against their oppressors. They were in the forefront (the avant-garde) of the union builders, attended rallies to protest Jim Crow laws, and generally considered themselves champions of the working class. But yes, they felt that probably capitalism was not going to be the wave of the future, because they believed that workers were frequently exploited and that capitalists were only interested in profits, not people.

My father was one of them, and I liked what my father had to say about it. So that was his self-educated Marxist rationale as well as a well-read one to boot. My mother was also concerned with fairness, but one could tell she was not an ideologue. She just loved to feed people, to sing and dance and bring joy to the world. When I got older I began to understand that my father was a Marxist not only because he hated the untold amount of unfairness that certain people were dealt, but in a more personal way, and as I've noted, he was terribly risk averse, especially when it came to owing anyone any money.

When his friends from the old country invited him to join them in their successful business of manufacturing straps for wristwatches (which they imported from Switzerland), and told him they would set up a partnership with him in a small factory requiring them to fund it with $5,000 (which he would repay gradually), it was really an irresistible offer—yet one which ultimately he could not accept. He said he would not be able to live with not being able to pay them back if the business failed. Thus, with my father, pessimism and anxiety controlled him—especially with that enormous sum (at that time) of $5,000.

In contrast, with my mother, the sky was the limit. It is in this respect that I took after her. Yet my sense of pride, fairness, as well as my sense of integrity was and is, I believe, identical to his. Thus, my father's Marxism was nurtured by his sense of the importance of fairness as well as by his risk-averse nature. He knew he couldn't be an entrepreneur.

In any event, these three Jewish subcultures within the larger Jewish diaspora all created their own cultural clubs, vacation spots, children's camps, choruses, orchestras, newspapers, and magazines, published books, and also founded little Yiddish schools that were generally not religiously based. They were secular, so that in all of these subgroups, these shulas, as they were called (meaning "little schools") were therefore secular. They provided children with classes of Yiddish-language study, Yiddish literature, Jewish history, songs, and dances, and wherever they found themselves, also staged performances in the available concert venues all over major cities. I participated in these performances in many cities even other than New York City, including Los Angeles, Miami, Philadelphia, and various other cities of the Northeast.

All in all, these disparate groups were nevertheless solely unified in the goal of bringing to America some continuity regarding who they were. This meant speaking Yiddish, which they all loved. In Yiddish it's called "mammeh lushn"—mother tongue. And they wanted their children to speak, read, write, and to live it kind of generally in Yiddish—like how they lived it.

As a matter of fact, I also felt this continuity need as it corresponded to my growing family with my wife, Linda, and our four boys, and to this point, we and three other couples formed a secular Yiddish shula so that our children could be connected to their roots, and as a way to broaden the scope of their lives. The children had classes every Saturday from 10 a.m. till 2 p.m.—with classes in Jewish history, Yiddish language, literature, singing, and dancing. It became for them a little, yet important, subculture. The shula had a lifespan of about a decade, with a student population that reached seventeen or eighteen kids (including our four). Then it gradually dissipated, largely because in America, popular culture swallows things such as foreign languages. As my friend, the historian and author Rick Brookhiser, put it: America is omnivorous with respect to foreign cultures and languages. The additional truth is that America beckons children who are growing up with an entire array of opportunities that then take them here and there—including taking them to college, and also away from their ethnic roots.

However, the other contingent of Jewish immigrants in America was the Orthodox Jews, who generally kept themselves separate from the secular Jewish population that I've been discussing. Interestingly, these Orthodox Yiddish-speaking Jews are actually the ones who are, en masse, keeping Yiddish alive.

Even though my wife, Linda (whose family was Jewish), grew up in an environment where this sort of cultural orientation (with Yiddish as the centerpiece) was not a focus, nevertheless she joined me in the sense of offering our children an opportunity to touch their roots. I believe the experience of attending this little shula in fact contributed to an expansion of a worldly outlook for these children, as well as seeding a further deepening of their development generally. As it turned out, our sons pursued this "Yiddish thing" by studying Yiddish in college, by attending the Oxford University Summer Yiddish Program in Oxford, England, and also by attending Yiddish-speaking weeklong summer retreats in New York State.

In America, all of these people (especially the grandparents) in each of these political and cultural subgroups—in this case, of the Yiddish world—were originally immigrants who spoke English typically with a Yiddish accent. The Jews from Spain, Portugal, Iran, Turkey, Syria, or Egypt spoke other Jewish languages, such as Ladino, and were not particularly involved in this explosion of Yiddish culture. Incidentally, over millennia, the total glossia (the possession of a specified number of tongues) of the variety of particular Jewish languages spoken throughout the world equals about twenty or somewhat more of such languages—of which the most spoken language (especially up and into the twentieth century) was Yiddish. At the Yiddish Book Center in Amherst, Massachusetts, their collection of books written in Yiddish is beginning to approach more than a million and a half of such publications.

Despite their political differences, these disparate Jewish groups were united in one way: that is, they all understood, as Jews, that the world was poisoned with anti-Semitism so that it would be impossible for any of them not to be, so to speak, political. It all meant that these people (including those on the left) would always be attuned to issues that could negatively affect their lives from the premises and behavior of authoritarianists or totalitarianists.

We, of the Ashkenazi Eastern European Yiddish group, were all proud that in the latter part of the twentieth century and early twenty-first century, this Yiddish Book Center at Amherst had amassed that huge collection of Yiddish books, and many of us Yiddish language lovers are also quite taken with the fact that Yiddish became the first fully digitized language in this new technological world of the twenty-first century. Along with this pride in Yiddish, my son Max declared in his interview with Christa Whitney of the Wexler Oral History Project of the Yiddish Book Center that "Yiddish is transcendent and didn't just belong to this time and place." I loved Max's comment. By the way, Max is a nationally and internationally known tv and radio broadcaster.

With this thumbnail historical sketch in mind, I return to my mother, who tugged at my sleeve when I was playing marbles in the street with my friends. She started dragging me another block further north from Claremont (along Washington Avenue) and across the street from the Bronx House, a community center. I asked where we were going and she said to a Yiddish shula. I told her I didn't want to go, but she insisted, and so I went. I entered a storefront and was confronted with a teacher standing at the head of a group of about twenty or so children who were more or less my age. They were sitting at desks. The teacher was speaking to them in Yiddish, and of course I understood it all. I remember that I stopped protesting—I guess because I could see that in this class I'd be a fish in water. And here was where I became the atom.

It was here, that is, that in short order I became the tip of the spear of the Yiddish movement—on the left sponsored by the IWO (International Worker's Order) and its cultural division, the JPFO (Jewish Peoples Fraternal Order)—so that I became the template, so to speak, of how this idea of Yiddish cultural continuity with respect to its young people in America was envisioned as having a reasonable chance to materialize.

How wrong in that prediction they were! What I mean is that this hope of continuity of Yiddish in America was, ultimately, an abject failure. I mean that as Rick Brookhiser said to me, "America is omnivorous to other languages and cultures."

Therefore, here and there, an organization forms that tries to rescue such continuity. And they are, in a token sense, successful. But it's in a token sense. Such an organization for the rescue of Yiddish is the Yiddish Book Center, located in Amherst, Massachusetts, which is a gargantuan success story with respect to an international ingathering of approximately a million and a half volumes of published Yiddish material, supplying full Yiddish libraries to numerous colleges, creating a Yiddish learning center, and creating a library of over one thousand interviews with people who were part of this immigrant population, along with their first-generation children as well as their grandchildren. I am happy to report that I as well as my son Max were two to be interviewed among this over a thousand.

This then became my second career. My first career was throwing and catching with Richie, and playing punchball, stickball, and softball, which I, with pleasure, pursued until I was thirteen to seventeen. Thus, this second career could be characterized as Henry Kellerman who became the progenitor of a kind of inspiration to the immigrant Jewish left-leaning public involved with declaring a Yiddish-speaking hopeful continuity of this culture—and no less, in America.

And here's how it happened.

4
Yiddish and Kamen

My Twelve-Volume Performance Archive

At this first happening, when I personally as a seven-year-old entered the new world of Yiddish school held twice a week (after regular grammar school), my mother told the teacher, Mr. Nathan Kamen, that I was two weeks shy of my seventh birthday, and asked if she could make a party for me there. She said she would bake several cakes to feed all the children—about twenty in all. Khaver Kamen readily agreed. ("Khaver" is the Hebrew word meaning "friend," used in Yiddish as the polite form of "Mister.") He then asked me a question in Yiddish, which I answered in Yiddish. He said to my mother that my Yiddish was clear and authentic and it would not be possible for anyone to think I was American-born. Then he volunteered to write a poem in Yiddish that he wanted me to recite at my birthday party in the shula. On a blank sheet of paper, he extemporaneously wrote a rhyming poem in Yiddish:

> **Hynt bin ikh zibn your alt.** (*Today I am seven years old.*)
> **Zynen fraylikh tatteh mammeh mishpokheh oon gootteh frynt.**
>   (*So my mother, father, family, and good friends are happy.*)

Khaver Kamen then told my mother to teach it to me so that I could recite it from memory at the party. To me that seemed instantly unnecessary because I had it already memorized as he was writing and saying it, and then also instantly recited it immediately after he wrote it. When I returned for the next class and again recited the lines to him, I could see he was again impressed. He continued writing:

Dank ikh eikh far'n yum-tov zayer hartzick oon fine,
   (*So I thank you for this celebration from the bottom of my heart,*)
Oon zug tsoo zikh lehrnen oon oikh a gooter bukher zine.
   (*And promise to study well and also to be a good boy.*)

Again, a few days later, at the next class, I recited the entire poem to him. Khaver Kamen took a few moments, looked at me, then turned his attention to my mother and declared in Yiddish to her, "Eekh deynk az meer hubn epess doo" (I think we have something here).

What it turned out to be, regarding "having something here," was that Khaver Kamen then had me accompany him to visit the director of the entire Yiddish organization of that particular subgroup of Yiddishists (all political persuasions of such subgroups were unified in their love of Yiddish; hence they would be referred to as "Yiddishists"—lovers of Yiddish). He introduced me to such people and said almost the same thing to them. I remember him saying with certainty: "We've got something here." And that was the beginning of my anointment as the one who was going to bring Yiddish to the burgeoning progressive Yiddish-speaking population of America, and especially as an example of how their own children could live with Yiddish as their language of cultural continuity in America.

At some point I had also known the Goodhearts, who were my parents' dear friends. It was Sam and Maria Goodheart and their gifted son Eugene, who was about seven years older than I. Eugene had been another of these special Yiddish-speaking kids who performed in Yiddish at various events. He also had that special Yiddish diction that belied his American-born identity. His was a shorter-lived Yiddish performing career than mine was. Gene eventually found his true American career as a distinguished American literary critic (professor Eugene Goodheart), and published a number of books. Gene's memoir was especially interesting to me because of the numerous parallels of our lives, and I've read and fully immersed myself in his memoir on two separate detail reads set apart by an intervening decade. He too, as I did, retained a love of Yiddish (he but somewhat at a distance, and I very interested in getting my sons to understand our roots). But apparently Gene, like I, relinquished the early persuasions regarding all the assumed political notions associated with any totalitarian system with its putative yet declared promises of fairness for all.

In this sense, reality was all too visible to us both. Under it all, I believe we were both gifted with an insatiable intellectual curiosity, along with valuable and profound encounters with many of those who were not part of our progressive entrenched home-base population: Gene with his immersion in the language of the academy and literary world, as well as those who were more so, educated in other progressive, although nonradical, cultural environments; and I in the scientific psychological and psychoanalytic world, looking inward at more ubiquitous human survival mechanisms along with my foray into the wider world of America. For me, I danced away—literally.

I believe it occurred to each of us that altruistic value was not solely the domain or purview of left-wing Yiddish-speaking individuals. Thus, regarding Yiddish, what was not yet understood by the leadership of our progressive Yiddish organization, or by any other leadership of the other political Yiddish subgroups, was that in one or two generations, American popular culture (as I've claimed) swallows it all; that is, no matter the ethnic cast of any family, descendants of such cultures will not be speaking the language of their ancestors. What this means is that essentially no ethnic population in the United States of America will have grandchildren or great-grandchildren speaking their ancestral language. And that includes those in America who are here from all the other continents—including those speaking Spanish or any of the Asian tongues. The only exceptions to this phenomenon of the erasure of ancestral languages in America are in those subgroups that are outliers, such as Orthodox groups or those that keep themselves deliberately encased and thus isolated in subgroup, sect-like compartments. The joke is: What do you call someone who knows three foreign languages? The answer: Trilingual. The second question is: What do you call someone who knows two foreign languages? The answer: Bilingual. The third question is: What do you call someone who knows no foreign languages? The answer: American!

Regarding Yiddish as a language to be counted as respectively one of the world's multitudes of languages, the Yiddish writer and poet Yuri Shul said it well in a little poem titled "Foon Land tsoo Land" (From One Country to Another). I had rendered this poem many times over decades and in all sorts of Yiddish-speaking venues. It claims the virtue of Yiddish along with all other languages. My granddaughter Esther rendered it at her secular Bat Mitzvah.

Der yam is shtill, oon eekh bime breg (*The ocean is calm and I'm at the shore*)
Loif nokh der vitekite mit mine blick (*I chase the distance with my glance*)
Oon four mit yeder shif aveck (*And with every ship I leave*)
Oon koom mit yeder shif tsoorik (*And with every ship, return*)

Der yam is shtill, oonee eekh bine breg (*The ocean is calm and I'm at the shore*)
Farvarf foon land tsoo land a brick (*I build from land to land a bridge*)
Oon trug a groos aheen aveck (*And carry a greeting to all there*)
Oon brayng a groose foon dort tsoorik (*And bring a greeting from there to here*)

Der yam is shtill, oon eekh bime breg (*The ocean is calm and I'm at the shore*)
Nem oif foon yedn lannd zine klang (*I hear the song of all the lands*)
Oon zing mine Eeiddish leed arine (*And I sing my Yiddish song along*)
In khor foon veltlekhn gezang (*In the chorus of all the world's songs*)

My Yiddish teacher, Mr. Nathan Kamen, who started me on my Yiddish performing career in 1945 when I was seven years old. I dedicated my book *Curing Psychological Symptoms* to him. In the dedication I wrote: "To Nathan Kamen, teacher, dear friend, great pathfinder." I loved Nathan Kamen. He was clearly one of the most important influences of my life.

Me at age twelve in 1950, at age seventeen in 1955, and at age seventy-five in 2013.

My identification and love of my parents was what started me on this performing career—along with my love of Khaver Nathan Kamen, the Yiddish teacher into whose class I was originally delivered when I was seven years old. Yet that connection was not all of it. What I mean is that I began to notice and to feel that I had virtuosity in delivering the message of such Yiddish progressive content which I was consistently conveying to like-minded audiences.

I could feel this virtuosity as though it was a strong muscle that needs to seek its expression, in the sense of the strength and art inherent in how the rendering of the poem or prose is done. It's kind of like an addiction that concert violinists or pianists or other instrumentalists have. They have this addiction (or need to perform at a high virtuosic level) because they learned to do what they do by a series of successive approximations over many years—and then they find that they need to do it again and again because it's wonderful to be able to give the artful gift. Then the venues in which one performs in this way begin, in time, to multiply, so that eventually greater and greater experience across decades ensues.

In my case, these venues included every major stage in New York City prior to the construction and debut of Lincoln Center for the Performing Arts. By the time Lincoln Center became a fact of New York City geography and culture, I had already made an acute retreat from my consistent contribution to the Yiddish cultural world. This meant that I began this second career at the age seven, continued till seventeen, and essentially from that point on began to reduce what had been my unabated participation. In that first decade my performance total

New York Times and *Herald Tribune* notices of 1955.

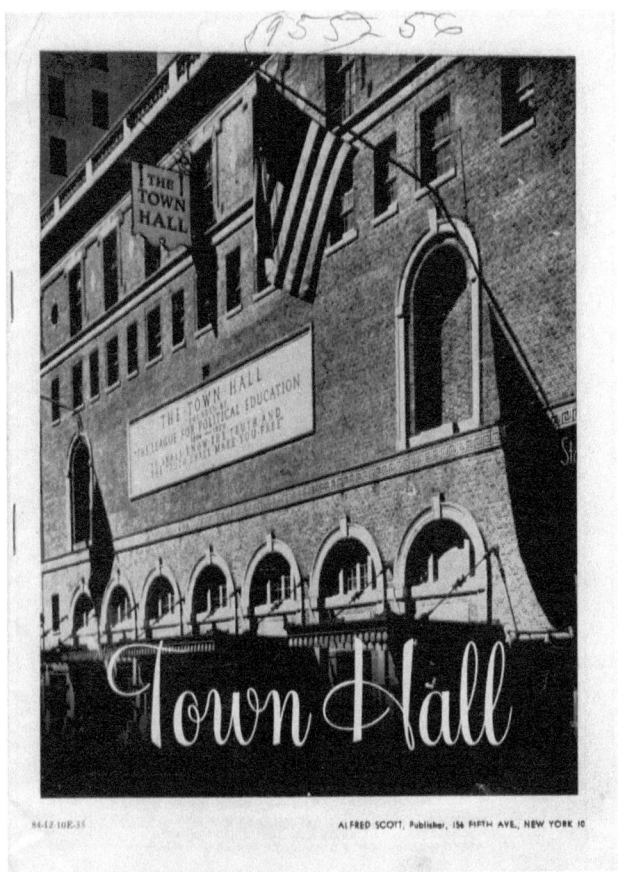

Town Hall playbill of 1955.

included about seventy or more performances per year, for a ten-year count of approximately seven hundred or so performances.

As stated, it was a ten-year cascade of performances in all major venues in New York City, as well as appearances in other cities, such as in various cities of the Northeast as well as the ones I've cited earlier like Los Angeles, Philadelphia, and Miami. These venues in New York City included Town Hall, Carnegie Hall, the old Metropolitan Opera House, the Grand Ballroom of the Waldorf Astoria, the old Madison Square Garden, Brooklyn Academy of Music, Bronx Winter Garden, Carl Fisher Concert Hall, as well as all other major and notable arenas of the city, such as the vast venue of Manhattan Center Hall.

All of it, for example, included theater performances like with Maurice

Brooklyn Academy of Music playbill of 1962.

Schwartz (the most important Yiddish performing personality in America) at the Second Avenue Theatre, and at the Barbizon Plaza Theatre with the Yiddish Ensemble Theatre. Over the years and in most of these venues, I appeared multiple times.

The nature of many of these performances included my participation as narrator of a cantata, which means that I was the leader of an organized performance comprised of a narrative piece of music for voices with instrumental accompaniment, typically with solos, chorus, and orchestra. At times such an event was devoted to honoring a great Yiddish literary figure, or at other times in an annual event such as a commemorative event. An example of such an event was a memo-

With Maurice Schwartz in the play "Competitors" (Kunkorentn) at the 2nd Ave. Theatre, New York City, 1949.

rial or commemoration of the Warsaw Ghetto uprising. This particular event was held in the late 1940s, to a capacity audience in the old Madison Square Garden of a touch under twenty thousand people. Incidentally, it was at this event that, for the first time ever, I felt rattled onstage.

The issue at this event was that when I walked up to the microphone to speak, Madison Square Garden was filled to capacity, and was dark except for the spotlight directed at the stage. Suddenly what struck me were the reflections of light coming from all over the audience based on whatever metal was visible on anyone's clothing. This meant that I was seeing the reflection of light on metal buttons, or tie clasps, or whatever was reflecting light, so that I was confronted with what looked like thousands of fireflies flitting in an irrepressible random dance. It was giving me a disorienting and distracting sense, and it was what rattled me. But the audience was silent, and the contrast between what I was seeing with respect to those flitting fireflies and what I was hearing—the deafening silence—was what was unsettling.

Playbill for the opening performance of Rivals at the Second Avenue Theatre, December 15, 1949, when I was eleven years old.

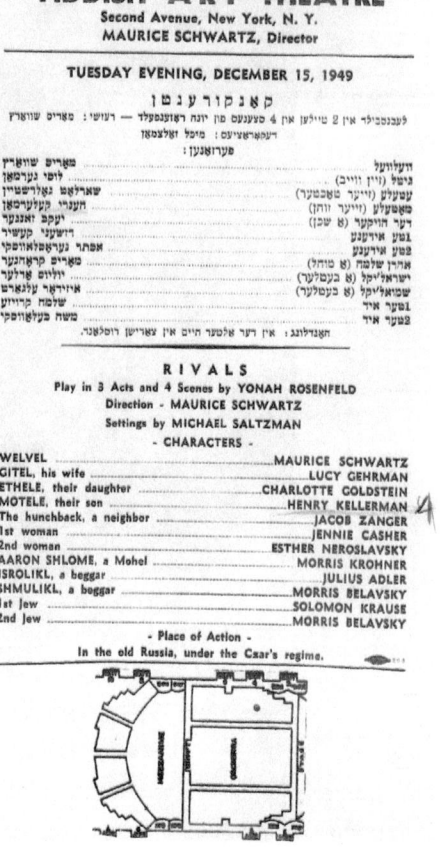

Suddenly and seemingly out of nowhere, I heard from the audience what was definitely a man coughing once and then loudly clearing his throat. Yes, it was unmistakably my father. I was absolutely sure it was him. And it was hearing that it was him that automatically and instantly settled me down. My father was an honest man, so that there was no artifice in him. This also meant that when he needed, for example, to clear his throat, he would do so without hesitation no matter the environment—such as in a packed and silent Madison Square Garden.

Then with certainty I began presenting my part in the program. You see, I knew beyond a shadow of a doubt that although my mother was the major force in the family, it was my father who was my strength.

I stared into the darkness of this standing-room-only darkened arena and slowly, but with deliberate intonation, began. Here is a snippet of the narration in Yiddish transliteration and in translation. It is a poem by Binem Heller titled "In the Warsaw Ghetto Is Now the Month of Nissan" (the month when the Jews came out of Egypt).

In Varshever Ghetto is itzt khoidish Nissan.
(In the Warsaw Ghetto it is now the month of Nissan.)
Foon shukhn tzoo shukhn vert ibergegebn,
(The word is passed from neighbor to neighbor,)
Dos Nazisheh bloot zul nisht oifhern geesn,
(That Nazi blood should not stop flowing,)
Kulzman s'vet a Eed in der Ghetto nokh lebn.
(Even if there is only one Jew remaining in the Ghetto.)

As a twelve-year-old, and with my strength and conviction of delivering these lines, is an example of how I was embedded and infused with the idea and feeling of never yielding to tyranny, and especially to the sense I took from it that Jews needed to fight and were not to be passive. This is an example of how my acquaintance with such material was an emotional world different even from those friends of mine in the left-progressive shula movement who were also familiar with the historical persecution of Jews. The difference is that I was steeping in the soup in which my understanding became emotionally knitted with steel yarn.

With respect to the variety of cantata performances at which I participated, it was the musical virtuoso Maurice Rauch who conducted these programs, which were performed each year either in Carnegie Hall or Town Hall. Each of these presentations would contain a literary script, usually written by Itche Goldberg, who was also the director and leader of this Yiddish cultural organization. Edith Segal was the one to choreograph when dances were required. Participating at these presentations were two or three Metropolitan Opera singers, a noted pianist, a hundred-voice chorus, and I narrating it all—in Yiddish. In addition to these performances, I was also called upon to appear at what were referred to as branches of the broad shula movement, and even its sister associated organizations of the left-leaning progressive Yiddish cultural outlets such as reading circles, meetings designed to plan future events, and even typical Friday night scheduled get-togethers of what was referred to as Yiddish clubs.

In fact, I was in such demand that there were many such Friday nights when I performed in the Bronx starting at 7 p.m., was then shuttled to Manhattan for a performance at about 8:30 p.m., and then also shuttled to Brooklyn for a final performance at about 9:30 or 10 p.m. I would usually and finally be home in the Bronx somewhat before midnight. It was a whirlwind, and these trifectas occurred often. What I remember about these multiple evening excursions was the driver of the car who was getting me from borough to borough (Bronx, Manhattan, Brooklyn) on such a Friday evening. He was typically a short, elderly Jewish man who would be straining to see over the steering wheel in order to approximate the road in front of him. Each of these drivers spoke with an exaggerated English/Yiddish accent. There were several different elderly men who shared this responsibility of getting me to these venues—and on time.

I have no memory of ever having a conversation with any of them while we were existing in our trajectory and hopefully aiming toward our destinations. I seem to remember rehearsing to myself and working through in my mind how I would decide to phrase certain things with respect to accenting them and/or pacing them, and/or oscillating them. All of the material was serious and related to Jewish history, discrimination, and mistreatment of Jews, to the Holocaust, the Warsaw Ghetto, the Spanish Inquisition, the Maccabean revolt, and in contrast also concerning the need for peace and understanding in the world.

So it was not that I only proclaimed the bitterness of oppression or the need to fight. Some of the material that interested these people concerned issues of love and peace—although in the context of overcoming oppression of any people. For example, the following is a little excerpt from a poem by the writer Sorah Barkan. Her poem is called "Faygalakh" (Birdies):

Hoikh oif mine dakh, voinen faygalakh a sakh
   (*High on my roof there live many little birds*)
In aynem vee breeder oon shvester. (*In a sense like sisters and brothers.*)
Doorkh freemorgn dem shtiln, nemen zay shpeeln
   (*In the early quiet morning they being to play*)
Inaynem vee ayn groiser orkester. (*Together like one great orchestra.*)

Ikh derher zayer nign dem zeesn. (*I hear their sweet hymn.*)
Verter nem ikh tzoo dem shrybn. (*I begin to compose words to it.*)
Dee moozick oon grammen veb ikh tsuzamen
    (*The music and grammar I weave together*)
mine leed zul oif aybik farblybn. (*So that my song will be forever memorialized.*)

Zingen leeder nyheh, dee foigl getryheh (*These loyal brethren sing new songs*)
Bagreesn dee boimer oon bloomen. (*That greet the flowers and trees—*)
Azoi vee tsoo a Kalleh—farnoign zikh alleh (*As to a bride they all bow*)
In a karahoud aroomgenoomen. (*And in a circle around, embrace.*)

Ven rabin roit-broost hut a bloi-djay gekoosht
    (*When robin red-breast kissed a blue jay*)
Hub ikh sholem gezen in zay baydn. (*I saw the peacefulness in them both.*)
Eekh bin geshtanen a shtilleh, far zay gettun tfilleh
    (*I remained still as though in prayer*)
Az a shtoorum zol zay nit tseshaidn. (*So that no storm would interfere.*)

Hoikh oif mine dakh voinen faygalakh a sakh
    (*High on my roof there live many little birds.*)
Zay zingen leeder foon freedn; (*They sing songs of freedom.*)
Zay viln nur shpeeln, az der mentsh zul derfeeln
    (*They only want to play so as to influence people*)
Oon trakhtn foon leebeh, sholem, oon freedn.
    (*That these people should feel and think—of love, peace, and freedom.*)

Thus, this was an example of both sides of what had so importantly influenced me. On the one hand, there was the spirit of rebellion against injustice (which made me angry about such injustice, and put me on the side of Malcolm X). On the other hand, there was the spirit of imagining peace in the world and agreeableness among people (which mollified my anger, and simultaneously put me on the side of Martin Luther King, Jr.).

Each of these appearances lasted twenty minutes or so, in which I would simply convey in my delivery of the material the meanings of various literary forms—poems, essays, excerpts from books. From the age of seven to twelve I would render such material from memory, and then from twelve to seventeen, as the material became more and more complex, I would read rather than do it all from memory. And incidentally, wherever I could, I would clip photos of these writers of such poems and prose and paste them onto the material I was reading. I loved seeing the faces of the authors of such material as I was performing their words and works. My favorite photo was that of the beautiful and soulful Dora Teitelbaum, who wrote a heartbreaking poem of an orphaned boy called "Shmooleek" (Samuel).

Many authors of books written in Yiddish would send me books they had published and would ask me to include, in my repertoire, parts of their works—which they would indicate by marking sections they felt would be effective for me to read. These authors would inscribe something of appreciation to me on the inside cover page of the book—and because of my dramatic presentation of their work, I began to know many of them personally.

Eventually, when I was already in my early seventies, I created a twelve-volume archive of all of my work. One of these volumes contains quite a large sample of such inscriptions on books that were sent to me. In this particular volume of my archive, I include excerpts and facsimiles of the front cover of each book, the title, the author's name, the inscription to me on the inside cover, and the date of publication (that is to say, a copy of the copyright page).

When I was a child, growing more and more into my role as the "tip of the spear," the task of organizing all of this material into a scrapbook soon became impossible for my mother to undertake. The material was massive and growing exponentially, and it seems to me that she must have felt that this avalanche was quickly becoming more than she could handle. Therefore, all of this material wound up in three large suitcases and three plastic bags, randomly stuffed and therefore minus any consideration of chronology of events or of the unity of germane categories. This particular treasure trove of suitcases and plastic bags languished literally for decades in repositories such as basement storage facilities, then later in closets of apartments, and still later stored under beds.

I knew that someday I would need to collect it all and construct more than just a simple scrapbook. When I was in my very early seventies—probably in 2005 or 2006—and after I had finished writing a book, I kind of knew it was time. I retrieved the suitcases and plastic bags and emptied all of the material contained in these golden receptacles onto a huge and wide dining room table—a table that could seat twelve to fourteen people. The material occupied the entire table and was piled in tiers—stack after stack after stack. Then I went to work.

Gulp—it soon became apparent that what had been three plastic bags was now two plastic bags. After carefully sifting through all of the material on the table, it further became clear that the one plastic bag missing was the one packed with material from when I was seven and eight years old—when I began this career. Yet, here and there, material that had been mixed into the other plastic bags and suitcases was where material that was dated 1945 and 1946 in fact still survived—although not in any sense voluminous for those initial years.

It took me six months of solid work—working approximately five hours per day, three or four days a week—to complete the task. As a psychologist/psychoanalyst/author, my professional private practice was at that point in my life a three-half-days-per-week office responsibility. All of the other time was spent constructing the archive. And it was an archive that ended up as a ten-volume collection on DVD (although in the original pasteup its bulk made it a total of twelve volumes).

This entire archive is now in the permanent collection of the New York Public Library's Dorot Division, devoted to Yiddish performance art. ("Dorot" is the Hebrew word for "generations.") The archive was also accepted by the YIVO Institute for Jewish Research in New York City. This organization acts as a repository for millions of print material, letters, and all else related to the art, history, and culture of the Eastern European Jews. My archive is also part of the archival collection of the Yiddish Book Center, in Amherst, Massachusetts (the Yiddish-language collection and educational institution mentioned earlier).

The table of contents of the original twelve-volume archive (transformed into a ten-volume set when digitized) is here listed as it was in the bulk form of the archive, in the original pasteup set of twelve volumes.

Volumes 1, 2, and 3 are devoted to reviews and presented chronologically, starting in 1945 when I was seven years old. My mother had clipped all the reviews in which I was mentioned. Specifically, what she clipped was the review of the entire event. She would indicate with a red mark where in the review of the event my name appeared. In this way, my archive contains a history of Yiddish progressively "inked" culture of the last half of the twentieth century and into the early first phase of the twenty-first century. These volumes also contain playbills.

Volume 4 contains only advertisements of each event (also chronologically listed) in which my name (as well as others listed) is included as part of the printed program.

Volumes 5 and 6 are devoted to letters of appreciation I received throughout the years, from the widest array of organizations.

Volume 7 contains my entire repertoire of material, including prose and poetry.

Volumes 8, 9, and 10 are collections of all the scripts in which I narrated shows of cantatas and other forms of performance that were always presented at major venues such as at Carnegie Hall, Town Hall, Manhattan Center, the Waldorf Astoria's Main Ballroom, Metropolitan Opera House, and even, as I've noted, at Madison Square Garden (for a Warsaw Ghetto memorial). Sample playbills of dramatic theater (stage plays) are included.

Volume 11 contains inscriptions to me by Yiddish authors on their published books. These authors would point out which parts of the book might be suitable for me to consider using in my repertoire. I had about ninety such books, and the archive contains a sample of about a bit more than a third.

Volume 12 is a compilation of biographical material, family photos, copies of diplomas and achievements from the shulas, awards for my dramatic contributions, music I composed to the author I. E. Ronch's poem "Hent" (Hands), essays I've written concerning Yiddish in America which were delivered at conferences about the state of Yiddish in America, and finally, material regarding my parents—also representing work and essays that they had done. My father was an excellent writer and storyteller, and my mother was, as you already know, a great singer—"geshmack" is the Yiddish word meaning something like "taste" and "charm"—soulful. With that smoky alto of hers, had she been born in America she could have been a hell of a torch singer. Also as noted earlier, she was a great dancer, and she was the one to help me understand how to present material to the kinds of audiences for whom I performed. This meant utilizing high-caliber literary material for a sophisticated, progressive European immigrant Yiddish audience—with an acquired American sensibility.

The entire twelve-volume original pasteup bulk archive is 1,143 pages in length.

5

Never Say Never

Dancing Away

In addition to my slice of Yiddish left-leaning ideological audiences, the Zionist Yiddish-speaking groups also heard about this child who was called a "vunderkind," and they also contacted me, so that during my full career as a Yiddish cultural performer, they too frequently called upon me to perform at their Zionist events, including one for the Hagganah (the Jewish fighting force) in Sharon Springs, New York. This event called out onto the streets of Sharon Springs an estimated fifteen thousand Jewish people in support of the creation of the State of Israel, and I was one of about a half dozen luminaries on the program. The event took place in the summer of 1946, when I was eight years old. The official notification of this event—a playbill—is included in the archive and is one of the pieces that survived the disappearance of one of the plastic bags.

Interestingly, the so-called progressive, left-leaning Jews were not quite entirely politically supportive of the Zionist agenda regarding the fight for the State of Israel, and yet in their hearts they couldn't resist supporting it. Most of this progressive Jewish population were not members of Zionist organizations. I was discerningly different. Much of the material I presented at performances was very connected to oppression of Jews—especially the oppression and genocide of Jews during the Holocaust. As a young child, it would have been impossible for me not to be swallowed up by the truth of "the unarmed Jew" and consequences thereof.

Thus, when it came to supporting anything regarding Jews who were fighting, I was for it—Zionist or not. And to this day, and as a Jewish atheist, I remain

```
              UNITED JEWISH APPEAL - MASS MEETING

        Sharon Springs, New York    July 21, 1948   8:30 PM
                         IMPERIAL BATHHOUSE


                              PROGRAM

        1.  National Anthem and Hatikvoh, led by the combined
            Sharon Springs orchestras.

        2.  Invocations by: Father John Casey, St. Mary's
                            Catholic Church, Sharon Springs, NY

                            Rabbi Solomon Sigal, Congregation
                            Sons of Jacob, Springfield, Mass.

        3.  Prayer for the Dead; intoned by Cantor David Brodsky
                            Cantor, Jewish Communal Center,
                            Brooklyn, New York

        4.  Overture:       Combined Sharon Springs Orchestras,
                            Conducted by Yasha Kreitzberg.

        5.  "My People Israel": Recitation in Jewish by
                            Master Henry Kellerman.

        6.  Eli Eli          Sung by Mrs. Celia Stern.

        7.  Address by Mr.  Louis Saphian, United Jewish Appeal
                            guest speaker.
            - - - - - - - - - -
        8.  Selections from Grand Opera by the combined Sharon
                            Springs Orchestras.

        9.  Kol Nidre        Bernard Kugel, Violinist

        10. Play Fiddle Play  Special arrangement by Hotel
                            Adler Orchestra. Henry Nelson
                            conducting.
```

United Jewish Appeal for Hagganah playbill of 1948,
in Sharon Springs, New York.

committed to fighting back. In this sense, and as part of my understanding of history, it becomes clear that Jews cannot engage in passive resistance.

So to be clear about it, if someone attacks you because you're a Jew, you need to answer in kind and hit back—or, if necessary, fire that gun. That's right. I said it: Fire it! So you see, when you're a child infused with the memory of all of this helplessness in the Jewish historical experience, and additionally as an American, and additionally like having a father like mine, and in addition growing up on the streets of the Southeast Bronx of New York City, the answer to being attacked is, for me: it is not possible to be passive.

So when my first encounter with any Zionist organization was for the objective of, no less, supporting the Hagganah, I realized that my interest in Jewish strength triumphed over whatever was the agenda of any so-called progressive political stance. Even though I didn't fully understand what the objections were of the progressives regarding this State of Israel situation, I instinctively knew I was with Jews arming themselves and, if necessary, fighting—and, by all means, winning. What I did realize was that the progressives were always championing those who had been historically oppressed, and so my sense of it all was that the oppressed plight of Arab people (including Palestinians) was not to be ignored.

However, in my guts I knew that even if that were true, nothing could place in second position the plight of Jews who had survived the Holocaust and who were determined to have a homeland—and further, to be armed to the teeth. To say the least, I was for it!

I've mentioned the issue of winning because the history and literature of the Jewish experience exposed me necessarily (and truthfully) to understanding such experience of Jews: fighting and winning has always meant survival, while fighting and losing has correspondingly and fervently meant helplessness and explicit extinction.

So who were these people, these Jewish people whose shoes were stacked higher than the Alps? Here is Moishe Shulshtayn's part answer to that question, as I continue to quote, chronologically, stanzas from his poem " Ikh Hub Gezen a Barg" (I Saw a Mountain):

Hert ois, hert ois dem marsh (*Hear it, hear the march*)
Hert ois dem heemen, (*Hear the hymn,*)
Foon sheekh farblibineh, der letzter simmen.
   (*Of these remaining shoes—the last sign.*)
Foon klayn oon grois, foon kind oon kate
   (*Of those small and large, of shackled children*)
A varreh far dee ryan far dee pourrn, (*Material for the rows and pairs,*)
A varreh far dee doiress, far dee yourrn, (*Material for the generations and years,*)
Dee sheekh armay, zee gate oon gate. (*The army of shoes continues to march.*)

This following poem is the answer. It is a song written by Hirsh Glick, who was a partisan and escaped the Vilna Ghetto during World War II. He was twenty-four years old, and was eventually caught and killed. His poem "Zug Nit Kaynmul" (Never Say Never) became the Jewish secular national anthem of World War II. It was sung here in America at most Jewish memorial events. It was translated by Aaron Kremer, a noted translator of Yiddish poetry. Here are sample stanzas:

Zug nit kaynmul az doo gayst dem letsn veg
(Never say there is only death for you)
Ven himlen blayeneh farshteln bloyeh teg.
(Though leaden skies may be concealing days of blue.)
Vayl koomen vet nukh oondzer oisgebenkteh shuh
(Because the hour we hungered for is near:)
S'vet a poik ton oonzer trot meer zaynen duh.
(Beneath our tread the earth shall thunder: We are here!)

Another stanza of this poem contains a reference to what can be done in the midst of all this horror:

Geshribn iz dus leed mit bloot oon nit mit bly
(This song was written with blood and not with lead.)
S'iz nit a leed foon Zamerfoigl oif der fry
(It's not a song that summer birds sing overhead.)
Nor s'hut a folk tzvishn fallndickeh vent
(It was a people among toppling barricades,)
Dus leed gezungen mit naganen in dee hent.
(That sang this song of ours with pistols and grenades.)

Thus, as the years passed, I had two distinct political audiences: the progressive Yiddish-speaking audience and the Zionist Israeli fighters for a Jewish state. In the years since I was a performer for both of these audiences, I also now realize that I'm not always in agreement with the Israeli state. However, I'm also from time to time not in agreement fully with the politics of the Arab coalition or with the United States either. But totalitarian states are clearly the worst.

The main point about the USA, however, and as I've said earlier, is that America gave my parents a chance, and so I've always loved America despite, for example, America's original sin of the stain of murder, torture, and racism toward Black people, as well as the overall genocide against Native Americans. The point here is that we all know that no matter the nature of the state, corruption, disgraceful behavior, and political conflict exists everywhere. To our misfortune, these kinds of horrors also happened and continue to happen here in America to all sorts of groups (especially toward Black people), and now in the twenty-first century to immigrant groups as well.

Thus, rationalization or not, I'm going to support the Jewish state—also in the hope that it will be a light unto nations. And I must say that in the major negotiations with its neighbors, as well as with its Palestinian indigenous population, the Palestinian leadership has consistently snatched defeat of proposed treaties for a two-state solution out of the jaws of victory! In addition, I'm going to support Jews everywhere, along with being critical when it's called for.

Some years ago, I attended a conference at YIVO (the Yiddish Institute of Knowledge or Yiddish Scientific Institute). The symposium at this conference focused on spies in America in the service of the Soviet Union roughly related to the 1940s and 1950s. The alleged reported factoid was that of all the spies apprehended, I believe they said that about 46 percent were Jewish. That percentage is enormous, but no one attempted to ask: Why is that? Why is that number so high? Isn't that a profound indictment of Jews generally? Doesn't that support all of the nonsense of how the Jews are not to be trusted? The truth is that I became incensed that none of the professional presenters bothered to tackle the issue of the reason for it all.

Since then it has been known that the most disgraceful spy of the FBI as well as the one from the CIA were both Christians. Robert Philip Hanssen was a high-level FBI agent who spied for the Russians and is considered the one responsible for the worst intelligence disaster in United States history. Simultaneous to his spying activity, he was an active member of Opus Dei, the most sobering sect of the Catholic Church. Members practice what is known as corporal mortification—self-inflicted punishment meant to create suffering of the self—essentially to nullify sin.

Parallel to all of this, Hanssen perverted his relationship with his wife by getting his friend to secretly observe Hanssen and his wife in their sexual relationship. Hanssen is serving a life term in a federal supermax prison without any chance for parole.

The CIA counterpart to Hanssen's crime was Aldrich Hazen Ames. Ames was a double agent who was responsible for spying for the Soviet Union and later for Russia. He compromised more highly classified CIA assets (meaning people), which resulted in their deaths, than anyone else. Until Hanssen of the FBI was detected, Ames of the CIA was the most important spy ever caught. Ames is serving life imprisonment without parole in a federal medium-security prison.

I cite these cases, who were not given any death sentence, as compared to the Rosenbergs, who were both also caught for spying but were executed despite the undeniable fact that what the Rosenbergs gave the Soviets concerned small matters of mechanical engineering information and nothing about atomic bomb information—about which they were not even in a position to know—in addition to not having anyone else compromised or killed.

Despite that, I definitely reject what the Rosenbergs did. Nevertheless, to execute them was nothing less than a misguided act and a tragedy. I leave it to the reader to ask whether the Rosenberg capital punishment case was inspired by the eruption of Cold War fever over any other concern—along, perhaps, with the fact that they were Jews!

Now back to the symposium and the ostensible claim that a large percentage of spies were tabulated to have been Jews. At the Q&A after all the discussion, I raised my hand and asked the question that was hanging in the air like a lead balloon—defying gravity. There was no answer, and the moderator indicated they were going to end the meeting. I wouldn't let him finish his sentence and said that I would like to try to answer that question. The moderator didn't stop me.

As I started to answer it, I could feel I was angry because of the pejorative implication that remained concerning Jews. Therefore, in my "boogie-down Bronx attitude" (Parish, 1984), I started on the high ground with respect to Jews because I knew those on the dais, who were all, I believe, Jewish, wouldn't like anything that could be interpreted as some kind of theme that made Jews seem superior. In that case, I said:

"It's true that at the very top of each and every profession there are an inordinate number of Jewish people—at the very top. That goes from engineering to medicine, from the legal profession to the specific sciences, and from the humanities to the arts, including of course those who are our literary geniuses, as well as easily eighty percent of musical composers and lyricists who are mainly responsible for the American Songbook as well as for the creation of Broadway and Hollywood. I believe what this all means is that in Jewish culture exists the implicit mandate of 'contribution.'"

I paused for a moment.

"Furthermore," I continued, "therefore if there is a cause that Jews feel is worthy and valuable, they probably would want to contribute. And since there are an inordinate number of Jewish people at the top of any field of endeavor, this might explain the inordinate percentage number of spies who may have been Jewish—because deeply etched within Jewish consciousness is the message that doing something seen as 'of value' and in addition seems something greater than the self, then participating in such an endeavor may seem to be an important contribution."

And with that little interposed moment, I stopped. The response I got was no response. However, at the end of the discussion, when the audience was filing out of the auditorium, a group of about five or six people gathered around me and congratulated me on my little speech. What I didn't say then, but now wished I had said, was that it was a Jewish Navy admiral who was the only one in the United States government to argue for the construction of an atomic fleet of submarines patrolling beneath the Atlantic and Pacific Oceans—each of which would carry a large number of atomic missiles, and which in fact would make the United States invulnerable to attack from any other state. And, yes, it was a Jewish man who made it all possible—Admiral Hyman Rickover.

In this respect, I become incensed when Jews are directly accused or even implicated in wrongdoing unless I research the situation and either confirm or reject the accusation. And this applies also to lots of criticisms of Israel—much but not all of which, I believe, is anti-Jewish.

I should pause for a moment here and say that the Palestinians very definitely should have their own state, but I think the Palestinians are waiting too long to accept compromises, and the longer they wait, the less the opportunity becomes viable. So far, and at the last minute, they've walked out of two out of two compromise negotiations *to which they had already, seemingly at least, partially agreed.* The program for negotiation presented by President Trump that was composed by Jared Kushner was, in my opinion, a nonstarter. Yet, I would have hoped that the Palestinians would sit with the Israelis and adjust it all. It needs to be fair all around. With this overall issue, I bid my far-left friends a farewell.

Also, in this sense, I should also say that the six to seven million Jews killed in the Holocaust for sure took with them, at the very least, what many people feel was the cure for a variety of diseases, including cancer. Given the enormous contribution that Jews have made in the discovery of cures to diseases, I believe it is not unreasonable to think that the cure for any number of diseases lies in the ashes of Nazi crematoria and in the killing fields of Eastern European shtetls.

And by the way, who were these Nazis? They and their families had been churchgoers who were fed the utterly ridiculous blood libel, which told a preposterous story of Jews drinking the blood of Christian children. And apparently: They believed it! They wanted to believe it! They believed it! They wanted to believe it!

Yes, they were taught to want to believe it. And the Vatican echo that the Jews killed Christ still vibrates throughout Christianity. For example, Pope Paul VI continued giving sermons during the time when the Church was seeking to renounce Jewish accusation of deicide (that of declaring that the Jews killed Christ). But this pope refused to renounce such accusation. And the unmitigated answer to the question as to whether Jews could ever believe this about any other group who are accused of blood drinking is beyond ridiculous! Yet, in the mid-twentieth century, in the town of Massena, New York, the disappearance of a girl was attributed to Jews who were accused of such a blood libel—that they killed her to drink her blood.

Since I feel myself to be a soldier in the service of protecting Jewish integrity, my fervor regarding Israel was added to in my contribution to the Zionist agenda, although I was not in any way a committed Zionist. In my performance archive are included letters of appreciation sent to me after each of my performances over all of the twenty years of my active as well as less-than-active participation. These letters of appreciation that I received occupy two full volumes in this performance archive and of course include all letters I received from progressive organizations as well as from the Zionists. Also included in this archive is the fact of my being written into Israel's Golden Book of important contributors to the cause of statehood, as well as a multiplicity of trees planted in my name by such organizations.

Referring to my performance archive, I say "active" and "less-than-active participation" because although after I turned seventeen I had relinquished my typical availability for such work, nevertheless as a result of the enormous numbers of special people I had met, I still needed, correspondingly, to do special favors for those particular individuals, and therefore I continued to perform for about another ten years, until I was twenty-seven. Thus, from age seven to seventeen was when I was in the eye of the hurricane, doing about seventy or more performances per year. The next decade, from age seventeen to age twenty-seven, I significantly reduced my participation as the go-to person of this Yiddish movement (both from the progressives as well as from the Zionists), so that from seventeen to twenty-seven about six or seven or somewhat more performances per year could be counted. I was essentially retired from this second career.

In contrast to performing as a solo performer, I was also active as an actor in plays, as for example on the Yiddish stage in 1949 when I was eleven years old, with Maurice Schwartz at the Second Avenue Theatre, or with the American Yiddish Ensemble at the Barbizon Plaza Theatre, in the play *The Sonnenbruch Family* in 1951 when I was thirteen years old.

My theater work is reviewed in the multiple-volume collection of *The Lexi-

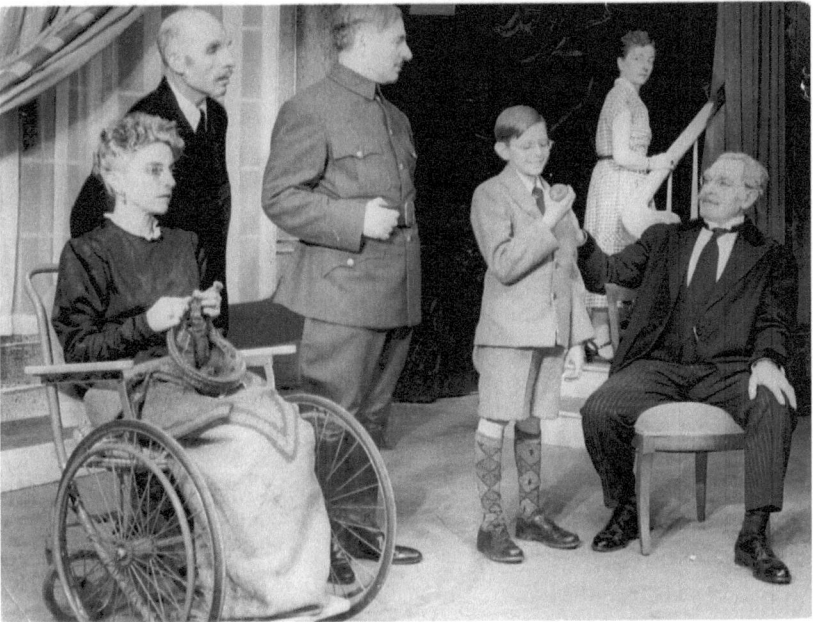

Stage play: *The Sonnenbruch Family*. A play in three acts. I played two parts. In the first act I was a Jewish boy caught in the woods by a Nazi soldier, and eventually shot. In the third act I was the son of a Nazi officer (which was not my favorite thing). The play opened in 1951 and ran for sixteen weeks.

con of Yiddish Theatre, Vol. 6, edited by Z. Zylbercweig (1969). Yet, even beyond my twenty-seventh year, and to this very day, the only venues that remain are memorial services of people I had known and/or whose families would request that I read something in Yiddish at funerals or at such memorial services. Thus, in the past more than fifty years, I have now read to audiences at about twenty of such events.

The one memorial service that gave me the most difficulty was the one for my beloved first Yiddish teacher when I had turned seven years of age—my Yiddish teacher Khaver Nathan Kamen. I recited two poems at his memorial service and in both cases needed to hold down my terribly choked feelings.

Taking a Breath

Now, for a moment—for you, my reader, to take a breath—meaning to move for a moment away from very serious, ponderous matters, I'll briefly report on a rather special little contrasting career that was also ongoing during all of this time, especially crystallized at its start when I was about age fifteen. As it turned out, I was a naturally gifted social dancer. This means a ballroom dancer. Never having taken a single dance lesson, all I needed was to see the dance and/or hear the rhythm/melody of the dance and I could dance it naturally. It wasn't that I was good at it. Rather, the truth is I was really *very* good at it.

Through the years, people have approached me at affairs where dancing was the point of the event, such as at dance ballrooms, and have said the same thing to me: "You dance like Fred Astaire, and you look like Frank Sinatra." I've heard that over and over. I was thin like Sinatra, and had that similar Sinatra smile. And people would comment on it. As for Fred Astaire, the best I can say about myself is that I'd never taken tap-dance lessons, so that I can assure everyone that Astaire remains incomparable.

At one point when I was about eleven years old, I was rehearsing for a play at the LeTang Studios in Manhattan. We were rehearsing on a high floor, but I kept hearing great swing music and tap dancing coming from two floors below. At the break I dashed down the stairs to the second floor and saw several boys and girls tap dancing to that great swing music which I found irresistible. Yes, I loved and knew I'd be good at it—that I'd be a perfect person to learn it.

I asked my father if he and my mother would give me such tap-dancing lessons.

In a rare no, and with no reason to it (except his own untutored understanding of physical exertion), my father said: "It's not good for your heart." In other words, my father actually was trying to protect me, even though I was in perfect health and there was never anything wrong with my heart. Goodbye to tap dancing. Yet, as a swing lindy dancer, mambo, rumba, pachanga, and cha-cha (general salsa) dancer, as well as a beautiful waltzer, once, when I was about thirty, a man walked over to me after my partner and I had won the dance contest, and asked: "Tell me, when I try to dance, I never know where if I put my foot it will be the right place to put it. How do you know where you put your foot is the right place?" My response to his question seems to me to have been unfortunate and not meant to be as terse as I believe it was. I didn't mean it to come out that way, but I think perhaps it did come out that way. I answered: "I don't know, but wherever I put my foot, it seems to be the right place." I know it sounds dismissive and even smug, but the truth is that that was the only way I could express it because that's what faithfully reflected how I felt—and also that it was, in an automatic dancing sense, true. The greater truth is that one doesn't really dance with one's feet. It's the beat in the heart and in every fiber of your body.

Since age fifteen when I entered my first dance contest at a Jewish community center, I've entered, all told, fourteen such contests, and won them all. The last one I entered was at a hotel when on vacation. I was in my early forties. My trademark was always to give the bottle of champagne or trophy to my partner. I've never kept a single winner's prize. To me that was the cool thing to do. Coming, as I've said, from the so-called boogie-down Bronx, the cool thing to be was cool. And I could see and feel that being, walking, and talking cool had rhythm to it, so therefore, it got a hold on me and so I understood the whole "cool" thing in my bones.

In any event, I actually don't remember all my great dance partners (some of whom I simply met on a dance floor and never even exchanged names), but I do remember Judy, Iris, Deanna, Mary-Ann, Gloria, Maria, Myrna, Sue, Sandy's friend, and Helen's friend Blossom.

Again, I attribute this so-called "cool" thing to my roots on Claremont Parkway, along with a healthy boost from Sinatra, Astaire, and Brando (in that order of greatest influence). That sort of influence was also born from my diverse neighborhood of all the cool guys who could really play ball. It was easy for me to identify with these guys in our everyday contact because I was one of them who could play ball, and do it not just well but really, shall we say, in a way that even looked cool. And with respect to this issue of coolness, years later, when I was attending a psychoanalytic conference in New York City, a Saturday night social with a live dance band was scheduled. Of course I attended the conference but was more looking forward to the night of dancing. Linda and I attended and although Linda is not a dancer, nevertheless she would usually consent to do a foxtrot with me. It's not my favorite dance, but at least we danced.

We were sitting at a table for four. The man of the other couple was a well-known and respected group therapist. Unfortunately, he was suffering with some kind of crippling disease and walked with difficulty. He was actually quite compromised. I could see that his wife loved swing music because she was watching it all with great interest. One song they played was a rather slow foxtrot, so that Linda and I danced to it. When we returned to the table, the man had gone to the restroom. As we sat at the table, the woman leaned toward me and said: "You move beautifully." I knew what she meant, and I've never forgotten those few words she parenthetically said. I think I appreciated what she said because whenever I see someone who moves (dances) beautifully, I also feel like telling them so, and I usually do.

In the genesis of this issue of how to be of the "coolness" image, my father was my earliest and true identification figure. He was cool in the sense of having an unselfconsciousness about it—about himself. As I've said, I even imitated his gait, his stride, his posture, and his humor. He was without guile, and in his straightforward manner, also without artifice whatsoever.

To continue, other notable dance contests, as well as these certain dance venues, were quite famous in the decade from the 1950s to 1960s. During that time I won contests in a wide variety of venues, including two at hotels, both in Miami Beach. These also included two contests I won at Grossinger's, in the Catskill Mountains (one dancing with Myrna T. and the other with Iris). I became friends with the professional dance team of Nortie and Iris, and eventually danced with Iris, who was a fabulous ballroom dancer. After we did a swing dance and a rumba, referring to my dancing, she said to Nortie: "Silk." He nodded yes. I also won two at the Adirondacks, at a place called Golden Acres. At Golden Acres in the Adirondacks I also met Mary-Ann P., the dance director there, who is a great dancer, and we danced an awful lot. I've always enjoyed dancing with her as I always did also dancing with Judy, Maria, and Deanna. Deanna and her husband

and Linda and I were once at an affair that had a dance band. Deanna and I began doing a rumba to a great beat from a great band. Gradually, the kitchen helpers (all who happened to be Hispanic) began wandering out to watch us. One could see that they were understanding it, and loving it.

Winning of dance contests was a far distance from my Yiddish cultural environment and also from my Claremont Parkway neighborhood. Further, with respect to distance, these other environments were far afield of my High School of Music & Art life, where I was required to attend operas at the Met, as well as encouraged to attend Carnegie Hall symphonic orchestra performances. In fact, when I was in my senior year, at age seventeen, I attended fifteen Broadway stage plays in that year alone with tickets that were gifted to me by other theater people.

Interestingly (for me at least) were, shall I say, furtive assignations with girls and women who seemed to turn up wherever I went. For example, when I was about twenty-two years old, and in an impulsive moment on a Friday night, I hopped a plane at LaGuardia Airport and transported myself to Miami Beach because I knew that the Al Escobar band was playing at Harry's American Bar at the Eden Roc Hotel and I wanted to dance to guajira music.

I could do this impulsive thing because I had just finished field directing a presidential poll for a motivation/marketing group where I worked while in graduate school, paid for by the John Kennedy political organization. The Kennedys were interested in ascertaining whether Kennedy's religious affiliation as a Catholic would negatively affect his election to the presidency. I had been paid quite handsomely for this job, so that suddenly, for the first time in my life, I had spending money.

The point I'm making here is that while doing all this other dazzling stuff, it was a world where at times I would even have a flash of: "What in the world am I doing here? Do I belong here?" These were moments when I was instantly aware that my existential other life did not have the slightest resemblance or synapse with my Yiddish progressive world—where I was truly a progressive guardian at the gate of the life of Yiddish in America.

The poem by the Yiddish writer Ber Green states that which I at least knew that Jews felt—or rather that they hoped was true about the future and fate of Yiddish. It is a lengthy poem, but in one of latter stanzas, this future hope of the life of Yiddish in America is almost taken for granted as to its so-called probable achievement. The poem is titled "Mizmer Sheer L'Eedish" (The Story of Yiddish):

Eedish, lushn nekhtn, lushn hynt, lushn murgn
   (*Yiddish, language of yesteryear, language of now, language of tomorrow.*)
Geshtikt hut men dikh, dervorgn (*They choked you, they strangled you,*)
Geplukt, gematert. (*They tortured you, they depleted you.*)
Oon doo, shtraliker voonder (*But you, miraculous wonder,*)
Vee a foon hust zikh tsevlatert. (*Like a flag you unfurled freely in the wind.*)
   [Meaning the flag of Yiddish burst forth victoriously]

And despite my devotion to Yiddish, in any event, I was planning to dance to the Al Escobar guajira band. I landed, and made it in plenty of time to Harry's American Bar, located on the ground level floor of the hotel. I sat at the bar waiting for the band to end their break and start in with their great guajira sound when suddenly a woman approached me from the blind side, touched my elbow, and said, "Hank." It was my friend Gloria, who happened to be a great dancer. With my inner-circle friends, they all called me Hank. Gloria and I were actually surprised to see one another. Gloria wound up at Harry's for the same reason I did: she wanted to dance to the Escobar band. But we didn't dance very much because the event was overwhelmed by celebrities who had also attended. These included the actor Richard Conte, among others. So the audience was entranced listening to celebrities being introduced. This included Sophie Tucker, known as the "Last of the Red-Hot Mamas." Tucker took over and held forth so that the band was on a hiatus.

So we didn't dance as soon as we met at Harry's. Instead we had a long conversation while at the bar and then danced one or two dances later. I don't remember how it all ended for the evening, but we eventually bid each other farewell at about two in the morning and retired to our respective rooms. So even though Gloria was and remains a very good friend, she, along with my other good friends, were not at all familiar with my Yiddish world and knew absolutely nothing about my Yiddish performance life nor, at the time, my semi-radical political views.

I was obviously living a compartmentalized, sequestered, insular life, although at the same time, a life that was, here and there, rhapsodic—along with my wandering in what seemed like alien worlds.

6
Girls and Women

Promiscuity?

And this brings me to girls. I was always interested in girls. And I mean interested! I can remember feeling it since I was very young. Along with this, and with respect to my amalgam of qualities: innocence, worldliness, coolness, shyness, dancer, Yiddish speaker, boyish looks, and, I guess, cute, I began to notice that girls and women were attracted to me. My close friends also noticed it, and more than one of them said to me they thought it was because these girls and women wanted to mother me.

I knew that that probably wasn't the only truth (even if that might have been, perhaps, somewhat true), especially because the things these girls and women were saying to me—and actually doing—was nothing at all like that which my mother ever said to me or how she behaved toward me. These things that were said and done were sexual things with not an iota of embarrassment on their part, while whispering to me what they wanted from me and what they wanted to do with me and wanted me to do with, and to, them.

When I was nine years old and on one of the days of the Yiddish shula, a girl who was fourteen, and also a student there in an advanced class, would consistently be near me wherever it was that I moved. On one of those days when no one else was in the room, she started chasing me until I dove under a couch, thinking that we were having a game and that I was winning. To my surprise she followed me by also diving under the couch. She pinned me down, with me lying in a supine position. Then she looked at me close-up, squarely face-to-face, and with determination, planted a long kiss—lips to lips. I distinctly remember not moving. She did all the moving.

Even during my sophomore or junior year at the High School of Music & Art in New York City, one day while walking down the stairs with many other students (going from one floor to the other), while I was at the top of the stairs a blonde girl at the bottom of the stairs suddenly wheeled around, ran up the entire stairwell directly toward me, and planted a love kiss right on my lips. I could smell the bouquet of her scent (and that actually sent me), and the kiss was not a peck. It was a real, heartfelt love kiss with her full, beautiful, soft, luscious lips into it. She then quickly ran back down the stairs and disappeared. I never really knew who she was, and over the years I never could find her picture in any of the yearbooks of graduating classes of the school. And I did look for her. She may even have been a student teacher. I was never sure.

Several years later, while I was seated at a cafeteria table at the unheralded but rigorously oriented Hofstra College where I wound up going to college, she passed me by where I was sitting with my friends, spotted me, and stopped. There she was. Beautiful as ever. We talked but I don't quite remember what we talked about. I believe her name was Carol, but I'm not sure.

In addition to this up-the-stairs luscious, memorable kiss, several other similar experiences come to mind. Therefore, in my recounting of such experiences, I've included here only a rather small sample of these experiences, first with girls and then with women. For example, when I was about seventeen, a young Hispanic woman (perhaps mid- to late twenties), who was a salesperson in one of the stores in my Bronx neighborhood, walked past me on the street and delivered an unmistakably flirtatious sexual smile at me. She and I had seen one another in the street several times before that particular occasion, and each time I could see she was interested.

On this occasion she stopped me, and without any hesitation said she'd like me to take her for a drive. I told her I didn't have a car but that a friend of mine did, and would it be all right with her if he drove us? I wasn't at all embarrassed by this impending arrangement, primarily because she was knockout gorgeous and really beautifully endowed. She agreed he could drive.

My friend, Hank B., drove, but the odd thing was that an hour before Hank was to arrive, my cousin Melvin paid me a visit. I couldn't just leave him stranded because he came from Brooklyn, so lo and behold, we took Mel along. This saleswoman and I did everything we did in the back seat of Hank's Plymouth, while Hank was driving with Mel sitting in the front companion seat. Neither she nor I cared about this particular arrangement in the car.

In that same year, and on one of my visits home to the Bronx, my blood brother, Richie, and I wanted to catch a movie but our neighborhood movie theater was playing a Spanish-language double feature, so we were out of luck. However, the manager of the movie theater, who also was a beautiful Hispanic woman (about perhaps in her early thirties), walked up to us on the street. She and I had seen one another in passing several times before. She simply asked us to accompany her into the theater, which we did. She told us where to sit and she then walked to the front of the theater, climbed the steps, and disappeared into the side area of the stage behind the curtain. This was strange because we knew that she knew we didn't know Spanish.

So Richie and I sat there, not talking, just waiting for something to happen. Sure enough, a female usher came over to us and leaned directly toward me, saying that the manager wanted me to visit with her. This usher instructed me to walk up the stairs at the curtain that was drawn to the side of the stage (while the movie was playing), and to slip in on the very edge to behind the curtain. She said the manager's office door would be directly in sight. And she walked away without the slightest acknowledgment regarding what appeared to me to be the initial stage of what I could see might be then defined as an impending, again let's call it, furtive assignation.

And that's what it turned out to be. She was not at all, not in the slightest, shy about it. The unadulterated fact was that I was already a bit experienced with this sort of thing even at my newly young seventeen, but it made me feel that my burgeoning social life was taking me into untethered territory. This was also true because I could (as I was frequently told) look more like a fourteen year old when I was seventeen, so that I was kind of usually feeling mixed; that is, that on the one hand it was a bit awkward to look so young and to be in such situations, but in another way I felt I was way ahead of the game. Yet again, to me it was like alien territory, having absolutely nothing to do with home base—which was my Yiddish world.

This sort of thing made me feel as though I was living two lives—though not parallel—actually asymmetric. Again, later on, when I was about twenty-three, my friend Alex K. and I were taking in the Latin sound in various nightspots around

New York City. One of these clubs was the Seclusion Room somewhere about West 46th Street or so near Broadway in Manhattan. Playing at the Seclusion Room that particular night was one of the best guajira bands around—that same Al Escobar band—along with the Cuban singing bombshells Celia Cruz and La Lupe, both queens of Latin charanga music. Charanga music features violins and flutes along with the other instruments. It was at that club where this gorgeous Hispanic woman of about forty-five walked over to me and, without hesitation, she said, "I'm taking you home." She did, to the far East Bronx.

It was there at her apartment, while we were sitting on the carpet in her living room, that she began to start what was obviously going to be some kind of sexual vortex. At that moment, what turned out to be her son's arrival (he was about twenty-two or twenty-three) stopped what was about to happen. He entered the room and in Spanish asked her something. She answered him and then, without ever looking at me, he left. At that point I felt out of my element. I could see he was more or less my age. I immediately thought: *What the hell am I doing here? I must be living in some alternate world!*—so I then left. And for the umpteenth time over the years, I asked myself: *Home base? Where* is *that?*

In any event, this sudden approach by this woman who, in a sense, hijacked me was reenacted about thirty-five years later when I was in my late fifties. I was about to visit my parents at their apartment, but first talked to the concierge of the building. Suddenly, an African American housekeeper to one of the apartments in the building walked over, interrupted my conversation with this concierge, and bluntly said, "I need your phone number." I thought she was looking for another job, so I gave it to her. She called the next day, but it wasn't for a job.

So in my adolescent years while I was going to regular school, to shula, while at my performing in my Yiddish career, now, at this point in my early adulthood, I was immersed in my Latin and swing dancing obsession, which was in full swing; I was also, and with alacrity, having a kind of secret and yet not-so-secret life with girls my own age and with women older than I, and then again, much older than I—also into their thirties as well as forties, and older.

I hadn't even seen it as an unusual phenomenon or that it was, in a sense, becoming a kind of habitual circumstance of my life, until one day one of my pals, another Hank (Hank H., a Navy veteran) identified it for me as something I was experiencing, insofar as he put it: "It's easy for you with married women—they're throwing themselves at you." It was only then that I began to also see it that concrete way. Hank H. and I had become great friends and we, along with other pals like Arty, Alex, Gene, and Hank B., became a social contingent connecting with all kinds of other groups in social events like parties, dances, trips to the Caribbean, and so forth. Yes, this good boy, Henry Kellerman, had already become "Hank K." to my friends, and had additionally added to this career list this perhaps bad-boy alternate career.

The issue with women also had several initial benchmarks other than when the beautiful blonde at the High School of Music & Art wheeled around from the bottom of the staircase, ran up the stairs to where I was standing and kissed me voluptuously on the lips, and then ran down the stairs. As mentioned, I had never seen her before that event.

These few other what I'm referring to as "benchmark" occasions included when I was fifteen and in a Yiddish stage play, when one of the stars of the play was a woman probably in her sixties, who at the time was lounging in her dressing room with the door ajar. As I walked by, she spoke to me in Yiddish, asking me to enter the room. She also motioned for me to come in.

I instantly sensed there was something strange about her invitation, but nevertheless I complied. Even though I was only fifteen, I as well as others in the cast could see that she was quite attractive and that she would usually wear tops that showed her considerable endowment to best advantage. She was reclining in a chair, looked directly at me, and in Yiddish asked me if her breasts were visible through the sheer blouse she was wearing—sans bra.

Despite my already budding experiences even at that age, I didn't quite know what to say, so I agreed that she was right, that all was visible. I don't quite remember how it all played out, but nothing actually happened. Yet although I didn't know why she asked me to come into the room, I also absolutely *did* know why.

In later years, I came out of my haze and for sure realized that she was trying to seduce me. Her usual hellos and goodbyes to me were always accompanied by a close embrace where I could feel our entire bodies pressed together. Yet, even though I was beginning to consider myself a cool dude with girls as well as with women, this was one time that I simply didn't know what to do. I was only fifteen. I think I may have been waiting for her to go further (which never happened), but in addition, her age was a definite oedipal thing for me, and because of that I believe my sense of her was also tension-filled (but even a bit anesthetized), so that rather than following through I was rather rendered emotionally and psychologically a bit unknowing about it all. The fact that she was surely in her sixties was certainly what made me feel strange.

Another similar benchmark demonstrating what I am here defining as how girls and women were, on what seemed like a regular basis, sending me signals of their interest, is this one. It occurred in the building in which I lived with my parents. I was sixteen. The super of the building was a woman of about fifty. She was not abundantly endowed and rather on the trim side. One day in the summer she was standing on the stoop with her dog and wearing a low-cut, loose blouse. I was talking to a friend in front of the house. She and I acknowledged one another by nodding. My friend left and I was standing alone on the street when she motioned for me to come over.

I don't remember what we talked about, but at one point she knelt over to pet the dog. Her blouse hung very low so that her breasts were completely and unalterably visible. Even at that age it was clear to me that she had done this deliberately so that I would then perhaps give her a sign. Again, I didn't follow through because I wasn't sure what to do. With an older woman I would have needed some additional signal from her. But there was none, and that was that.

In my mid-twenties, as I was entering greater maturity and experience, I was no longer even a bit naive. To that point at the end of naivety, I worked at a mental hospital where one of the clinic heads was a very attractive woman of about forty. She once asked me if I would perhaps offer a lecture on psychopathology to her staff. She asked me this in a way that was tentative, because I could see that she didn't want to seem presumptuous. I readily agreed, while returning her entirely innocent-seeming smile. After the lecture that I indeed delivered to her staff, she suddenly whispered to me, "I'd like you to follow me in your car. Just follow me." This hospital was located in a rural area and the lecture I gave was held in the evening. So here I am at 9 p.m., driving my car into a wooded area, and this so-called innocent woman is leading the way. She parked at a certain spot that was not easily visible to the road and motioned me to come to her. So here we now were in her car, in the woods, and neither of us was in the least behaving as though this was something unusual. And yes, she was married.

It was only later in my early career as psychoanalyst in training that my psychoanalyst pointed out to me that this thing with married women may have had direct implications to repeatedly winning my mother over my father and could be an oedipal problem. That particular insight instantly and permanently ended my activity with married women, although what remained unabated was my rather promiscuous life—though not entirely of my personal doing; that is, that this kind of life had become conveniently available, in contrast to actually or compulsively seeking it. I believe that in my case promiscuity was nevertheless finding me.

With respect to finding me, when I was about twenty-five years old I was in Florida on vacation. I was having breakfast at an outdoor café. One morning when the café was jammed, a rather full-bodied woman (not obese), probably in her mid-seventies, walked over to my table (for two) and asked if she could share it. I agreed. We talked a bit, but I was engrossed in reading my newspaper. When I was about to leave, she suddenly said, "Would you come home and sleep with me?" She just sat there seriously, staring at me and waiting.

Other than the myriad encounters not including those who, so to speak, took me home, one actually took me home, another took me into a car, another into the woods, another into a movie house, and this one home to sleep with her. Then it was a woman who was forty-four when I was twenty-six, which ended in an extended tryst. But jumping into when I was about fifty, a raven-haired beauty who was also about my age—and who, five years earlier, walked over to me on a beach in the Bahamas and said, "The man with me is not my boyfriend, and I'm not married"; we then bumped into one another in the gift shop of the hotel and talked for about a minute or two—then five years later, we ran into one another in New York City. Turns out she was a shrink. After knowing each other for a while, she said, "I was glad to have met you again. I had thought about you." She paused. "I want you to marry me. I know you're married, but." Sounds like fiction, but it's not. Again, nothing happened, and these are cited here as random events, not exploits!

In a sense, Eugene Goodheart was a bit smothered (as I see it diagnostically) by his parents, who insisted he be grounded in a contained space doing homework (also as an explicit demand), which then possibly generated an internalized sense that he was not a free person. Gene was raised by socially conscious, wonderful parents who, with respect to the aim of achievement and doing what they thought was the best for him, nevertheless, I believe, instilled in him a tyrannical superego (the thing that waves an accusatory pointing finger). This means that, psychoanalytically understood, Gene ingested or internalized a severe message regarding "responsibility" as a demand, as well as perhaps as a triumph over personal freedom.

Diagnostically, it could be hypothesized that such containment, along with a consistently smothered early life, may have been the issue that perhaps ultimately manifested itself in a terrible asthmatic condition. In fact, Gene's first severe asthmatic attack occurred in a circumstance where, as he reports in his memoir, he was already an adult and on vacation. He was visiting with friends who were in turn about to play a game of touch football. As Gene reports, about five minutes into the game was when he caught a pass and simultaneously was then struck—assaulted with a severe asthmatic attack.

Psychoanalytically, I believe it was a severe superego attack regarding the issue of Gene having no right to enjoy himself outside of productive work. The moment this superego-circuitry switched on was the moment Gene caught the ball. Catching the ball defined the click that he was free, especially because it was in the absence of first doing something productive—like homework. Apparently, the attack was so acute and so sudden that Gene needed to brace himself against a tree. Thus, Gene's moment of yielding to pleasure in the absence of even any notion of productivity could have been the mountain his psyche couldn't climb.

In contrast, my experience was quite the opposite to Gene's, despite the fact that our parents were alike in so many other ways. My parents had no interest in containing me, with respect to schoolwork. The only resemblance to such containment occurred with me starting about when I was fifteen. It was then that I began to resent the commitments of performances I had made with various Yiddish cultural and/or Zionist organizations. And in such a case, I myself cut it (the performances) during the next year by a significant factor.

The side effect of my relative absence of containment led to a kind of liberation, which then also enabled me to be available for all sorts of worldly experiences. In my tip-of-the-spear role within the Yiddish progressive movement I was, as mentioned earlier, of course the picture of the good boy. However, in my personal life I lived in another world. This other world was not particularly destructive sexually, even though I was in it in quite an active way. But it was anarchic. It was, as I've mentioned, untethered. It wasn't delinquent or lawless, but it was highly experimental and experiential and in the absence of any kind of supervision.

Two other similar experiences occurred: one when I was about eleven or twelve years old, and the other when I was about twenty-eight years old and still a single man. The first happened when I was an eleven-year-old camper at the Kinderland sleepaway camp. This camp also had a Yoongvarg division (Yiddish for "younger child" division). One day while I was sitting on a log near my bunk, a little girl ran up to me and before I even saw her coming, she swiftly appeared and planted a kiss on my cheek, and just as instantly turned and ran away. She must have been, more or less, about six or seven years old.

When I was already twenty-eight years old and still single, I was sitting in my office and the phone rang. It was a young woman about the age of twenty-three or twenty-four. I believe she must have seen me in those earlier years, but I believe I had only a slight acquaintance with her. In any event, she asked if she could come and sit in my waiting room. She just wanted to be close to me and to be able to see me—actually, she said, "to look at you." It took several explanations on my part to let her know that such a thing would not be possible, and I, practically and with an extremely apologetic attitude, asked her to not persist in her request.

She approached me again about ten or so years later at a gathering when she was accompanied by her boyfriend, and with ease and utter friendliness told me that her phone call to me those years earlier was based on a "tremendous crush" that at the time she couldn't shake, and so she figured that the only way to neutralize this obsession was to actually see me.

Finally, a conflicted feeling I was confronted with occurred when I worked as psychologist at a state mental hospital. I was trying to find a patient that I was assigned to interview on the admissions ward of the hospital. I walked in on the main floor, and for a moment stopped in my tracks to check my notes. Suddenly a patient approached me. I had never spoken to her before but had seen her there from time to time. I'll call her "Z." She was quite beautiful, full-figured and known to be a person of high intelligence. At the time, she was about twenty-two or twenty-three years old and I about twenty-five.

She walked over to me and, in a kind of familiar way, said, "I need to talk to you. Can we talk alone?" We went over to a quiet part of the corridor, but yet in full view of others who were milling around. She said, "I need to tell you I have a terrible crush on you."

This was a difficult moment for me because the one strict rule at the hospital (delivered at our orientation when we first arrived at the hospital) was to be careful not to fraternize with patients—especially with respect to romantic/sexual involvements. "Z.," I said to her, "I'm really flattered, and of course I've noticed you and could see how attractive and interesting you are. Here's the problem." I informed her that under other circumstances, any man would be interested, but the rule regarding fraternization made an invisible partition between us so that if anything happened, there would go my position at the hospital. We had no other interactions about that sort of thing.

However, I was, in fact, actually quite interested in her, and although I was dying to see her chart and read her history, I never did. I always felt obligated to honor everyone's privacy, and I adhered to this kind of stance despite my interest. Some time later that year, I left the hospital to begin my postdoctoral training in psychoanalytic psychotherapy.

As it turned out, the day I was leaving, it occurred to me to send Z. a note wishing her the best, and I stated that I was in a hurry to catch a bus, and a cab was waiting for me, so that I couldn't say goodbye personally. I gave the note to my departmental head, asking him to please deliver the note to her. Later on, I had a suspicion that it was quite probable that he never delivered the note. I've always felt bad about how it didn't work out, because I really liked her. The idea that she was perhaps somewhat troubled and a hospital patient didn't bother me.

There were other girls and women who appeared during important phases of my life. Some were short-lived, others more sustained. When I was twelve and at camp it was Jean, the girl even some of the counselors were looking at. The kissing was great and I liked her a lot. The next year at camp it was Annette, who was adorable. At fifteen, it was Phyllis, and this lasted a year. We first met at a party. The kissing with Phyllis was great. When I was twenty, it was this picture-postcard knockout, Lucy, who I really liked. That, too, lasted a year.

When I was twenty-one it was Roz. With Roz it was rapturous. It happened at the Stanbrooke Dude Ranch in Dutchess County, New York. She was about thirty-two or thirty-three. In the lounge that evening Roz began talking to me. I could see we were like-minded. It was New Year's Eve, 1959. My closest friend then, Alex K. (Al), and I were there for the four-day weekend. At that year-ending evening, with the band playing and the lights dimmed, everyone crowded onto the dance floor. I was also on the dance floor, looking for a partner to dance with, but it was too late to dance because at that point everyone began counting down from ten. Suddenly when the count was at three Roz happened to walk by, but didn't see me. I said her name. She turned, looked at me, and we both heard people shouting "one." Then "Happy New Year" was heard while Roz and I were already in a rhapsodic embrace, enthralled in a protracted over-the-top love kiss. And that was just the start of the evening for us. It was an unforgettable weekend.

At twenty-four it was Janet, and at twenty-six it was Cheri, both of whom were quite beautiful; and when I was twenty-seven it was Allison. With Allison it was for two years. Allison was very special. Then it was Carol, who was also quite beautiful and irresistible. Otherwise it was Stanbrooke (the classiest dude ranch), a couple of other such venues; as well as hotels in Miami, the Catskills, and Adirondack Mountains; as well as my childhood Camp Kinderland, when I would come to visit. In each of these places it was more of the same: girls, women, and in some of those places winning dance contests. All of these events were attested to by my buddies, Hank B., Hank H., and Alex K., where at least at each of these events one of them was with me and saw it all happen.

Over the years, from ten to twenty-seven, I had exactly three obsessions about girls and women. One was a minor one when I was seventeen. Of the other two, the first was when I was ten and the other when I was about twenty. The first when I was ten ended when I was about fifteen. She was an exceptionally beautiful girl of about twelve. Let's call it a magnificent obsession. The girl who was my age when I was seventeen did in fact rock me with her presence, but I can't quite characterize it as a magnificent obsession. Nevertheless, it still was not easy for me to shake my focus on her. It lasted only one summer. Then at twenty, I had a beaut. This one gradually evaporated over a few years. So, it was not that experiences with girls and women were only characterized as them coming toward me. I also had experiences of going toward them. Yet everything was not always hunky-dory; there have been incidents all along whereby my interest in a girl or woman was not replied in kind. Otherwise, here I'm relating rather limited samples of my libidinal life.

Then when I was twenty-nine it all reached a beautiful permanence with Linda, who of course I married, and then my so-called perhaps promiscuity was, at the least with respect to my feeling about the issue of such freedom, adumbrated and completely erased. With Linda it is now fifty-five years together and I've been, believe it or not, true-blue and feeling at home.

One of the Greatest and Most Memorable Events of My Life

An interesting story happened in Sharon Springs in the summer of 1946 when I was eight years old. To support the Yiddish shula, raffles were distributed to us kids, ten cents a raffle. The prize was a clock with a luminous dial. Our hotel in Sharon Springs was one of two hotels connected by a sprawling lawn. On each afternoon the lawn was to capacity with men and women playing cards while sitting around large tables. All were Jewish, so I thought I could sell all ten raffle books in a jiffy. I was sure my Yiddish would interest these people.

I began speaking Yiddish to them at their tables, but they ignored me. And as a beloved only child, I had no experience being ignored. Second, my only motive was to support the shula that I felt was a crucial cultural benchmark to the importance of Yiddish in America. Yet at the moment of feeling I didn't know what to do, I actually did know what to do. In a split second, I decided to recite a poem by Yuri Suhl, a noted Yiddish poet. I spotted an empty chair which was a few feet away from me. I stood on it, and facing this audience of about seventy or eighty people, and with power and assuredness, I shouted the title of the poem—of course, in Yiddish. It should be remembered that this was one year after World War II and the Holocaust. I shouted, "Es laypt dus Eedisheh folk" ("The Jewish people live!"). The gist of the poem is:

> **Vayn zeekh ois mine folk oif dine vaytig oif dine brukh**
> (*Cry it out my people—of your misery and of the **catastrophe**.*)
> **Sitz oup dee zex millionedikeh shiveh vokhn oon hoib zeekh oif**
> (*Sit through the six million shiva [mourning] weeks and **rise**—*)
> **Oon shtell zeekh oif dee fees tsooriek.** (*And get **back** on your **feet!***)
> **Oon kook tsum groisn murgn mit gloibn in dine blick**
> (*And look to the great tomorrow with **belief**.*)
> **Vee a denkmul far dee yourn shtell avek dine troyer**
> (*In memory of generations, set aside your **sorrow**—*)
> **Vile oif kine trern kennen mir nit boyen** (*Because we cannot build on **tears**.*)
> **Oon boyen darfn meer** (*And build we **must**—*)
> **Atzindert foon dus nigh** (*In the here and **now**.*)
> **Oon boyen veln meer,** (*And build we **will**, because—*)
> **Vile am isroel khie**
> **Es lebt dos Eedisheh folk!** (*The **Jewish people live!***)

[Note: I've italicized and bold-lettered words—even parts of words—in order to give you, the reader, a chance to feel the exact intonation of the righteous indignation and fighting spirit of the poem that I personally felt and thus tried to convey.]

After a split second of silence everyone from all the tables of this sprawling lawn rose as one. And after one or two seconds of silence, they stampeded toward me. I tried to open a raffle book but suddenly a lady gave me a small cardboard carton, and in Yiddish said to me that I should put the little book away and instead to fill up the carton with the money that people were already literally throwing at me. I didn't sell a single raffle. I took the carton to my parents' hotel room. In the carton was over one hundred dollars and some coins.

Included in this stash were three twenty-dollar bills. Please remember, this was 1946. When I finally made it back to our room, my parents asked what I had there, and when they heard the story, they both laughed and laughed. When I brought the $114 and change into the shula, I won the clock, but my main feeling was how serious I was in contributing to the shula.

I believe this incident may reflect my sense of knowing spontaneously what to do—a personality quality quite likely visible to girls and women as well as to my friends. It could be a quality of unselfconscious innocence containing a measure of assuredness—which also may, in some way, explain what had always been happening to me with girls and women.

In contrast and in addition, again, in my son Max's words when he was interviewed for the oral project of the Yiddish Book Center, he noted that Yiddish is like a "force" insofar as Yiddish is something transcendent and so not a slave to popular culture. And that's how I've always felt about Yiddish—in contrast to the nature of my social life, which, although exciting, was very much governed by the expectations of a certain segment of such popular culture.

For sure, I never quite understood why people always nominated me for president of my school classes. I never asked for it. Then again, this same doubt concerns why all these girls and women were attracted to me. I once asked one of them what it was that attracted her. She said: confident, innocent, cute. Along with this, she conveyed that I invite a sense of emotional safety, and that she liked the way I walked—my gait.

For me, these different facets of a person's life can be extraordinarily different; that is, my particular Yiddish world was far afield of my American world, and my social life was also, in a similar way, from another universe. To understand it all probably depends more on personality than it does on ideology. That is, ideologically, I should have primarily been focused on schoolwork and on my Yiddish cultural life. Yet, with respect to my personality (needs, attitude, impulses, emotions, and predilections), I think I just needed to dance away. So there I went.

7

College

Saved by the Bell

I graduated from the High School of Music & Art and I was college-bound. But I was facing a problem. My parents had no means of funding a private college education, so that I was scheduled to attend City College of the City University of New York. In my family it was understood that I would attend City College because of the tuition-free situation. My main problem was that if it was City, then I would live at home, which for sure I didn't want to do. At that point I was beginning to feel I needed to disappear from all demands coming my way from all those who sought me out for performance venues. In addition, living at home was not the environment I ever envisioned as a context for any college experience. So ultimately I wound up trading a rather prestigious City College for an unheralded suburban Hofstra College.

At my apartment where we lived on Claremont, there was no space for me to do homework. My bubba made working there just about impossible because the only place to do homework on a flat, hard surface was on the kitchen table. However, she first would spread a newspaper over the table to protect it; then on top of the newspaper would be spread a rather thin fabric large enough to cover the table, and then another tablecloth on top, and finally she would set place mats at each of the place settings. In other words, if one placed a glass of water on the table it might never be resting on a hard table surface, so that the issue of the glass tipping was always in play.

The first question was, How was I going to do homework on that surface? I didn't want to repeat my method of doing homework on the chair in front of the couch in the living room. The point of this was that throughout high school, that's how I did my homework—in a bent-over position, leaning down toward the chair on which I was working while sitting on the couch.

I first visited the lumberyard around the corner on Washington Avenue. There a workman gave me a wooden board, cut to the dimensions of my specifications, with two holes bored through on each side of the board. He never charged me for it. With that loving board, I laid it across a wooden chair, strung cord through the holes on each side of the board in order to tie the cord under the chair, with thick knots on each end of the cords, so that those knots would anchor the cords. Thus I made myself a desk, requiring me to sit on the edge of the couch and work as I was leaning down to the material on the chair, on this makeshift desk in the living room on the same couch that, with the chair removed, opened up as a full

My maternal grandmother ("bubba" in Yiddish), Pessie Pellis. She was born in 1864 (Civil War time in America) and died in 1958 at the age of ninety-four. She lived with us all my growing-up years. She died when I was graduating college. In my first published book I also dedicated it to her and my other grandparents (whom I never knew).

bed at night, becoming my bedroom. This was not an appealing thought as I was about to begin my college career.

But perhaps I could have managed were it not for the second problem. The unmitigated fact was that I needed to escape from any and all requests that would naturally be coming in from those who still needed my appearance at various Yiddish functions—both with the progressives as well as with the Zionists. And the only friends from camp with whom I had sustained an ongoing relationship were Bernie B. and Hank B. Otherwise, I believe I needed to feel free of it all. And I'm not saying it was a positive thing on my part, especially since I was entering alien territory (college). I think it felt to me as though I was orphaning myself—meaning my apparent need to be away from it all.

Even in the summers, when I attended summer camp at Camp Kinderland, I was always called upon to perform at the shula morning get-togethers and at the weekly Saturday night concerts. At this point in my life, however, I strongly felt it was enough. In addition, very many of these people were also going to, or already attending, City College. It just didn't sit right with me because truly, I felt I needed to become inconspicuous, anonymous, or even perhaps invisible. As a matter of fact, from the age of about fifteen to seventeen I was already beginning to feel compromised about my time being taken with weekend performance commitments; that is, when Wednesdays would roll around, I began regretting my commitment to appear here and there in my Yiddish performance capacity on the upcoming Friday and Saturday evenings, and sometimes Sunday afternoons as well. So, for that two-year period from fifteen to seventeen, as my dissatisfaction grew, by the time I was about to head for college, I felt a certain need to completely disappear. In fact, even though my Yiddish performance venues were very important and had great meaning for me, nevertheless, it all essentially left little energy or even less of an abiding interest, for example, even in my schoolwork. The prospect of college therefore felt as though it would be a relief not to need to confront what was becoming, to me, clearly burdensome.

Thus, the prospect of attending college and living at home meant that I would still be available to many who were continuing to call me at home in order to schedule a performance commitment. To put it figuratively as well as specifically, I just wanted to dance. In other words, I wanted to be away from the tip of the spear (that anointed position) whereby in the past, in order to reach me for a request to perform, the caller would need to get me to the performance venue where I would do my thing, and then after bidding all "ah gooteh nakht," I would then evaporate—completely disappear.

In my case, what I considered my greater need for leisure, fun, and freedom, I now realize was a function of my complete energic commitment of needing to "bring good news" to this segment of the radical Yiddish-speaking immigrant population (as well as to the Zionist organizations), who were really all good working people. And as I stated earlier, these were working people with Yiddish accents in their adopted English-speaking America. Many of these people were without any great formal education but were very culturally interested, and by the dint of experience acquired a thorough political orientation eschewing violence (but not necessarily embracing nonviolence); and also, of course, needing to counter unfairness and injustice, they fought for unions and against oppression of any people.

My performance oeuvre consisted of all such variants concerning largely this progressive, left-wing, so-called thinking person's agenda. I was committed to it, as were my parents; that is, committed in the sense that it was an idea about respect, fairness, and dignity for all people.

Thus, in high school I breezed through without much effort. I could easily have been a straight-A student, but my time was entirely hijacked (as I had begun to feel it) by the need for memorizing or familiarizing myself with scripts, with rehearsals and performances, which again, together, ultimately left only a smidgeon of time, energy, or even inclination to focus on schoolwork. However, later on I realized that school wasn't that crucial to me, largely because it didn't seem crucial to my parents. Where I actually was this straight-A student was in the arena that was important to them. And in that arena I was the equivalent of a valedictorian.

Along with this, all through the years I was paid a bit of money for my performances, which in fact I usually returned as a donation if it was only a pittance. That was my way of offering my support. When the fee was larger, I accepted it and gave it to my father. At the end of each year the larger fees added up to an average of about fifteen hundred dollars or a bit more, and so I was actually significantly helping with the expenses of the family since I was seven years old.

And here is where my experience with my parents diverged from Eugene Goodheart's experience with his parents. Gene reports that his parents were hell-bent on his regular school performance and did everything they could to convey to him the importance of it. In my case, my parents were not at all concerned about my regular schoolwork, and I assume (as noted earlier) they just felt I would handle that part of my life myself.

Thus, unlike Gene's parents, mine were very remote from anything involving formal schooling. All of their interest was invested, rather, in the Yiddish progressive movement and in making a living. For example, as I mentioned earlier, my parents never attended an open-school week or made time for teacher conferences. Not once! Therefore, in this sense of academic pressure from parents, I had none. Despite that, I still did reasonably well.

In later years, I realized that of course such absence of parental supervision had its positives along with its negatives, but surely was entirely opposite of the concerns these Yiddish-speaking progressive families had for their children (especially for their sons) with respect to ambition for them—as compared to the attitude of my parents. In my case, what I experienced as my particularized tip-of-the-spear issue was what essentially adumbrated leisure for me. Yet, despite explicit demands by people depending on me, as well as my own implicit demands in which I allied myself with the needs of these others, nevertheless, for whatever reason, this alliance of demands actually never erased my social life. In part, this was true because wherever I went, I found social opportunities which required only easy and rather immediate, shall I say, exploits. In this sense, my rather precocious social life was also unsupervised, so also as mentioned earlier, I can remember typically feeling unrestricted and untethered with respect to what I could do and experience.

Enter Hank B., my buddy who drove the car. Hank was a bunkmate of mine at Kinderland for about four or five summers. We had become very good friends. He lived in Hempstead, New York, in Nassau County, only about an hour and some from the Bronx where I lived. About a week before the beginning of what was to be my first day at City College, Hank calls. He tells me his mother would like for me to attend Hofstra College and room with him.

As it turned out, Hank's family was one of the only materially well-off families of anyone I had known in the Yiddish left movement, and certainly from anyone I knew in my immediate Southeast Bronx neighborhood. But his family was politically similar to my family, and our parents knew one another. Hank told me that Hofstra (a school I never heard of) was only a hop, skip, and a jump away from where he lived.

Hank's family lived in a private home with a finished basement that had a capacious bedroom with two beds and side tables at each bed, two closets, and two wide desks; one part of the room for him, the other for his sister, who was three years older.

Apparently the plan was for his sister to occupy one of the bedrooms on the main floor of the house, and we would share the basement bedroom. I remember thinking, *I could have my own desk!*

My parents agreed. The only problem was tuition, that nasty word. With no money in the family, how were we going to fund it all? My mother said I should go to the school and meet with someone of authority. I believe her sense of it was that anyone who would meet me would take me. She didn't know the phrase "dean of admissions," but I knew that was who she meant.

Sitting with the dean, who was an unmistakable Irishman with rusty-colored hair, I had an epiphany. You see, when I took the test for the High School of Music & Art, the music audition part of the test, given in the afternoon, was to play a piece on whatever was the instrument you were auditioning with, and then take a rhythm test. The morning three-hour first part of the test was a so-called "ear" test, where in a full auditorium of what seemed like a few hundred kids, I believe, we sat with earphones listening to a recording of different instruments playing a phrase or chord and we needed to tell whether the instruments playing the same phrase were the same instrument or different ones (I'm not sure if I remember this part clearly), and/or whether the chord itself was same or different. I felt on that particular test I had probably made a perfect score. But now in the very last part of the test I needed to play a piece on the piano and I had only started taking lessons (three dollars per lesson) for about six weeks prior to the test. But I had learned to play a little tarantella—an Italian folk dance with quick steps.

It was Mr. Lockett. He was also an unmistakably Irish man with rusty-red hair and an austere look on his face. I distinctly remember that the moment I laid eyes on him, I had the thought, *This anti-Semite will never give this Jewish boy a chance.* Yes, I had that thought!

As it turned out, this was my first lesson in stereotyping. He asked me to play my piece. I got into it for about five or six bars when he told me to stop. Then he motioned for me to stand by the piano while he tapped out a rhythm for me to repeat. I figured I had failed the piano test, but when it came to rhythm, no matter how old he was and how young I was, I was sure he could never get me on this one. *Rhythm is my thing, man, and I gotcha! If either of us will fail on this one, it won't be me.* And that's exactly what I consciously thought and felt.

He finished testing me and called in a monitor. He wrote something in red ink on the top of a sheet of paper, which he then enclosed in a manila envelope and gave it unsealed to the monitor to deliver it, and me, to the principal's office, which was the final stop on the way to being a Music & Art High School student or one who went to a regular neighborhood high school.

On the way down to the principal's office, the monitor says to me, "Want to see what you got?" That scared me. Was it a trick to see if I was an honest person? He repeated the question, and on his third try, I took a chance. He opened the manila envelope and pulled out the sheet of paper. What Mr. Lockett had written in red was: *98—highly recommended.* The monitor said, "You're in!" The cliché of "Don't judge a book by its cover" became instantly clear.

By the way, on the very first day of class at Music & Art, I was nominated for president of my official class. I instantly declined. The whole thing was pointless because all of us came from all the five boroughs of New York City, so that no one knew anyone else. To call for elections was therefore beyond ridiculous. I wanted no part of it and was not simply angry about it; rather, I was actually, I guess, flummoxed about the teacher not seeing it that way.

And now I was sitting with the dean of admissions at Hofstra College in Hempstead, New York, on Long Island. And like I said, he was a severe-looking Irishman. But now I was immunized against nonsense. I told him my money dilemma. He asked from which high school I had graduated and was impressed with my Music & Art credential. I could tell he liked me because we then had about a half-hour really good conversation. I liked him, too. He directed me to the psychology department because I told him I was interested in psychology, and he also directed me to the math department because I had mentioned I had graduated Music & Art with the high math Regent grades of 98 in intermediate algebra and 99 in geometry. In each of these departments (psychology and math) I was offered $150 to be an assistant to one of the professors, with respect mostly to office work. I took the psychology assistantship. In addition, he said that the audiovisual aids department needed someone to show films each Wednesday evening for various courses, and that they paid fifteen dollars for the evening's work. Then he said the important thing: "Don't worry about tuition." He asked me to send in all my Music & Art documents and said that I should make arrangements for lodging. In other words, in every respect, I was going to go to a private college away from home and away from everything I wanted to be away from—and tuition was perhaps going to be on the house. Tuition was twenty dollars per point, so that I paid only part of it and earned the rest with monies from showing films and from working in the psych department.

When the dean asked me to tell him what Music & Art was like, I told him about the cultural and academic high level of the school, but neglected to tell him what was most important to me. What was most important was the social life at Music & Art. Thus, I think my sense of high school was that it didn't mean much to me. It was the effort I generated in my Yiddish performance career that I considered to be the real thing. Actually, my wish, if possible, would have been to skip directly from junior high school to college.

However, at Music & Art, yes, it was the social life that interested me. And for me that meant girls. It especially meant this gorgeous one who I thought was most beautiful. She was an art student, and I would occasionally drift into her particular art studio just to more or less find her paintings. Actually, when I first saw her, I felt she took my life away. Her name was Linda, and we eventually became acquainted. I could never get close enough to her to tell her who I was (or who I think I was) and to explain what I meant by that. My first strident and grandiose wishful thought when I laid eyes on her was *I'd like to marry that girl*. However, with the excitement all of us graduating seniors had, these kinds of fantasies would simply evaporate. What did happen was that I phoned the office at City College asking to hold my acceptance for the following year, telling them I had decided not to attend in that present year. I was told to write a letter to that effect, but I don't remember if I made any promise for the following year. I had asked them to hold my placement because of the proverbial what-if. I guess I was needing some insurance. By then I had officially accepted the Hofstra offer and began packing for my Hofstra College adventure.

Then the phone rang!

It was Hank B., at whose house he and I would be roommates for the up-coming college four-year experience. He informed me that his mother had a change of heart and that I would not be able to live there. I guess she didn't feel about me the way others did. So here I was, without a place to live at Hofstra and without a compass—meaning no orientation regarding where to go and what to do. My first thought was to default to City College and living at home, but my mother instantly told me to take the train to Hempstead, get to the school, and speak to that nice dean. Thankfully I did just that. The dean pointed to a bulletin board on which were listed places to live in private homes surrounding the college. Apparently many students were doing just that.

I found one that was three very short suburban blocks from the back gate of one of the school's parking lots. It was a lovely little house, and the owners were a lovely couple. He, Carl, was from the island of Aruba in the Dutch West Indies, and she, Vera, was from Portugal. They lived on this manicured little block that was something out of a picture postcard of well-kept lovely suburban homes, each with a well-kept front lawn and backyard. Nirvana. Idyllic!

Upstairs were three bedrooms and a Hollywood bathroom. Not a cockroach in sight. In fact, no cockroach in its right mind would dare enter such a protected space. In any event, I remember thinking humorously that perhaps cockroaches only lived on Claremont Parkway.

Vera was meticulous in how she kept the house. I had now reached and gratified my wildest dream, which was to live in such a place, so that in the physical sense I thought that perhaps it felt what home wanted to feel like for me. It was right out of a movie, especially as compared to the physical surroundings of my growing-up years on Claremont Parkway—a gritty, wide-street cityscape with one four-story apartment building adjacent to another up and down the streets. Of course, the positive side of Claremont was that it seemed we all had loving families and definitely plenty of friends to play ball with, and we always had adequate heat in the winter. And that we always had heat was important to me.

Vera gave me a one-window bedroom with the promise that if I got a roommate, then I could switch to the front bedroom, with two windows in a cross-ventilation, and with that all-important table that had side panels that could be lifted, thereby extending the table. Thus, finding a roommate interested me; then the table with the side panels would be my own capacious desk, on which to keep my books, typewriter, and dictionary, and still have generous space on which to work. The issue was that other than Hank, I didn't know anyone at the school. But imagine that: my own large, beautiful table—even larger than a conventionally sized desk.

Vera only charged eight dollars per week for rent, and in addition, she prepared dinner each night for Carl and herself, and for me—and then, to boot, for my new soon-to-be roommate, Arthur (Arty) Libman. The fifteen dollars I earned Wednesday nights, working for the audiovisual aids department showing films, took care of the eight dollars rent per week, and I had enough left over for meals in the school cafeteria. My mother would send dinners to me with a man who worked at Grumman Aircraft on Long Island. He would stop at the house on Monday mornings, delivering dinners to me for the entire week, and then continue on his way.

Now I was settled. However, now only knowing Hank at Hofstra made me feel a bit less as though I was a stranger in a strange land. I remember the day before school started (before Arty and I met), I was sitting on the step of the front of the house at my new living venue at this 25 Hope Street address in Hempstead, New York. It was a warm, sunny day in September 1955. I was seventeen years old, and I thought, *Well, here I am; alone again. I'll do it myself. It's okay.* What I meant was that as an only child, I did everything myself, notwithstanding that I had many friends, no matter what the venue was in which I found myself. Nevertheless, this was a moment that my sense of anonymity gained an audience of one, and momentarily I realized that I liked it. I liked the anonymity of it. No one knew me here, and I liked the invisibility. Yes, I did.

Further, with respect to my need to be invisible, meaning not to be in the limelight and then also to keep my education in college as a primary motivation and direction, I also realized that Hofstra College qualified, both with respect to its absence as an arena of notoriety as well as my presence there in the further absence of no one knowing me. In no sense did I want to be the tip of the spear. Yet, as fate would have it, on the third day of college I won the dance contest, so that I guess, damn it, I became at once a bit popular anyway. I couldn't resist wanting to enter the contest (with twenty other couples), but I didn't know anyone. Then, suddenly, a girl touched my elbow. It was Sue G., my girlfriend from camp. We hadn't seen each other for more than four years. Sue was a great dancer, and we had danced a lot at camp. She said, "Let's dance." And that was it!

My college roommate, Arty Libman, and me. We became best buddies. I dedicated a book to Arty. It reads: "For Arthur Libman (Arty). It was the best of times." The title of the book is *Greedy, Cowardly, and Weak: Hollywood's Jewish Stereotypes*. It was the best of times because I was for the first time in my life in the absence of any supervision. For me this was freedom.

The photo of me in my Ph.D. doctoral graduation robe was taken in 1964 when I was twenty-six years old. Arty was twenty-eight. The photo of us both with gray hair was taken in 1998 when I was sixty and he sixty-two.

Although I knew I would see Hank on campus, I ultimately saw that his mother had changed her mind about my living at her house because Hank had a very troubled relationship with her and with his sister, and so his mother, along with his sister, were concerned that such information to an outsider would not be in the family's best interest. As a matter of fact, Hank mentioned that she had sabotaged another close relationship he had with a childhood buddy. Of course, I felt it was unconscionable that they had sprung the bad news (and at the last moment) that the plan of my living there had changed. Yet, as fate would have it, it could not have worked out better.

On the very first day of college classes, I had made a comment in my orientation class which prompted one of the other students to approach me during the break and introduce himself. It was "thank the Lord for Arty." He was from Brooklyn, New York, and per chance was looking for a place to live. He was Jewish, my height, a good-looking mesomorph type who, like me, really loved to play ball—and, like me, he was real good at it. And to top it all off, we had the entire upstairs to the house, and it was entirely private and separated from below.

Arty and I became roommates, and along with Richie, he became etched as another lifelong best friend. We hit it off. Personality-wise we were extraordinarily similar. Within the first week of living together, we had a long talk about our

(*Above*) 2002, Max at twenty-nine, Sam at twenty-seven, Jack at twenty-three, Harry at twenty-five. Linda in back embracing all. I call this photo "The Queen." (*Right*) In 1989, from left to right: Sam at fourteen, Jack at ten, Harry at twelve, Max at sixteen.

plans, and there and then we decided to graduate in three years rather than four. We had this talk while relaxing in my room and talking about our lives. Each of us was eager to get out into the world and do our thing—whatever that would turn out to be. So we each sketched out a program of credits that included two summers of coursework as well as the usual coursework of fall and spring semesters, with a few extra credits here and there.

And by the way, a great college roommate makes all the difference.

My reason for graduating in three years concerned the trials my parents were facing about how to survive. At that point, my Claremont Parkway neighborhood was changing. It was becoming more minority populated, and the businesses were similarly changing to minority ownership. Since my parents had this hole-in-the-wall luncheonette specializing in Jewish food, and since the neighborhood culture was also correspondingly changing, even their pittance of an income was also steadily declining, because a large percentage of their patronage was from the owners of the neighborhood businesses that had been mostly Jewish owned.

The question I gave myself was, *Who is going to save the day?* Because that day was rapidly approaching. The answer was obvious. I would save the day and bring "the good news." The thought was not burdensome. In fact, I was looking forward to it.

But back to beautiful Linda. As it turned out, after high school graduation, and as is usually the case (as noted earlier), people drift off to different objectives and pursue their future in their own way, and so people depart and leave each other's field of vision and even current preoccupations. So that's what happened to Linda and to me when we graduated from Music & Art. We didn't see each other again for more than a decade.

Then one day, we randomly met on a street in Greenwich Village, and we talked and caught up. She barely recognized me or even almost didn't remember me. I had to tell her who I was. She was surprised because I had been a short, skinny kid during our high school days, and now I was about three inches taller than she. She was the same height that she had been in high school—about five feet five inches—and where then I had been about the same, now I was my five feet eight inches and about a niftier twenty-five or thirty pounds heavier. Surprisingly, we talked and soon realized that we were going to the same party a few nights later.

To cut to the chase, we've never been apart since that night at the party. We started living together immediately. At that initial re-meeting, I was almost twenty-nine and she halfway to twenty-nine. As of 2023, we've been married fifty-one years and together for fifty-five. Before we married, we lived together for almost four years, and after we married we raised four sons: Max, Sam, Harry, Jack—the fabulous four.

8

Marriage

Linda, Me—All of Us

And so yes, I married the girl I wanted to marry even from the moment I laid eyes on her. She was not only beautiful but also multitalented. She was a self-taught guitarist and also tinkered at the piano, and she knew probably scores of authentic bluegrass songs, as well as knowing from memory lyrics to an assortment of Broadway musicals. In fact, she was a lyricist herself, insofar as she could consistently and without fail create a rhyming vignette at any time and on the spot. She eventually published a book entitled *My Animal Alphabet: Paintings and Poems*, authored with her professional artist's maiden name: Linda Mia Turkel.

In addition, I was very taken with Linda because in addition to her talents, she was someone with the highest integrity, and she had a wonderful fine-edge command of language along with a sky-high IQ, a great dry sense of humor, an unselfconscious modesty, deep beauty, an elegant stride when she walked, and I believe I felt, without being conscious of it, that we were quite similar in talents and abilities—of course, in different ways.

However, here's the bad news: she couldn't really dance (probably related to her modesty); and although she was Jewish, she didn't know a word of Yiddish. Oh my! She didn't have these particular two boxes checked off as my most important prerequisites. But the redeeming issue was that she came from parents who might be defined in their political philosophical underpinnings as unsullied liberals. And that was important to me.

And of course, she was my favorite painter—even more so than Jackson Pollack, who I discovered in the 1950s, along with Robert Motherwell. I'm also a bit partial to Motherwell because again, as fate would have it, we became friends, and he would send me copies of his work as well as books he would publish, and I would send him books that I published. Robert and I had wonderful and ongoing conversations, both in the building in which we lived and at his Cape Cod retreat. I was always proud to have known him. His elegies to the Spanish Republic were impressive and important. They were lamentations of the Spanish Civil War.

Once when he was exhibiting at the Guggenheim in New York City, I was drifting down from level to level in that spiral walk-down, checking out all the work, when he spotted me and waved me over. He was standing next to his art agent, and they were discussing how much he should charge for this quite large painting that was all black except for a slightly jagged, red-colored splotch in one of the corners of the painting. I believed the agent suggested something like $200,000. Motherwell asked me how much I thought the painting should bring, and I said $750,000. He laughed but liked the idea. I believe the painting sold for $600,000. In any event, he sent me his book, *The Collected Writings of Robert Motherwell*, edited by Stephanie Terenzio. I'm also fond of Renate Ponsold, Robert's wife, who is a noted photographic artist.

Sorry, I wandered. Back to Linda. Linda was never recognized in the class of Motherwell or Pollack, but nevertheless, her work was, for me, easily on that level. Linda's work contained deep feeling. As a matter of fact, she was a genius in creating textural composition in her paintings. As a psychologist I knew that in the Rorschach inkblot test, responses that subjects would give that would be assessed as reflecting a high percentage of textural responses were always correlated with deep feelings with and affective, emotion-filled indications of personality needs for affection, along with a tinge of anxiety. And I saw that such was also true of Linda; that is, that she was a very feeling person, and her textural excitational approach seemed to correspondingly reflect a person whose sensorium enabled her to feel things deeply.

But now comes the realistic bad news, because I instinctively knew, and also realized by dint of my training as a psychoanalyst—also over the years of treating many couples—that marriage is truly a battleground, even though it does not start out that way. It doesn't start out that way because love is an opiate designed in the personality to overlook anything negative in the other person. As the Notorious RBG said (attributed to her mother-in-law), "In marriage, it's a good idea to be a little deaf." (Of course, "RBG" is a shoutout to Ruth Bader Ginsburg, the late Supreme Court Justice—who, incidentally, should surely have resigned earlier.)

With love we get adoration, rapture, and yearning. Anything that is seen as negative in the partner is emotionally denied and disavowed. The honeymoon is over, however, when at some later point in the relationship, one walks into the bathroom and the toothpaste cap is off the toothpaste tube and one suddenly feels homicidal. That is precisely when the beginning of work in the relationship becomes crucial, because what becomes obvious (and in bold relief) is that two different personalities are now trying to live together and further need to work out their respective compromised freedoms. And in a large family, mother's helpers help. We had Dorian for a while, and then for the longest time we had Michelle, who was a great help to us.

I also experienced that my parents had numerous arguments about this or that, and so their difference in personality became apparent to me. However, with them it was kind of like spats. Nevertheless, I witnessed one blowup, so that I could tell that my parents, who actually had a good marriage, had it on a 7.5 scale out of 10, and as I've noted earlier, they were married for fifty-six years. My mother died first, at the age of eighty-two, and my father lived to the age of ninety-five.

The point is that when the rapture begins to wane—confronted by the easing off of the anesthesia that then awakens one's critical faculties—is when dissatisfactions with the other becomes manifest, so that then your loved one becomes "the other." The second truth is that no marriage is a perfect 10 on a 10-point scale. As a matter of fact, no marriage is even an 8 or a 9 on a 10-point scale. The best any marriage can be, assuming it's worked on, is a 7.5. The only time a marriage approaches a 10 is when you're both having dinner in a nicely low-lit restaurant with soft jazz playing and when the restaurant is not noisy, or when you're getting along well and intimacy gains the ascendancy. But this kind of positive experience is episodic, and not typical of the ongoing entire relationship. Otherwise it tops out at 7.5; there are no exceptions anywhere in the world—which means it's also true of Linda and me—rating at about a range of 6 to 7 to 7.5. It needs to be again noted that marriage is a condition in which each person's degrees of freedom is a bit abridged and then further, even pruned. That's a fact. And no one likes it. It's just how it is. That is also what generates "dissatispointment." The uncomfortable wisdom is:

That which initially attracts you is that which eventually kills you.

Thus, the ubiquitous phenomenon is the desire to have the other disappear. It's the wish from the unconscious to be free of the constraint of a commitment, and it is experienced with every partner in every relationship. It's referred to as the "disappearance daydream." Yet with Linda and me, I was very attracted to her modesty, her beauty, her stateliness, her talent, her intelligence, her artfulness, and her sense of herself that had both the appearance and truth of integrity. She also was a reader of books. In addition, she and our sons Sam and Harry were alike; that is, easily sociable in the sense that anyone and everyone could immediately like them. I early on discovered that Linda was a very good listener with other people and was actually interested in everything they said, on top of which she was also verbally gifted and very adept in such social conversation. In addition, as I've noted, her command of language was exquisite, and I loved to hear how she articulately talked. Also, importantly, she had a knowing understanding of the importance of fairness for all people. And this, too, was important to me; most of it, I later understood, reminded me of my father—including her particular looks.

Well, the question is, how or why did anything about her bother me? The answer is that after a while I got to see that like her mother, Linda was immovable with what she thought or wanted. In that sense, she had a controlling nature. Furthermore, her modesty hid an underlying shyness based upon a deeper kind of apprehension of things that could be considered or defined as a concern with "collisions." Thus, her inclination toward listening and getting along with others was exceedingly important to her insofar as such behavior nullified the possibility of any collision (confrontation). Yet she's not easily able to say she was wrong about something. It may be a gender difference meaning to be wrong is equivalent to being inferior. In addition to all of these possibly impossible traits, she's a beautiful soul inside out.

In addition, as noted, on the outside Linda is soft and agreeable, like Sam and Harry, but on the inside she's iron and steel, also like Sam and Harry; this despite her beautiful soulfulness. In contrast, I'm occasionally not so agreeable on the outside (a bit overassertive), more like Max and Jack, but like Max and Jack I'm also a bit too easy on the inside. In contrast, in a genetic sense and on the adult level, it seems to me that Max and Jack look more like Linda, while Sam and Harry look more like me. Go figure. Talk about Boolean algebra's logic gates!

Now, let me talk about myself in the relationship in terms of what might have been difficult for Linda to bear. I'm able to admit to being wrong, probably also because with respect to gender differences, men don't mind being wrong—whether you believe that or not. What men mind is being humiliated or reduced in stature. That's what's important to men. Women are much better at fielding humiliation, because perhaps they've been fielding it all their lives, also in so-called microaggressions that frequently don't immediately meet the eye. Therefore, I'm probably more defensive about any attack on my ego because such an attack for men (including me) is typically experienced as derision.

With respect to Linda's apprehension of any possible collision with anyone, I'm quite different. I'm not looking for collisions, but dear God, please let me have one once in a while—especially when I see an unfairness. However, the issue of fairness and the attainment of peace in the world as it is expressed in the progressive Yiddish literature also had a very important influence in my thinking, especially with respect to my vigilance regarding my protest against any form of tyranny. To this point, an example of the literary people who have focused on such material in the Yiddish progressive literature includes the writer Shmuel Halkin.

Khaver (Mr.) Halkin wrote a little poem that in a split second of its verse reveals the importance of seeing the world with clear vision and rejecting any focus on egoism. In a poem titled "Dus Gluz" (The Glass), he says it succinctly and with a simple Yiddish rhyme:

Dus gluz iz doorukhzeekhtic oon rayn (*The glass is transparent and clean.*)
Do zest doorkh eem dee gantzeh velt (*Through it, one can see the whole world,*)
Ver es vaint, oon ver es kvelt. (*whoever cries and whoever feels good.*)
Nor vee do hust ein zite farshtelt mit zilberfarb
  (*But should you silver one side of it*)
Vus hut dervert ah grushn gelt, tsoo etvos mer,
  (*[That costs a few bucks or maybe more],*)
Farshvint foon oig dee gantzeh ehrd. (*Then the whole world disappears.*)
Foon raynem gluz, a shpeegl vert (*Instead of clear glass a mirror forms—*)
Oon vee der shpeegl zul zine rayne, (*And no matter how clean is this mirror,*)
Do zest in eem nor zikh alayn. (*The only thing you can see in it is yourself.*)

I always liked that poem and felt it was like a balm to my rather conscious edges—and I used it as a little farewell whenever the audience insisted on an encore. In a sense, it must be difficult for Linda because I'm also like my mother, whereby my philosophy, like my mother's, is, to wit: "Where there's a will, there's a way." My mother actually stated that phrase to me two or three times during my formative years. Therefore, I'm a die-hard, and feel if it's done the way I believe is best, then it should be done that way, and that perhaps to that end I can help it a bit (said with a "bit" in my mouth). So, that's my way of coming across as controlling.

However, with respect to the personality of whom one marries, in a way it doesn't really matter, because whomever it is one marries, one really marries also the spouse's family, which each partner invites into the psychology of the marital interfacing and interaction. Thus, marriage is a complex intergenerational mix that is always manifesting itself, albeit in subtle though powerful ways. In some of these musings I've attempted to render something about how our personalities are actually quite different. Furthermore, even though Linda's also controlling, I might be even more so, given that in this respect I take after my mother, not my father. The point is that my father was not at all controlling, but my mother knew she needed to be careful because at a certain point he wouldn't take any unfairness. In this sense, I guess one can see how and why I can be exasperated with Linda as she can be with me.

Yet we managed to typically make a 7, and then pretty much a 7.5—though at times a 6! There have also been many 8s, 9s, and even 10s along the way, at nice restaurants that were not too noisy, and with soft jazz playing, plus nice walks and drives we took, as well as other things we did together, and also because we always coalesced with respect to the presence of our sons. There was also always romance between us, along with everything that goes with it.

Now, let me make this abundantly clear. Children always make it worse because they bring out the worst conflicts between their parents—an undeniable fact to which both Linda and I can attest. Therefore, in general, I say: In order for a relationship to be sustained indefinitely, at least one of the partners needs to be able to suffer inordinately. If neither can do it, then the relationship is doomed. If both can do it, the relationship becomes a sure thing. Even if one can do it, the relationship stands a good chance. A good mother's helper can be an impactful emulsifier. Thank you, Michelle (our mother's helper).

But back to marital relationships. Linda and I were invited to an opening of an Oscar-nominated documentary film on the lives of a Japanese couple, both of whom are painters. It was clearly obvious that the husband, Ushio Shinohara, was a tough motherfucker (I say that with some affection), but who is a noted artist and considered a national treasure of Japan. His wife, Noriko, is a beautiful, delightful, and charming woman and also a noted painter.

At the QA at the end of the film, both individuals were present and prepared for questions. Unfortunately, no one had a question or comment. It was a packed audience composed only of couples, all of whom had been invited, as we had been. The wife, Noriko, looked at me (Linda and I were in the front row) and motioned to me.

So I picked up on her cue and commented about the idea of inordinate suffering in a marriage, at which point the audience collapsed in hilarity. Why? Obviously because it was true of Noriko suffering with Ushio, as well as it hit the truth nerve in each and every one of these couples about themselves. The gist of it all, with respect to what is a basic truth about the psychological and empirical axioms of a marriage, is then also true of Linda and me. I've discussed this all in my book *Love Is Not Enough: What It Takes to Make It Work* (2009).

Despite all our differences and difficulties, the truth is that with Linda, I always knew and deeply felt that with her, home would be where she was. I'm also reminded that when asked who you would want to be your partner in a foxhole in order to safely escape, the answer of "my wife" or "my husband" might not be such a hot answer. The reason is that as relationships go, to have a spouse with you in a foxhole for your safety could be risky, because one might not know which way the spouse's rifle would be pointed!

Musings

But I'm not through analyzing how I might be controlling. As a psychoanalyst, I feel it's incumbent on me to seek that devil in the detail that might reveal a lot about anyone's personality. In my case, I believe it started with my mother's own musings concerning, as she would say, "Where there's a will, there's a way." For me, the implication of this "willful" phrase does not mean some sort of contamination of the self, or of ego, or of some even stronger pathological narcissism, or even of any ingrained grandiosity, or perhaps of even some infantile sense of anaclitic (infantile) omnipotence. Rather, let's look at megalomania—the idea of libido directed at the self; that is, as a magnificent obsession of self-love that then becomes transformed into one's wish to be even more powerful than reality.

In my case, if it is megalomania, it is probably based upon an incessant and impossible challenge I make to the challenge of changing fate! Thus, in my case I believe my fight with fate—having lost a child (an adult child), my son Sam, at age thirty—has been impossible for me to accept, despite that the reality is clear. So I take a half step and call it a "disappearance." It is this challenge to unfairness that I believe has me in the embrace of perhaps both a megalomaniacal refusal to accept fate, but at the same time, of a lifesaving vehicle enabling me to brace myself in the face of such reality.

And I feel I am a member of a father's club (no one should be in) called the Agon Club. *Agon* in Greek means "struggle" or "agony." And I'm in good company, including, as example notable others who have lost sons, Eric Clapton, Francis Coppola (my college roommate), Paul Newman, Gregory Peck, and Mike Wallace.

But here is an accompanied problem: I had four sons, and they, as most sons, experience the father as godlike—essentially and almost by definition—possibly enmeshing them in an identification with the father and family. In fact, if there was an enmeshment in my family, then I was certainly the chief enmesher!

This kind of identification with a dominant personality, despite its ability to endow strong egos, also has its deficits. It can be the generator of megalomaniacal consequences, such as feeling that what one does should not affect anyone else, even if those others might be suffering with whatever was done; or underachieving because the fantasy of greatness is impatient with the gradual and realistic attainment of any sort of achievement; or feeling that nothing but perfection will do; or even feeling one must do what one wants, come hell or high water.

Thus, when I think of good things my sons have perhaps gotten from me, I'm also always hopeful that they haven't incorporated any megalomaniacal sense that insists on compensatory internal needs as the essential mechanism of understanding the world—in contrast to what one should actually be struggling with in reality. In a nutshell (no pun intended), I'm always hopeful that such a megalomaniacal element is only something iffy in my personality, so that I could be spared the nightmare of thinking that something about me was toxic to them.

All of it brings me back to Linda, in the sense that whatever controlling nature she might have might pale in comparison to my controlling nature. I'm reminded what my son Max once said to me. He said, "Dad, you have an iron will." Yet the contretemps here is that even were my wish to be megalomaniacal, I'm also realistically fatalistic—meaning powerless to change anything, especially pertaining to correcting past events. So with this little bomb regarding some kind of megalomaniacal possible relevance, permit me to leave this rumination and return to the issue of *home*. And with respect to the importance of home.

I felt that at Hofstra College (which I positively loved) was another point in my life where I felt this *home* thing. This was also true because at Hofstra was the first time in my life when I was truly away from my home base on Claremont. Yet this different planet gave me pause in my assumption that my dominant boy-girl thing would always be a given.

At the age of seventeen, I still looked much younger, but by the end of my freshman year, I tipped the scale at almost a hulking 130 pounds and grew my final inch, standing at my full, towering height of five feet eight inches. Thus I was not physically equipped to play football or even basketball. I certainly could have made the baseball team because I was now strong enough to hit for average and power. Although despite that I now almost looked my age, a question mark entered my consciousness regarding whether I would still experience the boy-girl magic that seemed to be always finding me. As noted earlier, right off the bat I won the school dance. So, as mentioned, in a jiffy I had become somewhat known.

Arty was a witness to the dance contest, and said, "Man, you can dance!" As it turned out, Arty and I made many friends, and I did in fact still retain the power echo of how it used to be with girls and women. In fact, one of my female teachers smiled at me one day in the way I was experienced enough to notice. It turned into a kind of dormant flirtation. On the other hand, Rhonda (not her real name), who was a popular, attractive girl, happened to be in my poli-sci class. In that class, I was ahead of the game, primarily because of my left-wing experience with respect to the politics of the world along with my very good performance in my history class at Music & Art. Therefore, after two or three sessions of my participation in this poli-sci class, Rhonda would enter the class, look around, notice where I was sitting, and thereafter sit next to me. In that class I had a consistent give-and-take humor with the professor, and Rhonda seemed to have a good time with it. I had the distinct impression that she was interested in me, despite that she had a boyfriend. After graduation, we were no longer in touch. From time to time, even now, she pops into my head. And by the way, I never saw Sue again, the one with whom I had won the dance contest. She must have dropped out of school.

Robert Plutchik, Ph.D., and me, circa 1986, when I was forty-eight and he fifty-eight. Rob was one of the most important influences of my life. He is chiefly the one person most important in my scientific education. The book I dedicated to Rob is *Dictionary of Psychopathology*, published in 2009. The dedication reads: "To the memory of Robert Plutchik—scientist, teacher, friend, brother."

Yet, other than Arty, the most important person I met at Hofstra was Dr. Robert Plutchik, who was a professor in the psychology department, and who is the person largely responsible for my scientific education—for which I am forever grateful. He and I became good friends, and many years later eventually published clinical and scientific papers as well as books together.

I'll say it again, I absolutely loved Hofstra. The work was demanding and rigorous and the classes ever interesting. I graduated college in three years, and then six years after graduating was when I applied to an institute for a six-year postdoctoral training in psychoanalysis (which I finished in five years). At that time I had already gotten a master of arts degree in experimental/general psychology from Hofstra, and a master of science degree as well as a doctoral degree in clinical psychology in the psychology department at Yeshiva University.

The psych department at Yeshiva was not part of the religious orientation of the school; rather, it was in the same category as the Albert Einstein College of Medicine that similarly was not tied to the religious sense of the school. The five-year postdoc training in psychoanalysis at the Postgraduate Center for Mental Health was comprised of four years of training in individual psychoanalysis and two years of training in psychoanalytic group psychotherapy. It was these two programs that I, along with others, was able to do in five years.

However, I'm getting ahead of myself by jumping into postdoctoral psychoanalytic training. So let's return to graduate school. Getting to Yeshiva University was itself an adventure, because I needed to find a full-time psychology doctoral program and simultaneously sustain a full-time job. Therefore, I needed a program at some university (preferably in the Northeast) permitting full-time employment while also permitting full matriculation in the evenings.

As it turned out, that same friend, Hank B., was also instrumental here. He found the exact type of school I needed—one that offered permission to matriculate full-time in school along with working at a full-time job. And that's how I got to the Yeshiva University department of psychology as a doctoral student, with my major noted as a doctoral degree in clinical psychology.

I was a standout in this program because of my heavy load of psych courses at Hofstra, and was one of two students (out of sixty-four) who aced the comprehensive exam (a six-hour exam). I was then permitted entry into the doctoral seminar, leading to my thesis construction and to the oral defense of my dissertation.

In this doctoral seminar, I met one of the other students, who confirmed for me that I should immediately apply to the Postgraduate Center for Mental Health Psychoanalytic Training Institute, as he had already done. His name was Bruce M., and we had become good friends.

What prompted me to apply for psychoanalytic training concerned an interesting encounter with a staff member at the Middletown State Hospital, where I was on the staff as psychologist. After dinner at the staff house, many of the professional staff as well as some of the administrators of the hospital would, in the spring, summer, and early fall, congregate in a single file of about ten or so people sitting on rocking chairs across the long porch of the staff house. In a conversation with one of the aides rocking next to me, I asked how long he had been working there. He answered, "This is my twentieth year rocking in this chair." The next morning I submitted my four-week termination notice, which corresponded to when I had attained my doctoral degree, and which also came at the end of August 1964. I said goodbye to my great Middletown State Hospital, where I had a wonderful professional experience. I then called for an application to the Postgraduate Center for Mental Health Psychoanalytic Training Institute. Thus, from the time my rocking chair neighbor said he'd been at Middletown for twenty years, I didn't miss a beat.

When I called the dean's office for an application, I actually reached the dean, who told me in no uncertain terms that he was leaving the office in about twenty minutes, so that if I arrived in twenty-one minutes, he wouldn't be there. I jumped into a cab at 57th Street and 6th Avenue and told the cabdriver where I needed to go and that if he could do that in less than twenty minutes I would double the fare. With that, he took off, and I walked into the dean's office in under twenty minutes. He was there. I should again note here that at this point I had already worked at Pilgrim State Hospital, Kings County Hospital, and Middletown State Hospital, and also at two marketing/motivational companies, for a total of six years; and this was the point at which I applied for postdoctoral psychoanalytic training at the Postgraduate Center for Mental Health. In all of it I was always a full-time student and simultaneously always worked full-time.

This dean of training at the psychoanalytic institute was Dr. Emanuel K. Schwartz, a known international educator of psychoanalysis. He was not having what I wrote in the essay that he had asked me on the spot to write. I wrote that since I had gained expertise in psychodiagnosis by virtue of having worked in mental hospitals for four years (while simultaneously pursuing my graduate school studies), it was now that I wanted to deepen my training in psychotherapy, and I believed that Postgraduate Center was the way for me to go.

Dr. Schwartz started getting out of his seat, saying, "No, I'm not taking you because—"

I didn't let him finish his sentence, and said, "You didn't like that I said I have expertise in psychodiagnosis—with emphasis on the 'expertise,' right?" As I said that, I sat him back down with a sweeping wave of my hand as I also said, "Wait a minute!"

Then, while sitting, he said, "Right. I've been in this field for twenty-five years and I don't have expertise in psychodiagnosis."

My thought was but didn't say, *You may not feel expertise in psychodiagnosis, but I do.* But I did say, "Okay, here's the deal. Ask me anything in psychodiagnosis. If I get it wrong, I'll walk out. If I get it right, you must take me."

He gave me a long look. Then, not only did he take me, but after contemplating my challenge, said, "I like you, and I am taking you, and as well I'm giving you one of our two National Institute of Mental Health fellowships." The grant was for $7,000. The regular stipends that postdoc students were given was, if I remember correctly, about $2,500 or $3,000. He continued, "I'm taking a chance on you."

So Dr. Schwartz, also the dean at Hofstra, as well as Mr. Lockett at Music &

Art, gave me the same essential response that many friends and people generally—also girls and women—had been giving me all along; that is, joining with me rather than rejecting me—and at times even without my particularly asking for it—which, in this case, I did.

As it turned out, in the sixty-year history of the Psychoanalytic Institute of the Postgraduate Center for Mental Health, I would become the most prolific author of books at that institute. In addition, each year at graduation exercises I was the one to present book awards to those at the center (both staff and students) who had published an original book that year. I believe I turned the assignment into an interesting feature of the graduation program: after reading each book, I fashioned some fantastical story in which the theme of each book was knitted into the story. And in some years we had seven or eight books that had been published, so that the task I set for myself was, to say the least, not easy. The success of this idea of mine was attested to by several people who would come to me and ask whether the story I told was true.

In one of these presentations I fashioned a story about a medieval monk who wrote material that was stored at a highly classified Vatican archive, and that this monk had discovered many of the facets of what we today would identify as psychoanalytic metapsychology (essentially meaning psychoanalytic theory).

I derived a story about how I had contacted a radical priest at the Vatican, and told him that this monk's work, with the authorship listed as Sebastian of Livorno, was the work we desperately needed to see. This priest was agreeable to do the courageous thing of first locating this monk's manuscripts and then spiriting them out of the Vatican—the purpose of which was for us to compare Sebastian's work with what we already understood in psychoanalysis.

The priest got back to us and told us it was possible for him to do the transport, except that we only had forty-eight hours with the material. He could only replace it shortly after he'd retrieved it, otherwise it could risk his entire mission. However in the service of scholarship, he was opposed to all censorship and also opposed to the idea of hidden material—especially at the Vatican.

I told the audience that we got the material as well as getting it back to him, and how Sebastian's findings related to questions of contemporary psychoanalysis. I also related that we managed to store this precious material at the Postgraduate sub-basement but then pored over the material at the Postgrad library—also managing to have the library shut for the day.

Apparently, the story was so believable that many people were eager to hear more about it. One of the directors of a department at the center asked me to tell him more. I told him that the Postgrad law firm had issued strict instructions that no other information should be revealed. And each year for about fifteen years, I would fashion a new, fantastical story at these graduations that seemed plausible, but barely so. It became the intriguing part of each graduation.

In any event, at graduation from the institute when I became certificated as a psychoanalyst, Dr. Schwartz, the dean of students, who by that time was also

Newspaper article titled "The Contribution of Dr. Henry Kellerman," 1980.

a good friend, was the one handing out the certificates to all such graduates. When it was my turn, he handed me the certificate and whispered, "Some chance I took, huh?!" For some reason, that moment gave me pause, and I immediately associated to a surprise I got when my parents told me (it was in 1980) that they opened the Yiddish newspaper and were very surprised to see that the

Newspaper article titled "Henry," 1951.

writer Isaac E. Ronch had published an article entitled "The Contribution of Dr. Henry Kellerman." At the time I was forty-two. It was a full-page article on my contribution to the Yiddish art world. My photo was also included. He ended the article with the comment in Yiddish, "Salute, mine trirrehrer Henry" ("I salute you, my dear Henry").

About thirty years earlier, when I was thirteen, a first article appeared in the *Morgen Freiheit* simply entitled "Henry." This article, written by S. Davidovitch, traces my young career in the Yiddish progressive movement and commends me for my valuable contribution.

I guess that when Dean Schwartz said "Some chance I took, huh?!" it brought to mind that given the kinds of things I was doing (even as a child), I was confident that he was really not taking a chance at all; that is, I was always serious, first about my tip-of-the-spear role in the progressive Yiddish world, and then later on about my responsibility as an author and psychologist/psychoanalytic therapist/theorist. And to boot, I was, in spirit, never far away from the dance floor.

9
Friends and Dance Halls

Close Friends

At Hofstra, my roommate Arty was a finance major and I a psychology major. We took over the top floor of this two-story picture-book little house. With our doors open, we could see one another from our desks. Our rooms were separated by a small vestibule. Our work habits turned out to be that after studying and doing homework in the evenings, either he or I would look up and one of us would say to the other, "How much longer?" By this time it would be close to 10 p.m. and one of us would usually respond by indicating something like, "I need about twenty minutes." Then after about the last such twenty minutes of work time we would put our books down and split to the college hangout bar called Ryan's, approximately seven or eight blocks away from the house. We would do this twice a week.

The walk to Ryan's was a healing stroll. It was late at night and dark, and many of the private little houses along the way were also dark. Here and there a house was lit and it seemed to me that the people there lived nicely, warmly, and lovingly. Of course, with respect to *home*, it was something I had always dreamed about; that is, living in that kind of softly lit family environment that was truly a home.

When Arty and I did this little trek, it seemed like much of the world was asleep, and here we were rewarding ourselves with hanging out together and shooting the breeze. I should point out that I was also always, even as a young boy, looking into windows of apartments and houses to see if I could catch a glimpse of a nicely lit home. I guess I was always looking for something that was a facsimile of some image in my mind also as to something I yearned for. It was never a voyeuristic thing, such as in spying on women. For me it was something regarding trying to embrace something I'd always craved but never had—that I'm a bit embarrassed to say; that is, needing something like beautiful physical surroundings to match what I certainly did have: accepting and loving parents who I knew were doing everything they could, really for my sake. I think the spot of embarrassment is not wanting to identify myself with what might be considered a bourgeois need—if that's what it is.

In any event, at Ryan's we'd order a pitcher of beer and hang out until about close to midnight. Then we'd walk back, homeward bound to 25 Hope Street. The next morning, going to school, we'd stroll down the short three blocks to that locked back gate of the college and climb the fence. One of us would climb over, and then the other would hand both sets of books through the gate to the one who had already climbed, and then the one of us who had not yet climbed the fence would do so. Those fence-climbing and late-night treks became lifelong benchmarks of our experience going through college together.

I could swear there was never a lull in our conversations, not even once over that entire three-year period. When beginning our third and last year before graduation, Arty and I, along with two more friends we had made, rented a fully furnished house in West Hempstead, and with some sadness left Vera and Carl at our special place at 25 Hope Street. Yet some months before we left, one night we noticed a number of cars lining up at the house next door. A single man lived there, and after we noticed the number of cars parking there, we also noticed it began happening every few days. From the window in the third bedroom of our top floor, we could see a bedroom and bathroom in the other house where the shades were never drawn. We decided to get the binoculars.

And indeed we did. There, with the lights brightly on in the bathroom across at that other house, was this woman stark naked and the single man who owned the house doing what could only be described as sexual acrobatics, including everything sexual except perhaps screwing on the ceiling! Then after such nighttime viewing, we of course realized that he was running a brothel. No doubt. It was great viewing fun for us. We saw so much of this that we could easily identify that working woman. One day, Arty and I were having a catch (throwing a ball to one another) on the street between our house and the brothel house. As mentioned earlier, Arty was a good ballplayer, so that he could throw the ball and place it wherever he wanted it to go.

Of course, the moment he spotted our working woman about to leave her car that she had just parked outside of her—this working house—Arty threw the ball in a high arc, which then came down for me to catch as I was backing up into our working woman's arms, who was at that moment halfway out of the car. She embraced me as a way of balancing herself while catching me—as I caught the ball. She and I looked at one another, and I apologized, to which she smiled and then congratulated me on a good catch. "We both made a good catch," she said while laughing, as she quickly walked into the house.

A couple of decades later, when I was already writing books, I dedicated one of my books to Arty. The book was entitled *Greedy, Cowardly, and Weak: Hollywood's Jewish Stereotypes* (2009). On the dedication page I wrote, "For Arthur Libman (Arty). It was the best of times." I also had dedicated a book to Richie, entitled: *Love Is Not Enough: What It Takes to Make It Work* (2009), in which I wrote, "For Richard Grillo, lifelong blood brother. Love you, Rich." The reason it was the best of times with Arty was only noted because I was away from home and for the first time, as I said earlier, was not supervised by anyone. It was a truly first full phase of independent living, and I believe both Arty and I implicitly felt we were experiencing a strange land, fighting the good fight, and therefore in a foxhole together.

My childhood experience with Richie was, of course, something unparalleled. The only difference was that we were living with parents and were under their supervision—as are all fortunate children. Richie and I did everything together for more than a dozen years, starting from the age of four: movies, playing ball, hanging out (also in either apartment), trekking through new neighborhoods and discovering things. We both felt very lucky to have had each other, and we would discuss it. To this day, in both our eighty-fifth years, our blood brother-ship remains ironclad.

In my opinion, another detour here necessitates a brief note of my relationships with other very close friends. In the category with Richie and Arty is Henry Bender (Hank B.) and Bernard Becker (Bernie). Actually, Hank B. was instrumental in my life. He was the one to get me to Hofstra—arguably one of the best experiences of my life—as well as finding Yeshiva University as perhaps the only university at that time (1959) in the Northeast that enabled a student aiming for a doctoral degree in psychology to work full-time as well as being a graduate full-time student. The point was that I needed to work in order to make expenses.

Hank, Bernie, and I were bunkmates for a number of summers at camp. Bernie and I had been friends from the city, where during one of my performances at a Yiddish event that he and his family attended, he approached me and we talked. We hit it off and were great buddies during all of our adolescent years. I would sleep at his apartment on many weekends after we had gone to parties, hootenannies, and any number of other social events. I remember Bernie turning on the radio as we were going to sleep, and on two or three of those occasions, the radio was playing Ravel's *Boléro*.

Bernie, I, and another bunkmate, Ronnie G., were the ones involved in the only triple play in the history of camp softball in the summer of 1952. We were playing against boys in the group older than we. They had men on first and second with no outs. The next batter hit a rocket to Ronnie, who was playing third. Ronnie tagged the bag at third and fired a laser beam to me at second, at which time I pivoted and sent a missile on a straight line to Bernie at first. Bernie then gave me a fist pump, indicating that my throw was a strike and that it came in fast and hard (as did Ronnie's to me).

So with Bernie B., as well as with Hank B., I was in another foxhole, loosely identified as growing up together through adolescence. Being in a foxhole together is the detail that reflects the overarching context of such togetherness. It's because you go through a war together and thereby experience it together that it then becomes the glue, the context of the relationship.

Bernie and I, and Hank and I, had that kind of special togetherness throughout our adolescence. Of course Richie and I were in that foxhole together growing up on Claremont from the age of four to seventeen—and that was something indelible

(*Left*) Bernard (Bernie) Becker (right) was a lawyer and judge, and my closest friend during our adolescence. The book I dedicated to Bernie (and to Hank Bender, who is on the left), is titled *The Discovery of God: A Psychoevolutionary Perspective*.

(*Right*) Henry (Hank) Bender was a Ph.D. in human factors engineering. Hank and I were close from our summer camp years till the end of his life. Hank is the one person who had access to all of my career arenas.

In the book I dedicated to Hank and to Bernie together, the dedication is in memory of them both: "Devoted forever friends."

for each of us to this day. We always thought of one another that when we grew up we'd be the same height. However, that didn't quite work out. Our birthdays are in the same month and twenty-five days apart. I'm older. Richie is six foot five inches tall and I made it to my five feet eight unimposing inches medium. But the handwriting was on the wall from the beginning, because even at the age of four, Richie was a full head and some taller than I. His Italian Catholic heritage somehow gave him a height advantage, which wasn't true of my Ukrainian Jewish little-shtetl heritage.

It was interesting how Hank B. and I hit it off. It was highly unusual for me not to be able to sleep at night. Rather, it was typical for me to fall asleep instantly and sleep the night through. However, in camp one night I awakened at close to midnight and found myself wide-awake. I lay there for a while in my top bunk, looking around at this group composed of about a dozen boys asleep in their double-decker beds. Finally, I said to no one in particular, "Anyone up?" Hank looked up at me and answered, "Yes, me." And that was the start of our special friendship.

We took a couple of pillows and blankets, tiptoed out of the bunk, and spread the blankets on the grass. The counselor and the other boys were all asleep. We talked for about an hour, each of us took some puffs of a cigarette, and we decided we would be in touch when we got back from camp.

This was 1953. We were both fifteen. We did exactly that, and stayed friends for the rest of Hank's life. Hank died in his late fifties. His personality problems created traumas for him, and he was unhappy with his original nuclear family (his sister died in her early twenties). He also went through a difficult divorce from his first wife, the aftereffects of which left him bereft and traumatized for quite a long time. His second wife, Judy, saved the day. Other than that, his mother was the problem. She was a hovering, controlling person, who generated in Hank a simmering, irrevocable anger (see Kellerman, H., 2013b, *Anger: A Love Story*).

I dedicated a book to both Bernie and Hank, entitled *The Discovery of God: A Psychoevolutionary Perspective* (2013), in which I stated on the dedication page that I honored and appreciated them. Bernie became a judge and focused his efforts in the courts on behalf of Native Americans. Obviously his progressive Kinderland experience went a long way to inform his life. Hank attained a doctoral degree in human factors engineering.

With Bernie and Hank B. I was always feeling at home—especially since we three were bunkmates at Camp Kinderland for four or five consecutive summers, and we also sustained our friendship throughout all of the seasons of the year. All three of us had parents who were similar in outlook and all foreign-born, and all speaking and feeling very good about Yiddish and its hopeful prospects for the future.

This idea of Yiddish as it corresponds to feeling at home and also to feeling secure was very well illustrated in a Yiddish poem by the poet Rutka Veksler. The poem is entitled "Leed" (Poem/Song):

Vee der girrl zul meekh varfn (*Wherever fate lands me*)
Oo eekh zul in laybn zine (*Wherever I find myself in life*)
Nem eekh mit mine Eeiddish leedle (*My companion is my Yiddish poem*)
Bin eekh kanymul nisht alayn. (*So I'm never alone.*)

Hut men alts meer tsoogenoomen (*They took everything from me*)
Oon getribn meekh foon shtoob (*And drove me from my home*)
Hut mine mammeh meer gegebn (*But on the road, my mother gave me*)
Oifn veg ah Eedish leed. (*A Yiddish poem.*)

Khub gefeert es in vuganen (*I carried it in wagons*)
In dee lagehrn oif pine. (*In the ache of the work camps*)
Iz mit meer mine Eedish leedle, (*So because my Yiddish poem is with me*)
Bin eekh kaynmul nisht alayn. (*I am never alone.*)

In dee Daitchehsheh barakn (*In the German barracks*)
Nokh der shverer arbet—meed (*After slaving there—exhausted*)
Zeeng eekh kayner zul nisht hern (*I then quietly sing to myself so no one can hear*)
Meer a hartsik Eedish leed. (*My heartfelt Yiddish song.*)

Eedish leedle, leed foon benkshaft (*Yiddish poem and song of longing*)
Foon a mammeh, foon a haim, (*Of a mother and of a home.*)
Eekh gay mit deer in vytn leybn (*I accompany you along my distant life*)
Bin eeskh kaynmul nisht alayn. (*And thus I'm not ever alone.*)

For me, this poem was precisely how I always felt about Yiddish itself, along with how I felt about my close friends; these friendships were embracing, comforting, and nourishing. These were my nuclear friendships of Richie, Arty, Bernie, and Hank; I also shared a close pal-ship in junior high school with Stanley G., but then I shipped myself off to the High School of Music & Art. So when you're both that young and for such a brief moment of time no longer in the same foxhole, Stanley and I gradually were no longer in touch. Despite that, I still retain a very warm feeling of our friendship and still hope, one day, to see him.

In camp I was also in a best-friend relationship with Ray, who lived in Philadelphia, but that too was of a rather short duration—probably about a year or two. Other close friends included Henry Hoepker (another Hank), whom Arty and I met in the summer school abnormal psychology course. Arty, I, and this Hank rented a house for the three of us in West Hempstead for our last year at Hofstra. In short order, Hank B. joined us.

We also had another friend who roomed with us at that house, making it a contingent of five. It was none other than the future world-renowned writer, producer, director, and now wine connoisseur/entrepreneur of Coppola Wines, Francis Ford Coppola. In those days we called him Franny. He and I have retained our contact through the years, and to me he remains Franny.

Once when his film *One from the Heart* was playing at the Radio City Music Hall in New York, my wife, Linda, and I stood in the rope line along with scores of other people after the film ended and waited to see if he would emerge from the lobby. Sure enough, there he was. "Franny," I said as he passed me. We hadn't seen one another at that point for about a dozen years. He shouted, "Henry!" He grabbed my arm and pulled me under the rope line, at which point I grabbed Linda's arm and pulled her along. Up to the RCA Tower we went, to a lavish gala he was throwing, and at which point he held an interesting press conference. Of course I see all of his films, and whenever I publish a book I inscribe one and send it to him.

In the summer of 1969, after five years of not seeing one another, I visited Franny at the Warner Bros. studio in Burbank, California, and stayed with him for a few days. During those few days, a very interesting thing happened, which I've written about, but as of this writing, have not yet published. I believe it would make an interesting magazine piece.

I wrote:

It was August 1969. I was on a month's vacation, as is the tradition with shrinks during August. I left New York City and flew to Los Angeles to attend a conference on psychoanalytic psychotherapy. While I was there I visited a close friend/former college roommate who was now a successful Hollywood film writer/producer/director. I arrived at the studio and after our hellos, he gave me a grand tour of the studio. Then I was the first person to read his newest screenplay.

After that read, we spent a good deal of time talking and catching up. I reminded him of a time a decade earlier—It was New Year's Eve 1957—when in a blinding blizzard of a snowstorm we were on our way to a New Year's Eve party and were driving in his Peugeot on the West Side Highway. Sure enough, a flat tire. On top of that, his heater was on the blink so the car was ice-cold and we were freezing. He told me not to move, that he was going to change the tire. I saw he didn't have gloves, and I was worried his hands might freeze and adhere to the jack. Yet with no hesitation, he pulled the car to the far lane, jumped out, lifted out the spare from the trunk, jacked up the car, and changed the tire. In another jiffy, he climbed back in, saw me shivering, and assured me we would be at the party in ten or so minutes. I remember thinking, "This guy can do anything!"

Anyway, back to the studio. After I read the screenplay we had lunch at the studio commissary, where I was introduced to a number of celebs and to whom he announced that I was coming on as the company shrink. We all laughed. After lunch, he told me he needed to be at a meeting and wanted to drop me off at a park in order to keep a protégé of his company. This protégé was a young man in his early to mid-twenties who was working on a sci-fi screenplay that my friend was producing, and this protégé was spending time at the park sitting on a bench, writing. My friend told me he would pick me up in a couple of hours. He imagined his protégé and I would hit it off and that we would surely have an interesting conversation.

We got to the park, he introduced me and took off. His protégé and I actually did have an interesting conversation, also including a discussion of his sci-fi idea. At one point he told me that my friend was giving him ninety-five dollars per week as salary but that he needed another fifteen dollars to make it. He asked me whether I would lobby for him to get the extra fifteen dollars. I told him I would and that I was sure it would not be a problem.

Time zipped by and my friend arrived. My friend's protégé and I shook hands and I winked to him as though to say, "Don't worry, I'll see to it." Then my friend and I drove to his house where I spent the next few days. That was a bit more than fifty years ago. Ultimately, the protégé I met sitting on that park bench became highly successful—and are you ready for this? He recently sold his other franchise sci-fi series for $4 billion. Yes, "billion"! I've since heard that with other rights he had in the franchise, the total remuneration reached more than $20 billion.

The name of the protégé in the park: George Lucas of *Star Wars* fame. The newest screenplay that my friend had written and that I had read on that first day when I arrived at the studio was *Patton*. The name of my friend: Francis Ford Coppola.

Then in a footnote I identified myself:

Henry Kellerman, Ph.D. is a psychologist/psychoanalyst/author in private practice in New York City. His books include the novel *The Making of Ghosts*, published by Barricade Books, and *There's No Handle on My Door: Stories of Patients in Mental Hospitals*, published by American Mental Health Foundation Books.

Still another event is worth a story here regarding a midnight happening. Coppola was directing the play *The Rope* by Eugene O'Neill. At the time he was not quite twenty years old. The play was presented in the Little Theater, a delightful little structure in the middle of the Hofstra campus with a fully equipped stage as well as a nicely arranged, professionally done seating arrangement for the audience. Room capacity was approximately for sixty or seventy people.

Franny was so immersed in the entire process of the stage production that he was director, producer, stage manager, set decorator, costume designer, lighting expert, casting director, and so forth. In other words he could, and did, do it all. In this respect, one night a touch before midnight I asked the other guys where he was. Someone said he was still at school rehearsing the play. That didn't seem right to me because I knew he had school early the next morning. So I went back to the campus and directly to the Little Theater.

The building was dark, but I could see a light that was barely illuminating the stage area. There he was, lying asleep or simply resting on the wooden stage floor. We then went home.

These two events—the one about the park and this one—are the standout memories of our time together, except that we always discussed this or that about our lives, backgrounds, and potential careers. And by the way, Franny's production of *The Rope* was truly the best staging and directing of a play that I have ever seen, to this day.

The other associated memory is of Ruthie, who had the lead in Franny's play. She was a beautiful, blonde sophomore, and I had a crush on her. The other crush and close friend who I met in the abnormal psych class was this knockout Italian beauty who was twenty-one gorgeous years old named Maria. She and I have remained close friends over all these decades. I've also dedicated one of my books to her, entitled *Psychoanalysis of Evil: Perspectives on Destructive Behavior* (2014), where I referred to her as "beautiful Maria," my "forever friend." How it started: The first day of class (it was Summer Session) I was so interested in this subject matter of abnormal psychology that I took a seat in the front row center of the classroom.

Somehow right before the class started, and for whatever reason, I kind of felt that someone was looking at me. I turned around and there she was, two rows behind me, beaming a very warm, affectionate glance directly at me. It was the nicest hello I'd ever gotten. I smiled at her and took a long look.

During the break, many of us left the room to hit the coffee machine, candy machine, or bathroom. On the way to the coffee machine I walked past her as she was standing there not quite doing anything. As I walked by, I smiled at her—a smile which she returned. At the time I also was humming the song "Nancy (with the Laughing Face)"—a Sinatra favorite, written about Sinatra's daughter, Nancy. The song was written by Jimmy Van Heusen with lyrics by Phil Silvers. It happens to be one of my favorite Sinatra songs. I was singing it to myself, although audibly enough apparently for Maria to hear. It was probably about her.

The very next day, as I was approaching the building for the second day of that class, before I could enter the building Maria, who was standing outside of the building, approached me and handed me a square gift-wrapped, paper-thin package, tied with a bow on top. She smiled and asked me to open it, which I did. It was a Frank Sinatra album on which she used a yellow-colored magic marker to color over one of the listed songs on the back of the album. Of course the one she colored over was the Nancy song.

That was our romance, which by spontaneous combustion began that previous day in class, and that over time eventually transformed simply into a lifelong friendship. Maria was in high demand because she was such a showstopper. I guess she spotted me or was interested in me because, because, and because.

During the Maria time, another closest friend—in the category of Richie, Arty, Hank B., and Bernie—was Alex Kupperblatt (Al). Al's and mine was the longest ongoing friendship on a daily basis for more than forty years; that is, we shared the proverbial foxhole for all of that time, through thick and thin, girlfriends and marriages (mine and other friends we had). Al never married, was chock-full of experiences, but died in his mid-sixties. I gave the eulogy at his funeral.

Before Al died, he asked me to insert a small portable TV and a blanket into his casket, which I did. We were movie buddies, and went to several dude ranch weekends, parties, double dates, and trips to islands in the Caribbean. It was on the Stanbrooke dude ranch where I won another dance contest. When I walked off the dance floor and turned to give the bandleader an A-OK wave, he had been apparently looking at me as I was leaving and waved back. We had never spoken, but he could tell that I loved his swing band.

I dedicated a book to Al titled *Personality: How It Forms* (2012). My dedication to Al included some benchmark events of our decades-long adventures.

By this time Richie was out of the Air Force and living in San Diego; Arty was in Fort Lauderdale, Florida; Hank B. was in upstate New York working in what is referred to as human factors engineering; and Bernie B. was a judge living in the Midwest. Another close friend/roommate, Adrian A., was raising a family and working at two psychology-oriented jobs on Long Island; and Jerry Y., still another very close friend (we were colleagues), was living in Liberty/Loch Sheldrake, New York. Jerry and I were very close and worked together as psychologists at Kings County Hospital in Brooklyn, and after that at Middletown State Hospital. It was Jerry who got me to Middletown. He got the position there first and I followed.

Back to Al. Over decades we had an ocean of experiences. Of course, many of these were way outside of my sensibilities. For example, we went on junkets which were gambling gratis vacations—certainly a different planetary world far from my progressive shula/Kinderland Yiddish life, especially because on one of these occasions I met one of the higher-ups involved with the French Connection heroin-smuggling ring that was depicted in the Gene Hackman film *The French Connection*. It was not that I was relinquishing my sense of what the world was all about. Rather, I began finding myself living in a variety of environments—each one different from the other—and liking it, and yet also feeling a bit estranged in each of them except for home base, which seemed like the shula/Kinderland/Yiddish terrain, along with my Claremont Parkway home base, and for sure my freedom-home at Hofstra. Yet, even in all these situations, I'm still not really certain as to whether I was ever feeling completely what I would call "at home." These various environments, such as a few junket trips, were especially eye-openers to a sense of what the world was really like and what people were doing with their lives, and whether any such people ever had a notion of cultural influence other than pragmatism—that is, the idea that validity is governed only by some hedonistic factor of "solely if you like something."

All of these other environments were essentially antithetical to my original situation on the Yiddish-speaking radical left. These other environments included Latin nightclubs such as the Caravana Club and La Campana in the South Bronx and the Cabrahenio Club in the East Bronx, where I would dance till dawn to the bands of Johnny Pacheco, Eddie and Charlie Palmieri, and Tito Puente, and where along with Al, we may have been the only gringos there—albeit Jewish ones. Yet, at the Cabrahenio Club, whaddaya know—there was Richie dancing alongside me. We

Alex (Al) Kupperblatt. Al and I were best buddies from about 1959 to his mid-sixties when he died. The photo was taken circa 1970, when I was thirty-two and he thirty-seven. The book I dedicated to Al is titled *Personality: How It Forms*. The dedication reads:

> "In memory of Alex Kupperblatt, my buddy, Al; the charismatic Navy man who captained Velli, Kaye's Navy, and Vanilla. Here's to: movie lines, Stanbrooke, Sammy's Romanian, Caribbean jaunts, Montauk, Caravana Club Pachangas, and 40 years of laughing."

were in our early 20s and hadn't been in touch for a while because neither of us lived any longer on Claremont. Then about two years later, I was coming home from a party late at night and stopped on Claremont to visit my parents. As I approached the building at 493 Claremont, I hear Richie's voice saying, "Henry." Sure enough, we were on the same train, and he was also coming home to visit his parents. At that time it was about 2 a.m., so we both sat on the stoop and talked till 4 a.m. Then we entered the building—I going to my family's first-floor apartment and Richie continuing up the stairs to his family's fourth-floor apartment.

10

Different Worlds

Important Venues, Important People

In any event, the different environments in which I lived, I identify as: college, my dance world, my Richie ball playing, my world of Yiddish performance, my high school Music & Art world, my buddy-ship world—especially with Richie, Arty, Al, Hank B., Jerry Y., Bernie B., Adrian A, and Hank H.—and my heralded experience with women worlds. I managed to find time for it all—including hot vacation spots, Latin nightclubs, dance halls, and gambling junkets (I was never a gambler). And this was all happening while I was a doctoral student in graduate school, as well as still performing occasionally at Yiddish venues. Unreal!

I seemed to hit it off with best pals at each stage of my life. For example, Alex K. (Al) and I first met at a party at the house that Arty, Hank H., Hank B., Franny, and I rented in West Hempstead when the guys and I were at our last year at Hofstra. Al was invited by Hank H. He and Hank and another friend, Gene G., had grown up together in Belmont, a Bronx neighborhood not far from Claremont Parkway (on the other side of Crotona Park). Today, that Belmont neighborhood is famous for its Italian restaurants. Alex never finished high school. He was very bright, but school was not for him, and he went into the Navy during the Korean War. He and Hank H. were four-year Navy vets. After we met, Al and I had a tremendous lot of fun together over decades. Our friendship stood the test of time and we were important to one another.

Finally, there is Gerald Yagoda (Jerry). As mentioned above, Jerry and I met during our psychology internship at Kings County Hospital in Brooklyn, New

York, in 1961. It was a very selective internship, led by the Machovers, who were well-known in the field of clinical psychology. Karen Machover was the one who developed the Human Figure Drawing Test (1949) that became a standard unit of psychological assessment.

Jerry and I were two of five interns selected out of scores of applicants from all over the country. We were both doctoral students at the time, and we hit it off. For the following several years we were the best of friends, of course sharing a very important foxhole regarding our professional respective futures. After our internship at Kings County was when we also worked together at the Middletown State Hospital, in Middletown, New York.

At the time I was meandering, looking for a new position after the internship was over, even though I had been offered a position back at Kings County. Jerry had already landed a psychologist position at Middletown State Hospital and I followed him there. Jerry's beautiful wife, Marsha, made great dinners for us. I dedicated a book to Jerry and Marsha entitled *Hollywood Movies on the Couch: A Psychoanalyst Examines 15 Famous Films* (2011), in which I pointed out in the dedication just how important was the journey Jerry and I shared. We remain forever friends despite that we're no longer together in that foxhole.

In my experience of all my closest buddy-friendships, Jerry is in the category of Richie, Arty, Hank B., Bernie B., Adrian A., and Alex. I also fondly remember Stanley G., Ray F., and Hank H. Hank H. lived to his mid-sixties. Adrian A. and I are now again in constant touch, and though he lives now in Saratoga Springs, nevertheless he and I continue our phone contact and see one another once or twice a year. Adrian was also one of my roommates when I, Hank H., and Hank B. all had positions in 1958 at Pilgrim State Hospital located in West Brentwood, New York. The four of us rented a house in West Islip on Long Island which was a fifteen-minute drive from the hospital where we all worked in professional positions. I also dedicated a book to Adrian, titled *On the Nature of Nature* (2023), in which I pointed out our collegial and personal friendship.

At this point, Franny was at UCLA, and shortly thereafter ensconced in Hollywood directing his first notable feature, *You're a Big Boy Now*. Ray F. and I reconnected after many years (actually, after many decades) of not being in touch, and we continue an on-again, off-again email relationship.

There are three others whom I need to mention. These are friends whom I cherish, although not in the sense of being buddies who hang out together. The first is Robert Plutchik. Rob was the professor at Hofstra whose doctoral degree

Adrian and me. We were college friends and in 1958, immediately after graduation, we took our first professional positions together at Pilgrim State Hospital.

from Columbia University was in experimental psychology. As it turned out, I was one of his standout students. We hit it off, and ultimately became good friends and colleagues. As mentioned earlier, we published several clinical papers in professional psychology journals as well as publishing a psychological test, *The Emotions Profile Index* (1974). In addition, we published an edited five-volume set covering the entire field of emotions. Rob was clearly a genius. He had published several hundred papers and several books, and held positions at Hofstra, the Psychiatric Institute of Columbia University, and the Albert Einstein College of Medicine. He was a Renaissance man who also sculpted and published poetry. He died in his late seventies. Ultimately, he took the course I taught at the Postgraduate Center for Mental Health on projective psychology. Thus the professor (he) who taught the student (me) became the student (he) taught by the professor (me)—which is testimony to the issue of mentorship value. In fact, at Hofstra I became Rob's assistant, and on two occasions, when he was unable to teach, he asked me to take over the class. I was a senior at the time, and on both occasions I felt quite at ease taking over these classes, which in each case covered the area of the psychology of emotion theory (about which I had already become thoroughly familiar). At that point in my last semester I had the opportunity to also teach several sessions of an industrial psychology class. Of course, in my later professional career I taught the courses Psychological Diagnosis, Psychotherapy Process, Interpretation of Dreams, Developmental Psychology, and Experimentation in the Social Sciences—as adjunct professor at the City University, New York University, Postgraduate Center, and the New School.

I dedicated a book to Plutchik entitled *Dictionary of Psychopathology* (2009), where I honored him as the person most responsible for my scientific education—for which, as I proclaimed earlier, I am truly and forever grateful. The second person in this category is Eleanor Wheeler Wimble, who was the social work supervisor at Pilgrim State Hospital, where I worked for one year—1958 to 1959. Eleanor was an exceptional clinician and a wonderful person who had influenced scores of her supervisees, of whom I, as well as Adrian A., were two. We three became good friends which also stood the test of time. In my first book, entitled *Group Psychotherapy and Personality: Intersecting Structures* (1979), I indicated her value as a great supervisor and a wonderful, empathetic individual.

The fourth person in this category is Dr. Anthony Burry. Tony and I have similar credentials in the field (he is a Ph.D. psychologist/psychoanalyst), and when I was director of the psychology internship program at Postgraduate Center, he was assistant director. When I retired as director, he naturally was appointed as the new director of the program. As far as credentials, training, and theoretical interests in the clinical field, Tony and I were mirror images of one another. In addition, with respect to his intellectual stature, Tony is a finely educated individual; highly intelligent; and a competent, well-trained creative clinician, psychologist, author, and psychoanalyst-practitioner. We eventually coauthored six books, and we always found it to be a pleasure working together. We wrote these books on Fridays from 10 a.m. to 2 p.m.—a four-hour explosion of productivity that was ongoing for a number of years.

It was with Tony that I began to realize the importance of little details; that is, at times we both could identify and knew it would be important to stop writing and rather to discuss an ostensibly or seemingly unimportant detail which we both sensed needed examining. We could tell that this so-called seemingly unimportant detail might lead us to a better synthesis of the material we were covering, as well as possibly revealing something newly important. It was this kind of collaborative work that made it all exciting and valuable.

I dedicated a book to Tony entitled *Psychotherapeutic Traction: Uncovering the Patient's Power-Theme and Basic-Wish* (2018), in which I noted how I valued him as an equal partner in our collaborative work. As a footnote, Tony would always supply us with a thermos of tea. I've always felt about that thermos of tea the way Popeye always felt about spinach. Yes, yes, Tony is a special person.

Also at this point, Arty was gone. He became a stockbroker, soon married, and soon was raising a family. We gradually lost touch for about five or six years, largely because we were no longer together in that foxhole and each of us was busy building our respective lives—he starting a family and career, and I focused on career but not at all on permanence with respect to marriage and family. We regained our contact and have been again as close as ever for all these ensuing decades. Arty was two days shy of turning 86, to my 84, when he died.

Years after our work at Pilgrim State and for the succeeding numbers of decades, although Adrian and I hadn't been in touch, we reconnected after I read an obituary about his wife. I called him, and as I've noted above, now we've been in constant touch. In addition, during my professional career as a psychoanalyst, Robert Lampert, Ph.D., was my office mate at our Gramercy Park office for more than two decades, and we were very good friends as well as very much like-minded. He and I were also avid Knicks fans (basketball) and watched any number of games together (Willis/Clyde era). Abraham I. Cohen, Ph.D., was also a very special close friend and colleague during the period when he and I were in postdoctoral psychoanalytic training, and along with Linda, and Abe's beautiful wife, Julie, we four would occasionally meet for dinner.

Of that professional period, and of all the contacts there, the two classmates at the Postgrad Psychoanalytic Institute, Robert Marshall, Ph.D., and Arnold Rachman, Ph.D., remain close friends, and to this day Bob, Arnold, and I have a standing dinner get-together the first Thursday of each month.

Hank Bender, my Kinderland bunkmate and lifelong friend, was special insofar as he was the only friend who had a glimpse of all the environments in which I lived. As mentioned, Hank B. was the one who first got me to Hofstra (arguably the one place I considered to reflect where I experienced my greatest freedom), and also to Yeshiva University, where one could work full-time and still attend evening graduate school full-time as well. At that doctoral program I was therefore able to do all my graduate work on Wednesday evenings (two courses) and on Sundays (three courses). The school was closed on Saturdays.

It's interesting to me that none of my closest buddies knew all of my environments as well as all of my careers—except for Hank B. He saw it and experienced it all: my Yiddish performing life, camp life, college, graduate school, my dance life, my professional psychoanalytic life, my girl/woman extravaganza, my publishing life of books that I authored and edited, my early Claremont Parkway street life, my ball-playing life, my early nuclear family life, and my adult family life with my wife Linda and four sons: Max, Sam, Harry, Jack—my undeniably fabulous acronymic MaSaHaJa gang.

This characteristic partition of these various environments of my life—even with respect to what each of my friends knew or didn't know—gave me the sense that even here, I was also living a kind of life of *anonymity*. And it seems that perhaps this kind of partitioned anonymity made it better for me in the sense of providing greater peace of mind. I believe it may have been too much for most people to handle, in the sense of feeling that compared to them, I possibly was really an alien. I'm also a bit removed despite my gregariousness, and thus I can live in different worlds, and even in the sense of aloneness, even seek different worlds.

Thus, my untethered life, about which my parents only knew very little (except for the Yiddish performing part), was the element chiefly responsible for my sense of anonymity. This sense of anonymity enabled my liberation from commonplace expectations, so that I was free to follow my impulses and adventures into all sorts of different environments that would usually be unexpected from high-minded tip-of-the-spear individuals.

As it was, most people who only knew about my highly productive professional life (psychotherapy practice and writing of books) would variably say things to me like "When do you have time to do all of that?" Or "Do you ever sleep?" Along with this kind of perception that some people seem to have of me, others who were especially neurotically competitive would actually be angry with me, or find things to be angry about, because despite our friendship, when it came to the issue of jealousy or envy or simple competitiveness, I became for them someone to avoid, simply because it may have created a kind of failure in this neurotic competitiveness that they may have harbored. This is what I believe fractured the relationship that I enjoyed (that we both enjoyed) with a dear friend of mine who recently died (in 2023).

Professional Job and Sudden Affluence

In 1958–1959, immediately before entering my doctoral graduate program, it became important to land some kind of job that would be related to what I was ultimately going to do as a psychologist. With no money, I would need to have that job in order to make going to school possible—so that again, the problem was tuition. Lo and behold, I landed a position in a motivational/marketing research firm at the end of 1958 as a project director. This was more or less at the same time as I began studying for my doctoral degree in psychology.

At that time, Senator John Kennedy was preparing his potential presidential run, and Robert Kennedy selected the Simulmatics Corporation to organize a national survey poll essentially to ascertain the extent to which John Kennedy's Catholicism might be an obstacle for him in pursuing the presidency. Furst Survey Research Center, a motivational/marketing research firm, was selected to do the polling for Kennedy's potential presidential bid.

It was at Furst Survey where I was already working. By that time I had attained a Master of Arts degree in general/experimental psychology (1959), having gained expertise in measurement techniques as these techniques, for example, could be applied to perception—that is, how people saw things. Such measurement techniques would become the key instrumentality in gathering and analyzing data from these polling surveys. I was the only one on staff who understood how to do it all, so out of the blue, at the age of a touch under twenty-two, I became the field project director of the 1960 presidential poll for Senator and future President John Kennedy.

My particular function was that of computing the data which was collected and statistically analyzed out of the offices of Furst Survey Research Center in New York City, as well as supervising subcontractors in various states who were having difficulty with data workup. With my considerable total salary and bonus for the entire project, I was able to finance all of my further graduate school expenses to the end of 1964, when I had already graduated with a second master's degree (a master of science degree) and then, of course, with a doctoral degree in clinical psychology. At the end of that presidential polling project and with the financial rewards I received, I knew it was time for an acute shift in my professional trajectory—an internship in clinical psychology, and postdoctoral education in psychoanalysis.

As a postscript, apparently results of the polling were leaked, and we at Furst

Survey were told that Robert Kennedy wanted everyone to submit to a lie-detector test. I didn't leak anything, and nevertheless, under the threat of being fired, I still refused to take the lie-detector test. I was not fired, and eventually the leaker was identified as someone outside of Furst Survey.

However, and with some regret, I soon thereafter left my lucrative position with Furst Survey for more schooling, although at the time I had also consulted in the same capacity for another research firm as well. After completing all my coursework, I had also then completed my doctoral dissertation, which was the development of a personality-emotions index (test), and defended this more than one-hundred-page doctoral dissertation at an oral examination to an academic doctoral committee of five professors.

However, even before one could enter the phase of conducting the study and writing the dissertation, one needed to pass a written comprehensive examination, the structure of which comprised a two-hour short-answer exam as well as a four-hour essay exam.

When I confronted this very high bar, including my admission to the exam, a total of sixty-four students had qualified to take it. The simple qualification was to pass the entire curriculum of coursework, entailing a ninety-credit curriculum of courses. This meant completing the work and passing credits of thirty classes. At the rate of five classes per semester (for fifteen credits), plus twelve class credits in summer school for a yearly total of forty-two credits, I was able to complete this requirement in two years. The credits added up to eighty-four, and in addition there were another six credits for an externship clinical position. This made a total of ninety credits, and so at that point I was admitted to the comprehensive examination.

Counting time studying for the comprehensive exam, counting the time completing all coursework of the ninety credits including the time to achieve a second master's degree, and finally, counting the time it takes to conduct a study and write the dissertation, adds up on average to seven or eight years, or at times ten or even more years, that it would normally take to graduate. I did it all in five while still dancing on weekends at the Caravana Club—doing Latin dances such as the pachanga (a hard-core Latin dance featuring violins, flutes, timbales, piano, double bass, and guiro, a ratchet-sounding instrument for emphasis) with three hundred other fabulous dancers in this cavernous dance hall located at 149th Street in the South Bronx.

I even danced there instead of studying the night before the comprehensive exam, so that I and friends of mine (Alex Kupperblatt and Gloria Messer) danced pachangas till three in the morning to the four great charanga bands of Johnny Pacheco, Charlie Palmieri, Mongo Santamaría, and Tito Puente. Then I slept for about three hours, showered, and went to take the exam—which is testimony to the adage by George Bernard Shaw that youth is wasted on the young. Yet I was one of the two who passed the test without requiring extra coursework. This was also the case when I took the exam for Diplomate in clinical psychology and in psychoanalysis. I passed with excellent reviews. These exams indicate that the test taker has reached the pinnacle of recognition, with the highest-ranking mastery of the specific fields of endeavor regarding its subject matter.

The only other event where I was selected as in some way outstanding was at Camp Kinderland in the summer of 1950, when my counselor, Ben R., who we called "Hartford" (because he came from Hartford), identified me as the most outstanding camper of the bunk, where we had sixteen bunkmates. This counselor was my favorite over my five years at camp, and I learned an awful lot from him. He was a great model for me and he was a great guy.

My mother died of heart failure at the age of eighty-two. It was very difficult even to comprehend that she could ever be a person who could die. At that point I was forty-eight years old and my cathexis (a psychoanalytic term for "emotional investment") had already partially shifted to my wife and children so that I was able to factor her passing into my life with at least some equanimity. Thank goodness for her gift to me of optimism. My father died of lung cancer about a dozen years later at the age of ninety-five. Again, I couldn't imagine him gone—but there it was. He was my anchor and my strength. In the dedication to them both in my first book, *Group Psychotherapy and Personality: Intersecting Structures* (1979), I stated that they were the central guiding and caring figures of my life. I said: "I love you and embrace you, and dedicate this book to you both." In view of how I was fortunate to have very close friends and family, the following Yiddish poem, "Ahn Oitzer" (A Treasure), written by Sorah Fell Yellin, is one that I frequently have rendered at many memorial services for friends and family. It is a poem that values friendship above all else and is therefore a component of progressive Yiddishism in the category of valuing peace and consideration for all—and in Yiddish the rhyme is graceful.

Ver es shpourt hyzer, oon ver es shpourt gelt,
   (*Whoever values opulent homes and wealth,*)
Eekh shpoure meer oup gootteh frynt oif der velt.
   (*I value good friends in this world.*)
A vild fremdeh shtut, Ah fremder vugzall,
   (*Even in a strange place, a strange venue,*)
Oon plootsloong dergrekht meer ah varehmer shtrall
   (*I suddenly experience a warm feeling*)
A blik oon a smaykhl, men git zeekh dee hent
   (*A glance and smile and a warm handshake*)
Vee noenteh vous hubn zikh shoin yourn gekent.
   (*Like with close friends from long ago.*)

A nyer freint douh, oon a leeber frynt dourt,
   (*A new friend here and another there,*)
Eekh hub shoin an oitzer azah opgeshpourt. (*I've already assured such treasures.*)
Yedder bazoonder, varemkite khain (*Each one separately; warmth and charm*)
Mit zay vel eekh kaynmoul nisht blybn alayn.
   (*With such friendships I'll never be alone.*)
Kh'vel efsher fargesn a puhnim a shtreekh,
   (*I might forget a likeness or a characteristic*)
Dee fryntshaft vet gleehen oif aibik in meer.
   (*The friendship will be forever a light.*)
Fartooshn vet nemen dee rashikeh tsite, (*For sure, time will fleetingly pass,*)
Nour oitzer vet vern k'sayder bannite. (*But my treasure will be forever, indelible.*)

11

Precursor Career

My Psychotherapy Compass

My career was going to develop along the psychologist track, and then finally morphed onto the track of psychoanalyst. In a rudimentary form, a career in the general sense of psychotherapist was coalescing in my experience even as a seven-year-old. And here's the story.

The question becomes: Why did I pursue a career as psychologist in the first place, and then finally as psychoanalyst? Second, why this instead of pursuing an acting career based of course on my considerable Yiddish performance experience? That's the kind of question regarding the "why" of it that people ask themselves concerning their motive for entering the field of psychotherapy or, for that matter, any field of endeavor. It also becomes a question that others are curious about whenever they discover what I do for a living. And by the way, psychoanalysis is only one of the systems of psychology—it is the system of psychodynamic psychology.

The difference between a psychologist, psychiatrist, and psychoanalyst is that the psychologist has a Ph.D. doctoral degree in psychology, and a psychiatrist has an M.D. medical doctoral degree and is a physician. To become a psychoanalyst, either of these doctoral individuals must traverse a rigorous postdoctoral certificate in the psychoanalytic method—the one attributed to Sigmund Freud and others, which requires another four or more years to even seven or eight years of postdoctoral work. Certified clinical social workers and psychiatric nurses are among those also psychoanalytically certificated. The Ph.D. degree in psychology is a doctoral degree meaning a doctor (D) of philosophy (Ph) in the specialty of psychology.

Thus, the Ph.D. in psychology is considered a scholarly, philosophical, and research degree in the psychological sciences: in learning and developmental theory, psychology of motivation and perception, social and developmental psychology, group behavior, industrial psychology, in individual psychodynamics, in neuropsychology, as well as in a number of other subspecialties. A Psy.D. is a sister degree of later vintage, meaning doctor of psychology.

In any event, the general answer I've given myself, with respect to adding the title "psychoanalyst" to my psychologist credential, is that I thought I'd be good at it. But although that answer is accurate insofar as it's what I actually thought, it is, however, not specific. The specific answer would need, it seems, to have a genesis to it; to be part of a process that started very early in my life and that then created a path through life onto which I navigated directly toward the profession of doing psychotherapy. I never had the slightest intention of becoming a psychiatrist; the idea of medical school was never on my mind. That was true also of canceling any notion of becoming an actor.

When I was 17 years old and graduated high school, a producer contacted me. I don't remember his exact title. He had seen me in a Yiddish play and felt I would be very good playing a role as a teenager in a play that apparently would be opening on Broadway (on the American stage, not on the Yiddish stage). And the first thing he wanted to know was whether I spoke English, and if so, if it was without an accent. He actually said, "You speak English, right?"

So we had a conversation about various things when he again mentioned Broadway. I thought he mentioned Broadway as a good way to slay me with interest and motivation. How wrong he was. I had already made up my mind for a college education to be followed with a doctoral Ph.D. degree. In fact at that point in my life I eschewed any notion of being in a situation of memorizing reams of material as well as the inordinate suffering of needing to participate in endless rehearsals. In fact, I had always known that after high school I was ultimately headed to graduate school.

What I didn't know then, especially in a concrete, particularized way, was that the idea of anonymity in life very much appealed to me. The thought of being known on sight never entered my mind as something desirable. Therefore, as nicely as I could, and on the spot, I turned him down and discontinued any further conversation about any other possibility that would have had even a remote chance of it changing my mind. Psychology and psychoanalysis was what it would be, and I was planning to do all of it as soon and as fast as possible.

However, I think I know that there was another, very prosaic reason that drew me to the psychologies and not to theater. I believe it was the ingredient in my personality that craves relaxation, passivity, and convenience. In contrast, I abhor tension, over-excitation, and certainly inconvenience. My dream was to have a private practice of psychotherapy, and that the office needed to have proximity to wherever I lived. I've always sought to eliminate extra time traveling to and from work, and with respect to my need for anonymity (and proximity), a private practice was perfect. In fact, it is what I eventually made for myself: a comfortable office suite that I furnished so that it is somewhat less formal than an office and somewhat more formal than a living room. It is uncluttered, and all sorts of art adorn the walls of the office—including about a dozen diplomas and certificates of achievement. And over the decades I've reveled in the ease and comfort of it all.

My only regret (and I do have regrets) is when I see actors discussing their roles with one another, and also knowing that the experience of extemporaneous behavior onstage (even given the unadulterated fact that lines need to be memorized) is no doubt very interesting. The point here is that if I could have been typically placed in whatever role (while having read the script so that I knew the storyline and nature of the character)—but didn't have to memorize these lines and instead could just have winged it—then to be an actor may have been irresistible. Yet the chaotic-like process of getting a production to work always felt to me as a very busy and inconvenient undertaking, and one full of what to me also felt like a process characterized by over-excitation. When I take my tranquil, relaxing walk seventeen blocks to and from the office, it's quiet and unobtrusive, and a pleasure. My office is similarly quiet and without commotion. I think that I desire to always promote and manage to arrange my life so that especially with respect to my profession, I seek what to me feels like a low level of tension along with a bit of anonymity.

So, yes, there was a genesis to my interest in psychotherapy, psychopathology (neurosis, psychosis), psychoanalysis, and all the rest of it. In certain respects and without quite understanding it, I felt that my personal direction was, without any interruption, going to be something that I defined as needing a kind of academic intellectuality. Yet what was also visible to me was that art generally, and acting specifically, was infused also with emotional intellectuality and that, in addition, the entire structure and function of drama (about which, of course, actors are instrumental with respect to its interactive performance), is quite dependent upon an incisive intelligence and no less dependent on access to emotional truth.

Yet, with respect to my aim of developing a career in the arena of psychotherapy and psychopathology study, the unalloyed truth is that I'm in a thrall to idiosyncrasy, and always have been. It possibly could be said that I actually love pathology. Well, let me explain. It's that I love to be near it, to see it, observe it with a clinical eye, and, very importantly, with an empathetic eye. I feel strongly sympathetic with people who are severely and emotionally psychologically ill (disturbed). I can see what they feel, but what they think is, for me, where the mystery lies. I must also admit that observing pathology (and its implicit dynamics) is for me an aesthetic gratifying pleasure; it's like looking at something awesome, different, unusual, and deep—perhaps even, dare I say, beautiful.

The objective of psychotherapy, which I couldn't as a seven-year-old conceptualize, was this idea of the beauty and the essence of *struggle* —the only true understanding of the psychotherapeutic endeavor. In fact, my experience as an actor on the Yiddish stage, and as an individual performer of Yiddish material generally, was such that I could feel my personal struggle as defined by trying to pre-digest such material for the audience so that the audience could see and identify with the issues of the content of such material.

So, again, how did it all start, or where did it all start, or when did it all start, or why did it all start? The answer, as one might expect, started, I'm a bit reluctant to say, with a description that is usually assessed as a cliché; that is, with the relationship with my mother—and I believe I understand it.

It was not that she didn't love me or that I didn't love her. It was not that I came from a broken home. It was not that I was neglected. It was not that my father was cruel or an isolate or uninterested in me. I believe it all started because I felt sort of—betrayed. Yes, betrayed! And I felt this sort of betrayal when I was about two years old. That's right, even two-year-olds can feel such things.

The Family Psychodynamic

Up until I was two, my mother didn't work at a standard nine-to-five job. She was with me all the time. There were no stranger nannies or mother's helpers or babysitters—that is, there were no people around who were not in the immediate family. However, my bubba lived with us, and mine, as I've now repeatedly noted, was a Jewish immigrant family. My bubba spoke no English except to nod hello and wave goodbye—nodding her head up and down for "yes" and side to side for "no"—assuming she even understood the question.

Therefore, my first language as an American-born son was Yiddish. As mentioned earlier, I learned English on the streets of the Southeast Bronx in New York City—where we first lived in the Bronx, on Fulton Avenue, which was southeast of Claremont Parkway. But at home, especially with my bubba, I spoke only Yiddish. My parents learned "American" very quickly. So with my parents I spoke both Yiddish and English, but with bubba it was strictly Yiddish.

A pivotal situation occurred when I was this two-year-old who glimpsed this so-called betrayal. As I've said, my mother was my primary caregiver and was with me all the time. She was, and remained, a very loving parent. As I've also noted, she was an extraordinarily talented person and could do almost anything, and further, do it with great élan. She sang beautifully with that smoky alto, she was a great dancer, great cook, could sew anything, spoke several languages, and was an actress who could do accents and all sorts of roles requiring what she had—rhythm, perfect pitch for gesture, and unusual overall talent.

When I was two years old, and completely accustomed to her attention, love, affection, companionship, and safe harbor, she, one day, suddenly announced that she needed to go to work with my father in a little luncheonette that they were going to open—a store that was located at street level of the four-story tenement-like apartment building where we lived.

My talented, beautiful mother apparently thought that telling me she would be only a stone's throw away from our first-floor apartment (one flight up) would mollify my unhappiness about her departure—a departure that each day would bring her home in the evening. She reminded me that my bubba would always be there, and then she introduced me to two young babysitters who arrived at our apartment at the precise time my mother was telling me all this. Each babysitter was to alternate their babysitting stints during the week.

I wasn't shaken by the news, but I was definitely disappointed. Betrayed is really what I felt, but I couldn't put my finger on that particular word because, of course, I didn't know that word. I couldn't tag my feelings to that word until I was much older. And, of course, betrayed is a feeling, existing within the context of abandonment, and underpinned by disappointment, and the disappointment correspondingly underpinned by anger. So the fact of the matter is that I was angry with my mother, didn't know it as a specific, but nevertheless, definitely loved her.

Up to that early point in my life, I was a well-fed and chubby baby. And then, may I say hyperbolically, that after this catastrophic news of what I must have experienced as her disappearance, apparently I lost my appetite, or more to the point, I think I *decided* to lose my appetite. After that, and later on in life when contemplating it all, I realized that psychologically and emotionally I refused to eat until she nullified the ostensible abandonment and came home—which in any event she did each evening after working in the store. Then from a plump infant, I gradually became a skinny kid who, as the years passed, always looked much younger than his years.

To put it simply, I think I was angry and so I stopped eating. In fact, I really didn't even have an average appetite. Furthermore, later on, during the years whenever I was getting ready to perform, I was reluctant to eat because I was afraid I might belch during the performance. Therefore, over the years I missed a ton of meals. I also believe it would be accurate to define my situation as barely eating to live and not living to eat—or even never looking forward to the next meal. Essentially, I had a symptom; that is, I was in a protest!

As I look back, I can also see that my resistance to eating was also a result of the difficult situation I had. You see, with every moment of my parents' lives trying to make the store work, we would have almost all meals in the store because they were always working in the store. Therefore, perhaps I was too much of an aesthete and too much of a wishful person, so I didn't like eating in the store with all those people around. My idea was for the three of us to eat at the kitchen table at home without an army dining with us.

As I see it now, it wasn't just a simple protest I was in. Rather, it was a phenomenal protest. In fact, I vividly remember a dream I had in which I was standing with a machine gun spraying bullets at a row of mirrors that were mounted on one of the walls of the store. However, when I had that dream, about at the age of fifteen, I also instantly knew that despite my anger at the store (in which my parents slaved—the burden of which fell on my mother), it was that same store that kept us going.

Of course, as a shrink it then occurred to me that when one is angry, it is not typically or perhaps ever focused on an inanimate object like a store. Rather, it's always anger toward a person. Therefore, my great father, whom I loved, was also the reason my mother needed to work, and work, and work, and so he was the object of my anger. At the time when I was fifteen, I kind of knew it and I kind of didn't know it. Now I know it.

Yet I can't ignore the fact that in the dream I was shooting that machine gun at a row of mirrors so that while facing this row of mirrors, I was actually seeing *myself* being shattered. So what does that mean? I believe it means that in shooting, and thereby shattering those mirrors, I was in a way expressing my anger and obliterating myself (subtracting myself) from this entire issue of the store being my home. Since we had most of our meals in the store and since my parents spent most of their time in the store, then in a way, I fused the idea of home and store.

Interestingly, I began to notice that my appetite always and without fail would reappear whenever I was eating away from home. Again, in later years it gradually dawned on me that this eating symptom was an anger disguise because of what I considered to be that betrayal. Even later, it further occurred to me that my forgiveness index was very low, almost to zero. In that way, no one could ever confuse me with a devout and true Christian. This zero forgiveness index, then, was no doubt the birth of my personality trait of "protest"—to this day. But at this point I can say, "Mom and Dad, I forgive you." This near-zero forgiveness index was no doubt germinated and nourished on my full agenda, my full menu of Yiddish protest literature. I call it "my full menu" because it appears that the Yiddish literature was really my food, my nourishment—so I guess, at home, I didn't really need real food. For example, Ber Green, the *Morning Freiheit* associate editor, wrote the poem "Gedenk" (Remember). The gist of it, its essence, is in response to the Holocaust. Here is a fragment:

Gedenk. (*Remember.*)
Nikoumeh nem. (*Take revenge.*)
Mine farshnitn lebn nit farshem. (*Do not shame my shattered life.*)

This poem, which I had rendered many times, as well as others like it, apparently had its effect on me. That is, its message may have been for me overdetermined (meaning it probably also imposed itself as something self-referenced). Therefore, no, I was not immune to the messages I conveyed in my performances so that the reality of the material was also felt by the gathered. And I was part of this gathered. Yes, I was indeed very affected by what happened to Jews and others during the Holocaust. At the time I did indeed realize just how deeply it all meant to me, but did not realize how it all apparently *permanently* affected me. I wanted all of Germany and its people—destroyed!

This poem by Green expresses how I felt and continue to feel about the only truly tangible response to manifest and profound injustice. Here is the entire seven-line poem:

> **In shouwen heleh, in shouwen grroyeh** (*In hours of hell, in grayest hours*)
> **In mine zikorn, brent a tsevoweh.** (*A promise lives in my memory.*)
> **Mit bloot is geshribn oif ghetto vent:** (*With blood written on Ghetto walls:*)
> **"Zokhoir, gedenk, nikomeh nem!** (*"Remember, vengeance take!*)
> **Mine farshnitn lebn nit farshem."** (*Do not shame my shattered life."*)
> **In shouwen heleh, in shouwen grroyeh** (*In hours of hell, in grayest hours*)
> **Mit meer gayt oom dee tsevoweh!** (*In me lives the promise!*)

Yes, I believe that promise does indeed live inside of me, so that it becomes obvious that a child delivering such messages, specifically regarding the genocide of Jews, would become infused with the emotions attached to such content. Yes, I was shaped by what I was understanding and by what I was saying to these interested audiences.

But it could be that I was primed for it. The reality of it all was underpinned by what I knew about the pogroms in Yaruga. So, talk about remembering! In addition, I likely experienced my mother's working in the store with my father perhaps as an abandonment of me, so again, no less, talk about the sense of injustice, and therefore how I must have related it all possibly to my personal experience regarding this so-called betrayal.

Nevertheless, the so-called betrayal was also diluted by my sense that if my mother was doing this, it must have been important. I believe I also instinctively knew that she was doing it in order to save the family. That's right, two- or two-and-a-half-year-olds can understand or feel a great many things—things most people do not believe a two- or two-and-a-half-year-old can feel. But they can! However, my understanding of it all was not the entire psychological dynamic that I now feel as to what was more fully operating.

You see, my mother really was always in love with my father. And anyone who knew my father would understand why that was. Thus, when she told me she'd be working in the store with him, I now in retrospect understand that she truly always wanted to be with him—and tending to me on a full-time basis, while he was away somewhere working, would not be as good to her as her working full-time with him, shoulder to shoulder.

Thus, I believe my mother had a conflict and was ambivalent about not always being with my father. She may have been worried about his attractiveness to others and needed more control in the situation. She was also always crazy about him. And I believe that it could be that I'm in an oedipal dilemma; that is, the germ of my need for anonymity could be a function of a conflict. The conflict is on the one hand for me to be concerned that my mother would love me more than she loved my father. Or the more unconscious sense that, no, she actually couldn't love anyone more than she loved him. Thus, the solution for me may have been to seek anonymity as a way of disregarding and denying this kind of oedipal dilemma, or to be invisible as though not to count—not to be viable. This possible basis as perhaps the fount of my need for anonymity becomes, for me, a little theory not to be ignored—especially since it dovetails with my early sense of betrayal when she went to work in the store with my father and as I was left (abandoned?) in the apartment with my bubba. Remember, when it all happened I was two years old!

The fact of my bubba's presence at home enabled my mother to have a ready-made rationale that enabled her to have me entirely protected even though she herself wasn't at home full-time. I don't think she was conscious of it all—fitting the psychological tenet of the *unthought-known*; that is, somehow feeling it but not knowing why—having it not underpinned by a specific thought.

So that's the way it was, and this situation generated my first patient. No, it was not my mother. It was I who was my first patient. It was me.

12

A Seven-Year-Old Psychotherapist

I had a vague feeling that my father—handsome, intelligent, and the regular guy that he was—really couldn't make a living. Yes, even though I was coming out of my toddler stage, I still could sense that everything was all right in the family if my mother backed it all up. My father was (as I've noted) as honest as they come; he was loyal, and he had pride. As also noted, he could not tolerate unfairness, and had a sophisticated, democratic, even Marxist sense that equitable distribution of wealth should be the norm. However, his practical sense was essentially perhaps naive (perhaps he was in denial). Again (also as I've noted), he was maximally risk averse—the prototypical anti- or rather non-entrepreneur. He could not abide any thought that he might owe someone something and not be able to repay it.

Therefore, my father's ability to make a living was challenged, and so my mother with her can-do-anything attitude (who was, as also noted, always crazy about him) jumped into the fray, and they indeed opened that little hole-in-the-wall luncheonette, where she was in the back cooking all kinds of Jewish foods, and he was in the front serving and washing dishes and taking care of the cash register.

And that's how I grew up—with my bubba in the house and my parents in the store. Of course, I also spent much time in the store with them, at least until I went to kindergarten. I was only four years old when I was accepted into kindergarten because my parents could no longer afford even the pittance babysitters were paid in those years, and they needed to get me off the streets.

Okay, the first day of kindergarten arrived, and my mother ushered me into the classroom of the school, which was street level and diagonally across from where we lived. But I had another idea. I asked her to remain at the door and to not enter. All the other children had their mothers with them in the room, and these children, to the best of my recollection, were crying. I was not crying, not scared, and not at all caring about anything except going to the other side of the room to the windows in order to look out at the street, trying to see where my block would be in relation to the window through which I was instantly planning and doing some, shall we say, reconnaissance.

Sure enough, standing on a stool, I could see my building diagonally across the street from the school. Now I knew that if I needed to get the hell out of there, I could run out of the room, make an acute right turn, and head for the school door that would let me out onto the street. Then I would make a dash for it and run diagonally across the street, directly to my building where Richie would be, and the store where I knew my parents would be. I figured it all out in a flash, turned to signal my mother and waved her away. She left.

It has occurred to me that had I been living in a middle-class, all-Jewish neighborhood, I would not have had the burden of needing to secure extra safety strategies and tactics. I feel this as a certainty, and in retrospect as an ironclad truth. I also believe that this sort of implicit discernment about one's environment exists in one's personal calculus almost from the beginning—no matter the environment.

So here I was in kindergarten, and I was perfectly fine. I further see that because I had felt what I considered an abandonment when my mother went to work about two years earlier, I also felt a sense of independence, that I would need to take care of myself and perhaps also all of those around me. So at age four I was already getting set to do psychotherapy, especially with what I felt was my unusual sense of empathy with others.

However, decades later as a psychoanalyst, I also realized that my position regarding not needing my parent there at that first day of kindergarten reflected an unmitigated interest in being free; that is, I believe I was already escaping— and I believe I experienced an exhilarating sense of freedom about it all. I believe I was feeling the need to get into the world. And in that sense, I didn't need my mother to protect me in this new world—this kindergarten world. I could and even looked forward to doing it myself. It could even be that I may have unconsciously felt that if she could leave me, then I could leave her.

In fact, this idea of going it alone had other verifications of its possible truth.

For example, in my adolescent years, despite my virtuosity in a number of things, the other side of the coin was any delicious escape into *anonymity*. In addition, when I was a camper in the summers, I would need to be reminded that I never wrote home.

The additional possibility regarding escaping into anonymity is that even though I felt that my tip-of-the-spear responsibility was something I looked forward to because, as I consciously felt it, I was definitely making an important contribution to these hardworking immigrants whose basic motive was to make America more ideal; yet, unconsciously, I may have felt it as a burden—as something that was interfering with my normal curiosity concerning what weekend experiences, that I could have had, might be awaiting.

In addition, I guess my idea was that my parents' store was not a home, and therefore my protest about it all was, as an example, not to write home because the question was: Was there a home? Therefore, again, if I was angry, I didn't know it consciously. However, the director of the camp needed to remind me that my parents had called him because they had not heard from me. Of course, the classic example of it all was that I was instantly not afraid to be without a parent even on the first day of kindergarten when I was four years old.

Later, as a young adult, I loved flying places, and then even later on, when I bought a place in Napeague on the East End of Long Island directly on the dunes of the ocean, it was a most freeing feeling of being away (into anonymity)—possibly that I'd ever had.

At that early point I also felt—nay, I knew—I could navigate my life and perhaps help in the navigation of the lives of others. I believe my kindergarten teacher, Miss Dubin (whom I loved and who, I sensed, loved me), also felt I had certain special mature qualities and, without asking, and on that very first day, appointed me president of the class. It was a class of five-year-olds, and I was four.

All in all, I grew up with a bubba in the house, while at that time after school, I would hang out in the store. Those were three of my four venues (house, store, school). My fourth was playing ball in the street with my friends—especially Richie, my first and best friend (my lifelong blood brother). But there in the store was where I was essentially in training as a psychotherapist. The customers were endlessly interesting to me, and many of them had, to say the least, very idiosyncratic behaviors. And it was these idiosyncrasies that completely arrested my attention. It was there in that store where, in the sense of pathology, I was just beginning to understand the difference between idiosyncrasy and irrationality.

Mr. Jaskowitz

My next patient (as mentioned, I was my first patient) when I was in my early psychotherapy training (about six years old) was then leading to my first maturity as a budding psychotherapist a year later, at seven. This man was about sixty-five. I'll give him the name of Morris Jaskowitz. He was a Jewish immigrant to America, having arrived here at about the age of ten, in the early 1900s. At the age of twenty-something, he was a soldier in the First World War and was gassed during combat. Because of this trauma, he never recovered his normal mental functioning and was, from that time on, quite fearful and especially paranoid.

Mr. Jaskowitz's seeming only respite from worrying about the FBI was when he displayed his artwork. I thought he was actually a very good artist, and his sketchbook, although seeming to me to be quite artful (perhaps "quite artful" in my naive opinion), was loaded with, and contained features of what I could tell even then at my young age, what looked like suspiciousness, guardedness, and vigilance. It was in the eyes of the figures he sketched. The eyes were highly articulated. They were wary eyes, and the line quality around the eyes was an anxious one—shaded and overprescribed (staccato-like), as if the figure he drew was in a pronounced state of ominous apprehension.

It was interesting to me that even when I was that young, Mr. Jaskowitz spoke to me without feeling nervous; he didn't think that I was some kind of a spy or that I was out to get him. Of course, later on I understood more about Mr. Jaskowitz. I realized that he liked me and sensed that I was not malicious. He trusted me as a confidant and so would tell me stories about whom he feared and why. It was my first close-up view of a functioning paranoid delusional system.

Mr. Jaskowitz was full of stories of how the FBI was tapping his phone and following him. Of course I realized that the chief reason I had gained his trust was that even through his paranoid eyes, he nevertheless could see I was only a child; for me to be an FBI agent, or even an FBI informant, was obviously preposterous. Even with that sort of paranoid acuteness, he was not going to be preposterous. In that sense, he was normal.

Mr. Jaskowitz was a steady customer of the store, and, over the years, whenever I happened to be in the store and he would also be there, he would seek me out, and while he ate his meal, he would like to talk to me. It gradually dawned on me that I was beginning to understand what was happening to his thinking. It was a lesson in psychology.

What I saw was that one could never be able to argue logically with a delusion—no less a paranoid one. So I never tried to "logicalize" him out of his delusional thinking. I knew full well that if I tried, it would be the end of his trust in me and the end of our friendship.

The point is that even with such a well-meaning and positive motive (of logicalizing him), I still would not be even one iota closer to helping him, and certainly further away from that which fascinated me—being able to observe (close-up) his feelings and especially his mind. It hit me even then that a delusion cannot understand the language of logic and/or persuasion.

Over the years there were many other customers who would demonstrate idiosyncratic or neurotic behaviors (not necessarily pathological or irrational) and, without fail, these people would also interest me. Again, it occurred to me that without fail, I was helpless to the beauty (if I can say that) to idiosyncrasy, to the unusual—and not necessarily only in relation to pathology.

Then it hit home. When I was about fourteen years old, my bubba began displaying what in psychiatric lingo is called an *encapsulated delusion*. I only understood its basic meaning (and its reason for being) when I was in my thirties and already a practicing psychologist/psychoanalyst.

Bubba

My bubba, Pessie Pellis, born in Ukraine in 1864 (Civil War time in America), only really communicated with my mother (her daughter) and me, and infrequently with my father. My father and she never really liked one another, and they never addressed each other by name. They simply started talking to one another whenever necessary. That sort of interpersonal behavior also fascinated me. It told me something about how people are stubborn with regard to expressing pleasant behavior which they feel is equivalent to yielding—especially when angry with the other person. At the time I sort of knew what it meant, but not as a crystallized thought. I later considered this little non-interaction that my father and my bubba created as another important building block of my training as a budding mind pundit.

In any event, my mother, father, and I were always affectionate and warm, and my house was full of laughter and good humor. Yet my bubba was kind of a cool person—as in cold—and I could see she was somewhat hesitant in even embracing me or kissing me. Yet, she would do things for me, and took pleasure in making me her special salad. I could never figure out how my mother became so gregarious, growing up with a mother with that kind of austere manner. My Aunt Bessie, my mother's sister, told me that my mother was their father's favorite and he would always ask my mother to sing for him. I believe that's what likely saved her. And by the way, according to my mother, my bubba had nineteen births. My mother, two of her sisters, and five brothers survived—that's eight out of nineteen who survived. As a postscript, I remember thinking about the impossibility of my bubba being in a position of doing you-know-what at least nineteen times???

Thus my bubba was my third patient, starting when I was a small child, but gaining its full measure when I was about fourteen. My bubba was really alone most of the time. She had very little interface with neighbors. She would talk aloud to herself, even when coming from the market where she shopped for her special foods in stores run by Jewish owners who also spoke Yiddish to her. I would frequently see her speaking audibly to herself while she was walking. At home she would also talk aloud to herself.

Bubba was also a very stubborn person who could never admit to being wrong. Her feelings were more important to her than truth. I later realized that many people consider ideological positions more important than truth. And no matter how often their ideological positions may have empirically actually proved to be wrong, they still never take the position that they possibly could be wrong about anything. And that was my bubba. I quickly developed a sense that truth trumps ideology every time.

The trouble, I noticed, is that with delusion, truth means nothing. In a descriptive sense, a delusion seems to be the furthest extrapolation of the ideology—its apotheosis, the deification of something, or the most extended point of the ideology, and such a bona fide delusion is really something quite extraordinary.

From my later professional psychoanalytic vantage point, rather than its seeming relation to a belief, the delusion rather relates to the person's *wish*. As a belief, or even as an illusion, it would be expected that the so-called delusion could be confronted by logic and facts (except perhaps in the belief of the supernatural). But this is where the alleged connection between delusion and belief (or illusion) disintegrates. The delusion can only be reached (touched) by understanding the person's *wish*. My bubba's encapsulated delusion illustrates this point. And I believe here it is.

As mentioned, when I was about fourteen, my bubba developed this encapsulated delusional system. This meant that she was reasonably normal in her thinking about everything except one thing. This delusional, immovable and encapsulated thought of hers contained two parts. Her first claim was that I would sneak into her room when she wasn't there, open her trunk (which literally had not been opened for more than thirty years), and then, secondly, with a razor blade, slice the threads from the hems of her dresses, which again hadn't even been looked at or touched by anyone for all those years.

My thought was that the impossible situation here was that the threads of the hems of her dresses were with high probability burned away by age—if they were burned away at all. These articles of clothing actually traveled with her from the old country. They had been in her trunk for those decades. These were also articles of clothing she never wore. Second, she also claimed the same for the dresses and shoes that she always wore—the ones she had hanging and stored in her closet—those that were purchased for her here in America. In these cases the hems of her dresses and flaps of her shoes (that she claimed I sliced) were in perfect condition. But that didn't matter to her. It was a discrepancy she simply disregarded.

Despite my sense that it was not possible to argue with a delusion—especially with a stubborn person—nevertheless this got the best of me and I pleaded with her to believe me that I didn't do any of it. Of course she wouldn't listen. I reminded her that all I was interested in was playing ball with Richie and my other friends and that I had no interest whatsoever in her articles of clothing—and I said it all in Yiddish, of course, because that's the only way we could converse. I think I also felt (and most likely continue to feel) that if one speaks Yiddish, then how bad could it be?

On that note, it occurs to me now that my bubba never knew or was never apprised of my Yiddish performance career during the entire time it was happening. She just never knew about it. Amazing. As I think about it, I believe she was so much unaware of the dramas in America that I believe my mother didn't bother telling her things because of the filler (such as background history of things) that would be needed for her to get it all, to understand it.

Nevertheless, I pleaded with my parents to open her trunk in order to examine the alleged torn hems. At first they felt awkward about doing it, but at last when my bubba went shopping, they did open her trunk. First my mother went up to the apartment and opened the trunk. I was with her. Nothing was touched and not a single hem was sliced. Then she went down to the store and my father went up to examine the trunk. I remember insisting they both be in on the deal. I was with him, too. In addition, the shoes in her closet, which she claimed had been sliced with a razor blade at the flapped edges where they should have been bound, were, in contrast, in perfect condition. I felt entirely exonerated. We never told her about our findings.

In any event, and as I remember it, her complaints became dormant, and in short order I no longer lived at home. At seventeen I left for college and that was it for living at home. My bubba died at the age of about ninety-four. At the time I was twenty.

From a psychoanalytic perspective, and many years later, the meaning of her delusion became more obvious to me. She was very definitely a lonely person. She had no friends, despite the fact that there were two other elderly Jewish neighbors (widows) on our first-floor apartment house where each of the four flights of our building had three apartments. What was always interesting to me was that none of these three elderly neighbors ever had much interfacing with one another (all of course spoke Yiddish), and, in addition, they never even stepped one foot into each other's apartment. To this day, their sense of explicit partition puzzles me. The greetings they offered one another (in Yiddish, of course) were addressed with surnames. This may have been an old country cultural tradition.

I would occasionally ask my bubba whether she ever had girlfriends in the old country. She would then regale me with stories about her best friend Rokhl (Ruth). We would also occasionally sit by the window, and she would ask me about various people that were walking along on the street. I would tell her anything I knew about them, and these stories interested her.

Thus, my bubba wanted a friend. She was really *wishing* for someone to visit with her in her room, in her domain. It was that particular *wish* that she translated into a delusion. Freud said it: in reality wishes are frequently denied, but in the psyche no wish will ever be denied. That's why Freud also said that we love our symptoms. We love our symptoms because they are our wishes realized, albeit in perverse or neurotic form (Freud, 1926). Freud's word was "neurotic"; I added "perverse" to it.

And my bubba, by definition, must have loved her delusion despite the fact that it gave her a problem. She loved her delusion because as a symptom it represented a gratification of the *wish* to have someone actually be in her room—a familiar person with whom to break bread, with whom to talk and tell stories—a peer, a friend, a companion—a lover? But, as a delusion, she translated the wish so that her own psyche (a psyche that did the translation) would not permit her to know and focus on just how lonely she really was. She just didn't want to know. How about that for a perfect unconscious encryption?

However, as a psychoanalyst, I can see a deeper meaning to her delusion. The idea of someone having opened her trunk that had not been opened in decades can also be—are you ready for this—*a sex fantasy* (a wish), especially with the addendum of the ostensible tearing of the hems of her dresses. And the tearing of the hems of her dresses is likely also a reference to the tearing away of her privacy (*private* is the operative term here), and correspondingly representing a repression of such needs—notwithstanding such thoughts.

I know this may sound far-fetched for the uninitiated, but trust me, it is not far-fetched at all. The fact that she was a grandmother in her mid-eighties doesn't mean anything, because loneliness can be the mother of all needs and passions. And, it needs to be noted that even in very elderly people, these needs and passions are never, ever, sated. Of course they are frequently dormant, but never ever erased.

Thus, as can be seen, I was, early on, gestating an education in the psychology of the person's psyche (self to self) as well as in the psychology of interpersonal relationships (self to others). Further, psychoanalytically, her focus on me opening her trunk was again, in high likelihood, an extreme and oblique unconscious reference to a sexual need as "an opening"—the yielding of her needed secret. Even thinking or writing this is disturbing—and that slicing the hems of her dresses and shoes may also be an unmitigated reference to *vaginal penetration*—rape fantasy or not. Please, dear reader, as I've noted, again keep in mind that desire is never over, no matter the person's age and no matter who the other person in this ostensible drama might be—in this case, me! Even if such reference crosses personal boundaries such as family boundaries, unconscious motives of one's psyche disregard basic laws of civilization, and instead are always focusing solely on gratification of needs and of one's *basic-wish*.

As noted above, in the Freudian sense, a person's wishes are frequently denied, but in the psyche, no wish will be denied. Further, arguably the greatest insight regarding the infrastructure of personality was of Freud's discovery that "*behind the fear is the wish*." Therefore, in my bubba's psyche, she wanted "company," but knowing it consciously was impermissible. So, in her encrypted unconscious, she reversed it all; that is, that it was I who was sneaking into her room—as though she was a victim and I was the culprit. So consciously she felt threatened.

However, that's not the end of the psychological story here, because under the fear lies a layer of anger toward the "who," the person who is ostensibly responsible for it all—me! Because such anger is unconscious, it meant that she had internalized it (swallowed it).

The key here is that repressed anger will then attack the self, because that's what anger wants to do—to attack. Therefore, here are the axioms regarding repressed anger, to wit:

Where there is repressed anger, not only will there be a symptom, there must be a symptom.

Where there is no repressed anger, not only will there not be a symptom, there cannot be a symptom.

Ergo, my bubba had a symptom, which was the delusion.

All of these ins and outs of symptoms can be traced in my book *The Psychoanalysis of Symptoms* (2008), as well as in my book *Curing Psychological Symptoms* (2020).

Bobbeh, eekh feel a bissle shooldik vile eekh hub derklert farsheedineh zakhn—oikh derklert vegn dine pseekhahlogia. S'z nisht a shlekhteh zakh vile alleh mentchn in leybn hubn dee zelbeh zakhn in zeher s'korn. Eekh vayse az doo bist zeher a gooteh, a mentch mit a gooteh nishoumah, un eekh hub deekh leeb.

(*Bubba, I'm feeling a bit guilty because of the things I've discussed about you in public. Please forgive because the basic principles I've explained here are also true of every person on earth—no exceptions. I know you are a very decent person with a good soul, and I love you.*)

Simon

When I was about fifteen, I had my fourth patient. It was Simon. He also would come to eat in the store, and that's where he revealed to me what he considered his most precious thought. It was this: Simon felt that he was the only one in the world who understood how both animate objects (people, animals) as well as inanimate objects (chairs, tables, napkins) also felt. And one day while I was sitting at a table opposite to him, Simon pulled a napkin out of the napkin holder resting on the table, and looking at me, said:

"See, kid, I can't even tear this napkin apart because I can feel the pain it would cause the molecules being pulled apart."

Again, I understood many years later that Simon was very angry about the world (especially people in it—or some particular person in it), but it was all underneath, beneath his consciousness; his anger was repressed. As a repressed emotion, the anger he felt—in the assumed negative sense of feeling anger—was disguised as its positive opposite: a concern for all living things. And to Simon, live things meant all things—animate and inanimate. After I left for college I no longer saw Simon. But I definitely remembered him (and probably permanently retained a healthy respect for molecules).

But there was more. At the age of twenty-seven, I opened my private practice as psychologist/psychoanalyst at a Gramercy Park address in New York City. And, lo and behold, there was Simon. He was the daytime doorman of the building. We hadn't seen one another for a decade. The last time I saw Simon I was seventeen, and here I was now twenty-seven. The moment he spotted me he said, "Kid, it's you."

He was the same Simon with the same concern for molecules. Of course, by this time my psychoanalytic doubt index was at an all-time high—about how people can say one thing but really feel the opposite (frequently without really knowing the true feeling). In this respect, I knew that Simon was angry about almost everything and that he felt the world had dealt him a very poor hand. It was then that I coined an axiom actually based on what I could see was Simon's sense of his so-called fate. The Simon axiom is: "Life does not cooperate!" Therefore, Simon's concern about not even hurting a molecule had another more menacing, insidious, and even sinister meaning to it. To exaggerate in order to underscore this point, I would illustrate just how angry Simon really was with the world by saying that yes, he actually would not want to separate a napkin because the separation would hurt the molecules; rather, he would really, underneath it all, want to explode an atomic bomb; that's how angry Simon was—and didn't know it.

I then discovered that Simon lived in the underground garage of the building in a derelict car at the far wall abutting the building's boiler room. Obviously, he would be warm in winter. He sponge-bathed in the staff locker room/bathroom in the basement.

Simon was alone. He would be sitting or sleeping in that car against the far wall of the basement. There was not a single soul with whom he could share a common experience. Simon's aloneness reminds me that he could have been marching with those shoes that were piled higher than the Alps—primarily because he was considered an outlier, someone who could be ignored. In fact he was Jewish. It's almost as if he felt there was never any evidence of his existence.

Shulshtayn writes:

Meer zynen sheekh dee letsdeh aidiss (*We are shoes—the last evidence*)
Meer zynen sheekh foon ainiklakh oon zaydess
   (*We are shoes of grandchildren and grandfathers*)
Foon Prague, Pareez, oon Amsterdam (*From Prague, Paris, and Amsterdam*)
Oon vile meer zynen bloiz foon shtuff oon layder
   (*And because we're only made of cloth and leather*)
Oon nisht foon bloot oon flaysh (*And not of flesh and blood*)
Hut yeder gemeetn dem gehenem flam. (*So each of us met the Hellish fire.*)

Thus, with Simon, he may have felt that there was no real evidence of his existence; that he was an insubstantial person.

13

Professional Career

The Promised Land

In contrast, now here I was, sitting in a class of postdoctoral psychologists, psychiatrists, and master's degree clinical social workers in our first orientation day at the Postgraduate Center for Mental Health. The Postgrad Center was considered the largest psychoanalytic postgraduate training and treatment institute in the world. At that time in the mid-1960s (1964), when I was twenty-six years old, psychoanalytic treatment was in its glory, in its heyday—and Postgraduate Center, along with the William Alanson White Institute and the prominent and legendary New York Psychoanalytic Institute, was seen by many to be among the finest of the psychoanalytic centers.

We were a class of twenty, with ten in the full-time day program and ten in the evening program. I was one of the daytime ten. The dean of training, Emanuel K. Schwartz, was conducting one of the orientation groups with the attendance of five of us. Schwartz was the one who had almost rejected my application but then, in the end, accepted me, along with giving me the opportunity of gaining a special stipend and fellowship from the National Institute of Mental Health.

Without any other introduction, he called on each of us and began by asking what we thought about how psychotherapy treatment worked. Various points of view were heard. I was the fifth and last one called on to render my sense of it all. I'd always wondered why Schwartz decided to call on me last. The fourth candidate said something like establishing good rapport with the patient was the most important objective. "Well, Dr. Kellerman, how about you? How do you think psychotherapy treatment works?" I actually had been thinking about that sort of issue ever since I was seven years old and sitting and listening to the stories customers of the store were telling me about their concerns—as I was sitting across from them at a table in my parents' luncheonette. Then later on in my adult life, especially in the four years that I'd already worked in mental hospitals, I'd decided that the strongest substance in existence is not necessarily iron or steel, because there are certain combinations of atoms that would produce materials perhaps literally even a hundred times stronger than iron or steel.

In thinking about it, I decided that the exotic answer to that question had to be *personality*; that is, that personality can be arguably included in the conversation as to which material is the strongest—the one most resistant to change. Therefore, I started at that point and answered Dean Schwartz by saying that in my opinion, the best we can hope for regarding change in psychotherapy treatment is about two or three percent—out of a one-hundred-percent possibility. That answer invited some surprised reactions from the gathered. But I continued by saying that I've also considered the possibility that, therefore, the idea of *cure* as a goal of psychotherapy is pure fantasy; that *cure* is not relevant except perhaps in the curing of some emotional symptom such as, let's say, fear of flying. I continued by saying that therefore, the entire enterprise of psychotherapy depends on the patient's willingness to engage in one's personal struggle.

Thus, engaging in one's personal struggle means that the therapeutic endeavor enables one to create a bridge from the therapy room to one's outside life and will increase the probability that such a person will be able to work on this personal struggle—otherwise the therapy stays in the therapy room, and the therapy then translates into a simple catharsis but doesn't enter the domain of struggle.

I ended by predicting that empathy has an up/down personality, so that there needs to be some confrontation that also enters the picture of the therapist-patient relationship—otherwise, with perfect and uninterrupted empathy, the patient begins to feel that whoever they are and whatever they feel is not in need of any change at all, and certainly not even the two- or three-percent change that is really necessary for every person on earth. In this sense, the "up" of empathy is that it creates trust and an emotionally secure feeling. However, the "down" of empathy is that it may keep the patient on a so-called hamster wheel, going nowhere. Actually, this idea of the need for some confrontation in the therapeutic process was the essence of a book written years later by my colleague and dear friend, Abraham I. Cohen, Ph.D., entitled *Confrontation Analysis* (1982).

When I finished my prolegomenon, silence ensued. Schwartz then used what I had proclaimed as the theme of the rest of the orientation. In fact, it seemed to me that I took so much time answering his initial question that I experienced myself as someone who said a smart thing, but feeling also as someone who had spent a lot of time thinking about it all.

I believe I was simply translating what my feelings were in my own relationship with audiences for whom I performed my Yiddish material, which was characterized as sharing both the importance of Yiddish and also, of course, of the importance of the socially conscious material I was delivering. When I performed for such audiences, and in my delivery of the material, I invited the audience in with *empathy* for the content, but also challenged them with the idea of *confronting* injustice, which was usually the aim of such material in the first place.

I later also began to think that the therapy becomes a work in progress, and the therapist-patient relationship (if successful) becomes a verbal conversational jazz in progress—noted particularly by improvisational interaction but based on principles of feeling, thinking, and behavior—so that it's in the art of the psychotherapist that determines when and how to use psychoanalytic scientific principles artfully.

Professionally and in all of this, I always knew I was a serious person even though a lot of my free personal time was spent in those environments that many would assess as not being serious or sophisticated, or certainly not culturally elite—and probably about which no one would ever expect me to be a part—such as South Bronx salsa dance clubs, the Caribbean, and Las Vegas gambling casinos, as well as dance contests in the widest variety of venues; and, in addition, as well as it pertains to my interactions regarding romance and overall youthful exuberance. So it's not really possible to know anyone unless or until you really get to know them—meaning to be able to see the contrasts within as well as in terms of their whole personality landscape.

Then there were the more sophisticated venues, such as in the dolphin-communication labs located in Coconut Grove, Miami, Florida, and in Saint Thomas, Virgin Islands (which I'll describe later); as well as being staff psychologist in a few mental hospitals; not to mention my work for the John Kennedy presidential survey poll, for which I was its field project director.

In any event, a perfect example of this proposition I'm making regarding the nature of my sense of the vicissitudes of psychotherapy between patient and therapist—as it compares to performer and audience—occurred in a Town Hall concert honoring Paul Robeson, the African American artist/performer idolized by the Yiddish progressive audience as the courageous champion for civil rights and human rights. At this program in Town Hall, I was a featured performer, and rendered my interpretation of a poem by the Yiddish writer Z. Vineper, entitiled "Zing, Zing, Paul Robeson." The title says it: Sing, sing, Paul Robeson!

When I ended the poem, which reviewed Robeson's trials and tribulations by the American government (because of claims that he was a spokesperson for the Soviets, and by the racist reactions to him by bigots all over the place), in the last resounding line of the poem that counsels, nay, insists on resistance and perseverance in the fight for liberty, this last line of the poem gave me a chance to shout out:

"Zing, zing, Paul Robeson!"

As I resoundingly burst out with this line—proclaimed it—there was a split second of silence, after which the audience all rose up as one (as though someone had given them the instruction to rise), and gave me, as a surrogate for Robeson, a thunderous standing ovation. In addition, with respect to themes of social conscience, I also wrote music for chorus based upon Isaac E. Ronch's poem "Hent," a poem about the working man and his struggle. My ability to do that musically comes from my High School of Music & Art education.

To continue this detour from the question asked by the dean at the Postgraduate Center essentially referring to the relationship between therapist and patient, I can also validate that when one understands the ideology or nature of the audience, then the material performed is necessarily better identified with when reflecting that ideology or nature. When that happens, there becomes a congruence between artist and audience.

To this point, my audiences were largely composed of Yiddish-speaking progressives, so that the material I chose to present absolutely reflected what they believed: for example, poems and prose that embraced fairness, love of thy neighbor, the value of culture and work, and generally also love of Yiddish, and further, most importantly, the message of the essential fight against oppression of any people, especially informed by what happened to Jews during pogroms,

The great Paul Robeson with me at the microphone. Photo taken in 1949 at Camp Kinderland when I was eleven years old. When the program was over it was a privilege for me to have a conversation with him.

the Inquisition, and the Holocaust—as well as what happened in the plight of Africans during slavery, what happened to the Armenian population in Turkey, how the Native Americans were decimated, as well as many other examples that actually occurred later, such as what happened in the Cambodian Killing Fields.

In the art of it all, what happens as a result of the privilege the performer has is that if true to itself, what the performer does is to *reflect back to humanity its humanity*. This was a comment I once made to an audience when I delivered a lecture at the 92nd Street Y in New York City on Hollywood's Jewish stereotypes (2009). That same year I heard the lovely and talented actress Ellen Burstyn answer a question put to her by an interviewer, and she said the exact same thing—that art "reflects back to humanity its humanity." In my twelve-volume original rendition of my performance archive consisting of prose, poetry, scripts of stage plays, notices of all appearances with news coverage, playlists, playbills, and letters of appreciation received, are all collected and displayed regarding poems and prose in volume 7, and a sample of stage scripts in which I participated as actor or as narrator, as well as related material, is also contained in volumes 8, 9, and 10.

Yet as important as Ms. Burstyn's and my comment is, regarding how the performer reflects back to humanity its humanity, I never got around to including it somewhere in the archive. I'm happy to have remembered to include it here.

As mentioned earlier, the archive is a record of my Yiddish performance career which can be viewed in total either at the New York Public Library, Dorot Jewish Division, or at YIVO (the Yiddish Institute), both in New York City, and also at the Yiddish Book Center in Amherst, Massachusetts. I own a Yiddish Remington Rand typewriter, and on each volume of the archive I define its contents typed both in English and in Yiddish.

As exciting as was my contribution to the Yiddish culture, my initial entry into the psychoanalytic arena was also similarly very exciting. The opening of one's mind to psychoanalytic understandings was, to me, phenomenal. The truth is that I believe I'm addicted to extemporaneous performance, although as referred to earlier, I thought I would miss the conversations that occur in theater rehearsals regarding character analyses of roles, which indeed certainly parallel the analyses resulting from psychoanalytic insights. I also love the sense of camaraderie and fun actors have with one another, and the pal-ship that develops between actors has always been appealing to me especially because as an only child, my pal-ships were also singularly important to me. But I knew that the idea of people walking up to me in the street because they recognize my face, my fame, would be really uncomfortable.

I came to psychoanalysis as a novice and then ingested it whole, so that in the end it could do for me what I needed—that is, to further a more mature development as a person as well as a professional who could work intelligently and effectively. I distinctly remember carefully reading and dissecting Freud's most momentous volume, *The Interpretation of Dreams*, a six-hundred-plus-page masterpiece. I also read it a second time after a five-year interval. In addition, the plus for me was that in psychoanalytic training, analyzing character and understanding diagnosis and psychodynamics were the key issues of treatment (notwithstanding the importance of the issue of empathy).

Years later in my professional capacity as a psychoanalyst, I realized that apparently, when I feel transgressed upon or treated unfairly, it goes deep, and so it seems I have a tendency to be unforgiving. In retrospect, I also realize that my parents opened that luncheonette because then my mother would be able to help my father earn a living. She cooked, he served. Mom, forgive me. In reality I was never abandoned.

And so it went for more than an ongoing half century, whereby my private practice was successful, and as an unplanned side effect, contributed to making me quite affluent. But for me that wasn't enough. I never thought about doing it, but somehow one day I began to write a professional paper on the subject of group psychotherapy and group structure. It was 1974 when I started writing this paper, which in the long run turned out to be the seventh and eighth chapters of what morphed into my first book, published in 1979. Yes, it took me years to write it. It was the first science book in the group therapy field, and its title is *Group Psychotherapy and Personality: Intersecting Structures*. When I began writing that book, there were under thirty books in the entire group psychotherapy field, and just about all of them were "how-to" clinical practice books, meaning how to do group psychotherapy. In contrast, mine was an attempt to understand the science of it. This book has now been republished with the new subtitle (*Group Psychotherapy and Personality: A Theoretical Model*), in the year 2015, by American Mental Health Foundation Books (thirty-six years after the first print appeared). Several months after the book was first published, it garnered a Distinguished Book Award.

Writing books was not particularly on my mind. But one day I just started to write that paper, and suddenly the skies opened and I knew I would be spending the rest of my life as both a private practitioner as well as an author of books. Yet, my true clinical career, as previously stated, actually began in July of 1958 with my first professional position at Pilgrim State Hospital in West Brentwood,

New York (on Long Island in Suffolk County). My buddy Adrian Applebaum and I applied together. It was on a Hofstra College department bulletin board that we had found the notice that Pilgrim State Hospital was hiring in various departments, and that's when we decided to apply.

Staff Positions at Three Hospitals

Pilgrim State was a mental hospital that at the time was reputed to be the largest of such mental hospitals in the world. It housed twenty thousand patients, as well as another two thousand outpatients on convalescent care. These outpatients would arrive back at the hospital for periodic checkups or would have periodic visits by social workers at their places of residence. The hospital had its own farm, post office, and foundry.

It was at Pilgrim that I first met Eleanor Wimble. She was chief supervisor of the social work department and became my supervisor. At first I didn't like her, but then I started seeing that she was something special, and we became good friends. I learned a lot from her, and she became my first professional clinical mentor. It was at Pilgrim that I was exposed to the greatest variety of people who correspondingly exhibited the greatest variety of psychopathology that one could find anywhere. I saw it all—from simple schizophrenia to paranoia to manic and depressed patients, to the isolation rooms, to violence, to patients with organic brain trauma, and by the way, to the difference between male and female wards.

On the male wards, the men were in hospital greens, lights were out, there were no curtains on the windows, and the men were sitting and smoking. On the female wards, the patients were dressed in everyday clothing, were not smoking, lights were on, there were colorful curtains on the windows, and the women were interacting. It was social.

It was also the first time I was dealing with supervisory sessions, and I could feel the enormous learning experience—exactly what I had hoped for. Yet Adrian and I couldn't land positions as psychologist apprentice, because all we had were B.A. degrees, so we were hired with the designation of social worker apprentice in the department of social work.

Part of the position was having responsibility for visiting former inpatients who were now in convalescent care outside of the hospital at various locations in

Suffolk County of Long Island. For that, one needed a driver's license, and I didn't have one. I was twenty years old but had never driven. As soon as I was told I had the job, I quickly called my buddy Hank B. (the one who lived in Hempstead), and he gave me one lesson on his dad's Plymouth. With that lesson, I immediately took the driving test and passed on the first try. Now if asked, I could verify that I had a driver's license. I obtained the license in the mail about three or four days before Adrian and I were about to start our jobs at Pilgrim.

I had realized that commuting from Hofstra College to Pilgrim and back was not going to be a picnic. At that point I lived again at Vera and Carl's house near Hofstra, because immediately after graduating with a B.A., I began night courses for my master of arts degree in the psychology department at Hofstra. At that point, after graduation, my college roommate Arty was off doing his life.

Because the a.m./p.m. trek from Hempstead to the hospital and back was so inconvenient, I set my new plan in motion: I believed that my buddy Hank B. (the one from Hempstead), who was finishing his undergraduate work, would be accepted as a recreational therapist apprentice at the recreation therapy department at the hospital, and my buddy Hank H. would for sure obtain a position in the occupational therapy department. The problem was that by this time Hank H. lived and worked at Cape Canaveral in Florida. But I made the phone call and before you knew it, Hank H. packed his bags, and arrived at Pilgrim almost immediately.

And yes, he got the job in the occupational therapy department. Simultaneously, Hank B. also got the position as recreational therapist in the recreational therapy department, so that the four of us—Adrian, both Hanks, and I—then rented a fully furnished house near to West Brentwood, New York, where Pilgrim was located. It was a fifteen-minute drive from the hospital in a kind of desolate West Islip, so that Hank H. quipped that its location seemed so in the boondocks that the Viet Cong probably attacked at night. This, of course, was at the beginning of the Vietnam War. Hank H. was already a four-year Korean Navy vet, having done his duty on an aircraft carrier; Adrian, Hank B., and I had student deferments at the start of the Vietnam War.

The experience of living out in what seemed like a desolate West Islip on Long Island felt also unmistakably as though we were all on the frontier of freedom—as though we were the pioneers of a freedom country. And it felt like a home that was good, and it reminded me of a Yiddish poem by I. E. Ronch (Yiddish poet and novelist), whom I knew and whose work I had performed many times. His poem is actually titled "America," and it is an homage to America and how all sorts of people (including Jews) contributed to its greatness. Here, I'll quote from a few of the stanzas:

America—s'z aygnt meer dine gooteh erd
(*America—Your good earth feels close to me.*)
Meer hubn zee mit oonzer bloot genert. (*We nurtured you with our blood.*)
Tsuzamen mit dee kinder foon der velt (*Together with children the world over*)
Tsehackert hubn meer dine feld. (*We tilled your fields.*)

Atsind is rife dine frookht (*Now the fruit of all our labor is viable.*)
Dine gourtn bleet. (*Your garden is in full bloom.*)
Mine arbets hant—paast oif oon heet (*My work is visible.*)
Kh'bin aingevortslt teef—s'z vour, (*I'm deeply planted here—it's true,*)
Ikh bin shoin duh dry hoondert your. (*I'm already here three hundred years.*)

Doo fregst ver bin eekh ver? (*You ask who am I, who?*)
Eekh bin nukh altz der peeonner (*I am still the pioneer*)
Foon fryhite oon freed. of freedom and joy. (*I'm not tired. I'm never tired*)
Eekh bin nit meed. Eekh ver nit meed (*so that I clearly sing in the world choir*)
Tsoo zingen klour, in felker khour America, dine fryhite leed.
(*America, your freedom song.*)

On the first day on the job, Adrian and I were asked whether we could drive standard-shift cars. Of course, even though I had not gotten my license on a standard-shift car, nevertheless we both answered the question in the affirmative. The fact is, I didn't know how to drive a standard-shift car. Yet at the end of the first week at the hospital, we were taken to the hospital garage where state automobiles were garaged. Lo and behold, all were standard-shift cars.

We were given addresses of patients on convalescent care and were expected to make a single visit that day. On the way to the garage with our supervisor talking to another person and walking behind Adrian and me, I quickly asked Adrian how to use the clutch and to quickly also tell me how to shift. He did so with hand signals to me that no one walking behind us could see. Then almost in what seemed like a second or two more, here I was behind the wheel of a standard-shift state car, and with Adrian's instructions vividly etched in my mind, I slowly and bumpily edged the car out of the garage, while our supervisor was looking at me with some consternation.

However, off I went in third gear. When I got to the address, it was on a street that was a cul-de-sac, and I had the car pointed at the dead end. The problem was that I had not asked Adrian how to shift into reverse. To my luck, a garbage truck had pulled in some feet behind me so that I hopped out of the car, ran over to the driver, and asked him how to shift into reverse. He laughed, and simply gave me the instruction. I then went into the house, interviewed the patient, and backed out of the cul-de-sac and drove back to the hospital.

With the salary I was paid at the hospital (it was 1958), I bought myself a three-year monthly payout plan for a two-door, all-white Chevy Impala. With my weekly salary I started my payout for the car, kept a bit, and sent the rest to my parents.

I worked at Pilgrim for one year, and at the end was when I achieved a master of arts degree in general/experimental psychology from Hofstra. The clinical work I did at the hospital was good and, in addition, I learned an enormous amount about the experimental scientific method in the master's program at Hofstra.

The social life that I and the guys had was great, and we threw many parties. Yet it was still not the feeling of *home*. It felt as though I was on a train going somewhere—somewhere in transit; kind of like I was living in an alternate world and in a bit of anonymity. It seems to me that as a member of the Yiddish progressive world, everything else felt as though it was a world that was somewhat alien to me. However, if I was feeling productive and making a *contribution* greater than the self, then this probably made it possible to be reasonably okay in such a so-called alien world. To top it off, here and there, women appeared— and there I went.

My next stop was at that motivation/marketing firm, Furst Survey Research Center, mentioned earlier. I lived at my friend Gene's apartment on East Seventy-Ninth Street in New York City, and it was there when I first heard Erroll Garner that Gene had in his record collection. But before you knew it, I had applied to Kings County Hospital for a psychology internship.

As it turned out, applications from all over the country for that particular internship totaled over one hundred. Sadly, only five seats were available. In other words, only about one in twenty applications was accepted. So there I was—I was accepted.

The internship at Kings County in Brooklyn was great. There I made another lifetime buddy. It was Gerald (Jerry) Yagoda. The internship was a terrific learning experience, and Jerry and I were now in the psychological soup.

I had found an apartment near the hospital, and it was in that apartment that I constructed Robert Plutchik's index for his first book, *The Emotions: Facts, Theories, and a New Model*, published in 1962, which he asked me to do and which I accomplished by working in the evenings during the end of the year until August 1962. In addition to the privilege of working at the hospital, other than Plutchik himself I became the only person entirely expert with the ins and outs of the emotion model he had conceived and developed. This model of emotions became a smash hit and innumerable studies were generated from its conclusions regarding the structure and function of emotion.

My great friend Gerald (Jerry) Yagoda. Jerry and I became lifelong friends beginning in 1961 when we were psychology interns at Kings County Hospital in Brooklyn, New York. The book I dedicated to Jerry and his beautiful wife, Marsha, is titled *Hollywood Movies on the Couch: A Psychoanalyst Examines 15 Famous Films*. My dedication reads: "For Gerald Yagoda, Ph.D. My Jerry. From Kings County (and Lisa) through Middletown (and Florence), to the East End of Long Island. The journey was great and you always did it first. And for Marsha Yagoda. Beautiful Marsha; 'they were the best hamburgers.'" (Lisa and Florence are Jerry and Marsha's daughters).

The Kings County internship was an experience of a lifetime for psychology students (of which I was one), and by the end of it I had become quite expert in psychological diagnosis, having performed fifty complete diagnostic workups on the basis of about one a week. Each workup could take more or less about a total of eight hours, including a half-hour clinical interview, two and a half hours of testing, three hours of diagnostic analysis of data, and another couple of hours composing the report. Do that for fifty such exposures and you will see that such an amount of practice makes one ready for Carnegie Hall. It takes practice.

All of us five interns were also on a program of a rotating internship, meaning that each of us was on a six-week work basis for each service: mildly disturbed, severely disturbed, prison ward, children's ward, the outpatient clinic, and so on.

At the end of the internship, I was asked to stay on as a staff member. However, by that time, Jerry had gotten a position at the Middletown State Hospital in Middletown, New York, and I agreed with him that if we both worked there we'd have a great time. In addition, it was a top-notch state mental hospital with all the advantages of working with pathologies from A to Z. I took it and was appointed senior psychologist, same as Jerry.

At that point, when I was about to begin a senior psychology position at Middletown State Hospital, it occurred to me that I was already building a resume as a professional person. This resume was specifically in my chosen field as a mental health practitioner. I knew I would work at Middletown for the following two years, after which I planned to apply for postdoctoral training in psychoanalysis while simultaneously attaining my doctoral degree.

I began to have the reputation at the hospital of someone on the staff who could get things done and who was already well trained. In truth, I really was not already well trained. That happened in my postdoctoral psychoanalytic training at the Postgraduate Center for Mental Health starting in 1964. This was 1962. However, apparently it seemed to people that I was, in fact, well trained. I refer to how I was professionally seen at the hospital because of assignments I had gotten. These assignments were welcomed also because I had realized when I first felt I was so-called already knee-deep in my career (as a mental health diagnostic specialist) that my participation was seen as important by others as well.

It was in my psychology internship at Kings County Hospital that it first hit me, where all at once I felt I had truly morphed out of my zone of comfort as a Yiddish-speaking performer. It was my role as a Yiddish-speaking performer where it felt like I was most at *home*—as compared to what it felt like now, which was that I was in a different universe—not at all familiar to me, as though I was located, as mentioned above, nevertheless as somewhere strange or alien. However, as also noted, my specific assignments as well as experiences realigned me and I soon welcomed it all. In fact, I believe I loved being in a classroom more than I did being onstage. And I soon realized that writing books was to me just another way to be in a classroom—teaching and learning at the same time. I just loved writing books. It was my own designed classroom, and it called to me.

14
Assignments and Experiences

Treatment and Teaching

My experiences and assignments in the hospitals in which I worked (as well as in my private practice) enabled me to have varied and profoundly interesting experiences. This included also my postdoctoral experience at the Postgraduate Center for Mental Health's Psychoanalytic Institute, where the psychoanalytic curriculum was scintillating.

At Pilgrim State Hospital, I was tasked with doing home visits as well as doing psychological examinations of inpatients. At Kings County Hospital, I worked with all sorts of patients (from children to geriatric), and learned a great deal about graphic analysis, projective psychology, as well as learning how to construct a full psychological portrait of a patient based upon data collected from psychological projective assessment tools.

Finally, again, with respect to hospital work, at Middletown State Hospital, I was for two years able to work as a psychologist in the children's ward and in the adult admission wards, such as unlocked wards, locked wards, drug addiction unit, and outpatient clinic, as well as assigned to teach the abnormal psychology class in the nursing school affiliated with the hospital.

In the following, I'll list some assignments and experiences that I found exceedingly interesting.

1. The Grand Rounds

Grand rounds is defined as the entire professional staff attending an all-hospital monthly meeting, including all psychologists, psychiatrists, clinical social workers, psychiatric nurses, and other professional staff, where a patient is presented who has been examined by a member of each of these departments. Each staff member of each department then delivers findings regarding the psychological and psychiatric nature of the person's diagnosis and personality, with a focus on the patient's central problem that brought them to the hospital.

It was at such grand rounds presentations that I began having the reputation of delivering excellent psychological reports—so much so that various psychiatrists began inviting their spouses to hear me. It was possible to know who the staff member was who was scheduled to present by consulting a posted list, so that when my name appeared as the one presenting psychological material, the room actually filled.

It's true I feel that my material was good, insofar as many staff personnel read their reports on whatever patient they had worked with in a way that was not that interesting—largely because these people didn't know how to render material in a pre-digested fashion, whereas I was already expert in pre-digesting material for audiences. Therefore, I fashioned my material in a way that was considerate of the audience by making things understandable and by not throwing around erudite or technical psychological lingo. In addition, I also knew how to present material in a way that audiences could see I was truly interested in the material—which I was. Along with this, I had no fear of the audience, so that I could be actually conversational with them rather than read from notes in a less-than-relational way.

Of course, I attribute it all to my considerable experience with my Yiddish stage presentations, in which the key was to relate, not just speak. In addition, I believe I also had a natural inclination to relate.

I also was appointed to teach in the nursing school located on the grounds of the hospital, and in addition I was assigned to the drug addiction program that housed heroin addicts who were given a chance to be hospitalized and treated instead of doing prison time. There, too, I was seen as approachable, relational, not behaving in a superior way, and certainly not fearful.

In one instance when I was leading a group in this drug addiction unit, I talked to them about some delusional flight of imagination, and wove a fantastical story as an example that illustrated the point I was making. One of the patients, before I spoke, had also told some magical, improbable story. Then after she spoke was when I made my out-of-the-box point. When I finished my phantasmagorical musings, the one before me derisively shouted out, "Where did you get that from?" I instantly answered, "The same place you got yours from!" At that the entire room of about a dozen of these addicts broke into a cacophony of laughter, as did I—as well as the young woman who had challenged me. In this sense, my relationship on that ward was excellent, and because of the kind of interaction we all had, I could see that being extemporaneous was sort of natural with me and that it was really like dancing.

2. My Car with Leaves
When I taught the psychopathology course in the nursing school at the hospital I had about thirty nursing students (all female but one), and they were instructed by the director of their program to stand at attention whenever any doctor walked into the classroom. So the first day of the semester when I walked in, they all stood. I motioned for them to sit and introduced myself by indicating what my position was at the hospital, and in addition asked them not to stand when I entered the room. One of them simply said it was required of them to so honor any doctor who would enter. I thanked them but told them I'd rather they not do that with me. I had the thought that in fact I'd already known some doctors in the mental health field who, quite frankly, didn't deserve that kind of respect.

By the end of the semester they had given me excellent reviews. I had one more session with them the following day, so that I parked my car that previous day outside of the nursing school department in their parking space and left it there.

The next day as I was walking into the building to teach the last class, I noticed something funny about my car. I approached the car and looked in. What I saw gradually put a trace of a smile on my face. The car was filled with leaves from top to bottom and from front to back. It was late autumn, probably in November, so that the entire area around the nursing school was strewn with dead, dried autumn leaves.

I walked into class where all were trying not to smile, grin, or even laugh. I thanked them for the gesture but I told them in no uncertain terms that I needed the car that late afternoon and that I expected an equivalent gesture from them to match the first one, and therefore, to undo it all. When that last class ended, they applauded. I told them it was the best class I had ever had the pleasure of teaching, I thanked them, and left the room.

That afternoon I came back to the car. It was spotless in and out. They had not only thoroughly manicured the inside so that it looked like it had just come out of the showroom, but they also had washed and simonized the car so that it gleamed on the outside as well.

In that sense, even though it still didn't feel quite like *home* because I had originally identified *home* as my immersion in Yiddish progressive theater, nevertheless it felt like I was being forced by circumstance to adopt a newer or different version of *home*.

3. "I'm Goin'!"

At Middletown State Hospital in New York I was called in to do a battery of projective tests on an eighty-five-year-old African American woman from the Deep South. Let's call her Essie. She had been hospitalized because the friend with whom she had been staying died in her sleep and Essie suddenly experienced strange symptoms that included fainting at anything that scared her—and apparently a lot of stuff scared her.

The diagnostic dilemma faced by the psychiatrist on the ward was that it became difficult to see whether Essie was a malingerer or a classic hysteric. I was asked to take on the case because my reputation as a diagnostician preceded me. So there I was with my trusted Rorschach (inkblot test), my TAT (Thematic Apperception Test), and my white paper to ask Essie to draw the figure of a person (the Machover figure-drawing test).

But I also had a dilemma. Knowing how old she was, knowing that she was Black and from the South, I also had some suspicion that she was therefore probably educationally disadvantaged. I thought this would usually be the case with how the mores of the country—especially in the South—disadvantaged such people, and I had a feeling that this was not going to be a picnic. Everything that I was going to ask her to do was likely going to create a problem for her and that was certainly not fair to her largely because "race and class is inextricably linked in America"—as my son Max once declared on TV.

So what to do? I decided that rather than testing her with these standard tests, I would try to understand the diagnosis based on a simple conversation with her that I would try to make sure was not threatening. I waited for her in the treatment room that had a very wide table with a chair behind it and one in front of it. The door opened and an aide escorted Essie in. She sat in the chair opposite to me and we began. I introduced myself and told her my name and what my job was at the hospital, and further explained that I was asked to have a conversation with her in order to assess whether she was comfortable in her present circumstance.

Apparently she liked me because the first thing she did was to ask whether I was married. I told her no, I wasn't married, but hoped to be married someday. She said she thought I will marry because I was such a nice person. We then talked about her life in the South, and I was generally right about what might have been her overall circumstance there.

After about twenty minutes into our conversation, I realized that I would need to take a chance and show her the first Rorschach inkblot. People typically respond to that that card as though the image is that of a close-up bat. My feeling was that the moment she'll see the card, who knows what will happen?

I carefully gave her a brief rundown on what it was I was going to show her—that it was a picture of something—and that there are no right or wrong answers; that it's only about what she sees and nothing else, and that different people might see things that no one else sees and that's also good.

She nodded and said, "Yes."

Despite my concern, I held my breath and took the chance. I presented the first blot and said, "Now, in this picture, could you tell me what this looks like?"

Essie took one look at that bat, and with a kind of lilting intonation in her voice that implied *uh oh*, she said, "I'm g-o-i-n'." And with that she went instantly unconscious, as her head bent forward and her whole body started to collapse with her head about to hit the table surface with a huge thud, largely because at that point she was dead weight. I lunged for her, and as her face was about to hit the tabletop, I slid my hands under her face to soften the impact. It did soften the impact, but almost flattened my fingers. By this time, I was leaning over this very wide table, and in my awkward position of trying to hold her steady, she began to slide off the table—as did I. I shouted for the attendants and two of them came running in just in time to straighten Essie out and also prevent me from hitting the floor.

The attendants carried Essie (who was out cold) to her bed on the ward, which housed about a half dozen beds in one large room. At this time it was about one or two minutes before noontime, so that when the lunch bell on the ward would ring, all of the women would typically line up and walk into the adjacent dining room for their meal. Then, the very moment the bell rang, Essie got right up, out of bed, and led the procession of women behind her directly into the dining hall. Yes, she was first out of bed and first in line.

When hearing about it all, the ward psychiatrist said, "See, she's a malingerer. She got right up at the bell. She's faking it all."

My immediate answer to him was that he was wrong, because a true malingerer is full of paranoia and would never challenge logic by getting up at the bell. A true malingerer would lie there and think, *They think I'm going to get up, but I'm going to fool them all and just remain as though sleeping!* And I continued by saying,

"That means, with respect to a differential diagnosis here, that this woman is a classic hysteric."

The psychiatrist looked at me and said only one word: "Interesting."

It was in this sense that I felt almost at *home,* as though I had *contributed* something important—that is, I clarified someone's psychological situation, thus teaching something, inviting empathy and understanding, and most importantly, had a significant interpersonal interaction with Essie. I later apologized to Essie about showing her that picture. I almost was not sure if I should even mention "that picture," because I felt that as a classic hysteric, even mentioning to her what she considered the menacing stimulus might again affect her in the same way that it did the first time. It didn't. She said, "Oh, that's all right."

4. Breasts

This is a case of a full-bodied, attractive, and voluptuous woman with a rather obvious bustline who was hospitalized because of a depression along with an unusual symptom called a negative hallucination. Whereas a positive hallucination is defined as seeing something that in reality is not there, a negative hallucination produces a gap in reality so that the person doesn't see something that, in reality, is actually there. Her problem was that her negative hallucination concerned a perceptual gap between her neck and her waist; that is, she could not see her bustline. It was as though there was empty space between neck and waist.

I was called in to speak to her about it because two other staff members tried to reason with her regarding their objective in getting her to realize that it was only an illusion about not seeing the solid area of the space between her neck and waist. In both cases this woman became irritable and outwardly angry at both staff members—one a psychologist, and the other a psychiatrist. This was 1962, at which time this woman was sixty-two years old.

I knew that both of these staff members had not idea one about what constitutes a delusion. What they considered an illusion was basically a delusion, and the difference in illusion versus delusion is that an illusion can be reasoned with and logicalized, while a delusion can only be touched by addressing the person's *basic-wish.* Otherwise no delusion can ever be addressed with even irrefutable facts and logic. Delusion does not understand the language of logic, nor of logical persuasion. In that sense, I knew when I was assigned to interview this woman that I would not do two things:

1. I would never mention the word "breast."
2. I would not try to convince her of anything.

To summarize what happened here was that this woman hated her husband because he had an obsessional preoccupation and compulsive motive to always seek to caress her body (especially her breasts), but he would not at all be interested in the typical passionate interaction of sexual intercourse. At the third session we had, she told me she wanted to tell me something, but it was a bit awkward for her to talk about it. She said she would talk about "this thing" at the next session. In the meantime, all I did was to reflect her feelings about what she had said was an aberrant interaction with her husband, but never did I, nor she, specifically mention her breasts or what the aberrant interaction was.

The main theme of the sessions was revealed to be her stated wish for her husband to disappear so that she wouldn't need to comply with his compulsive, and what she felt was his peculiar, behavior. All I did about her stated wish was to repeat it to her and to let her know I understood what she meant, but I wondered whether she wanted him to disappear because perhaps she felt that she herself wanted to disappear. At that point she mentioned that her sister was encouraging her not to move away, even though the patient herself wanted to.

At the fourth session, she revealed that since our last session, a friend of hers had told her that her sister was having an affair with the patient's husband. Yet this woman, our patient, chose not to talk about anything related to possibly having angry feelings toward her sister.

At the fifth session, the patient was wearing a sweater on top of her hospital gown, and in the middle of the session she told me about the entire process of the sexual practice between her and her husband, and she indicated how much she hated it. She confessed that her husband only wanted sex with her breasts and never invited sexual intercourse. She then abruptly mentioned something that bothered her about her sister.

With that I only asked her to tell me more about her dissatisfactions with her husband (and in other ways as well), but I also referred to her sister and what this patient had told me about her sister's alleged affair with her husband. She then described all of it to me, and also told me that her sister was her older sister, and that she was apprehensive about her because this sister had always taken on the role of mother surrogate.

My comment to her was that a lot was riding, for her, on the possibility that she might want to take a chance and talk to her sister about it. When I then asked her how she felt about their alleged affair, she surprised me. She said it actually relieved her, thinking that her husband would no longer perhaps bother her with his obsession about her breasts, because he would be taken up with her sister.

Then in the middle of the next session, she suddenly looked down at her sweater, and while lifting and holding her breasts through the sweater said, "Oh look, I'm not wearing a bra."

And that was the end of her negative delusion, because in that split second, she was filling up the space between her neck and waist and no longer saw that part of her physical being as empty space. I believe it was feeling understood and expressing her anger at the "who"—that is, the person responsible for her hatred—that was the thing ostensibly and finally that did the trick. However, it was becoming clear that part of the problem was that the only thing she was angry with her sister about was her sister's attempt to hide the affair.

Apparently, her sister had been continuing to persuade this woman never to leave her husband. Our patient then understood that her sister didn't want the husband and our patient to separate because the sister was having this sexual contact with him and didn't want to chance him needing to reknit the relationship with the patient, thus likely challenging the sister's relationship with the patient's husband.

The true "who" culprit in this case was either the husband or the sister. The fact that this patient talked about them both meant that at least the one implicated in the reason for her symptom was in the conversation. Therefore, the lifting of her symptom was determined by her finally consolidating her consciousness regarding being angry at each of them; that is, at first, her anger was remaining unconscious, but at this time in our discussions, it all became conscious. In this case it wasn't crucial to identify which was the more important one with respect to the genesis of the symptom—the husband or the sister. The point is that her ultimate professed consciousness of her anger at each of them implicitly included who the culprit really was. It was likely the husband, so that her anger toward him, although conscious, also had an additional part that was unconscious. In addition, she hated her sister's manipulative behavior, but this information came to her after the appearance of her symptom.

Thus, it seems that her anger toward her sister was diluted because simultaneously she was almost grateful that her sister, who was occupying her husband's time, made it more possible that there would no longer be a need to endure his idiosyncratic compulsion.

The cure of her symptom lasted, and she was shortly discharged from the hospital. Again, working on this case brought me deeper into my new life, whereby I continued to feel pulled more and more away from my original *home* and into a different life that felt both valuable yet, in contrast, also "fremd" (the Yiddish word for "strange" or "as a stranger" or "alien" or even in a pejorative manner meaning "non-neighborly"). In other words, with my productive and *contributive* work, I dug deeper into a new identity, but perhaps also somehow feeling that I was abandoning myself. I think that was possibly it; that is, that I felt a bit distant from probably what I had considered my true self all of my life, more or less up to that point.

5. Bottles Under the Bed

Years later, when I was in private practice, a psychiatrist friend called me out of the blue saying that he wanted me to consult with his eleven-year-old son. I had known his son since the boy was born. In all his growing-up years, this boy and I had a consistently good relationship.

My friend told me he noticed his son was putting bottles under the bed because, as his son said, doing so would cure the funny feeling he had in his stomach. His son said that he hit upon the idea of the bottles kind of automatically.

After a number of avoidances, the boy finally arrived at my office. He repeated and confirmed what his father had told me. We chatted for a while, and I asked him when it all started. He said it started some time ago but didn't exactly know when. I then followed the formula I had synthesized to cure psychological symptoms and which I had already, some years before, published in my volume *The Psychoanalysis of Symptoms* (2008).

Before long, we had unearthed the genesis of this bottles issue. It was that this young boy had overheard his parents having a fight in which they shouted to one another something about divorce. The boy said he believed his father regarding the divorce issue, but not his mother. At that point he was fairly certain that the funny feelings in his stomach were related to this incident starting when his parents introduced the issue of divorce.

This boy was an only child, and the integrity of his family unit was paramount to him. I could understand that perfectly because I was an only child and the integrity of my family was also of primary importance to me. Of course I knew what the funny feelings were that he was experiencing. What I didn't know was under which bed he placed these bottles, and what kind of bottles they were.

I knew that the funny feeling without a doubt was only singular, not plural, and that the singular feeling was *anger*. He was angry about what he felt was a possible dissolution of his family. On top he was also fearful, but underneath his anger was primary. The question was *at whom* was he angry—that is, the principle is that all primary emotions take an object. With respect to emotions, an object always refers to a person, not a table or a chair. Therefore, who was the person toward whom this boy was angry?

The answer was easy, because when it came to the issue of divorce he said he believed his father but not his mother, meaning that perhaps it was his father toward whom he was angry, despite the unmitigated fact that he loved his father.

So after asking him under which bed did he place the bottles, and second, what kind of bottles were they, he answered without any confusion whatsoever that the bottles were all placed under his parents' bed. On which side were they placed, mother's or father's, was my next question. He naturally answered that they were placed on his father's side. To the question related to the type of bottles, he answered, "Anything related to sickness and to curing sickness." Then he itemized that these so-called bottles included even empty milk containers or band-aid boxes—in other words, anything concerned with care, health, and most importantly, cure.

Then the essential question almost answered itself. This boy was angry with his father because he felt it was his father who was threatening the integrity of his family. Second, he put the bottles under his father's side of the bed because then the imaginary fumes of these curative substances would waft up through the mattress (on his father's side of the bed) and cure his father of any divorce "sickness." And each time he performed this magical act, it was as if his father was then cured over and over again and all was then, in turn, okay in the family. Correspondingly, each time his father was "cured" was when his funny stomach feelings would also vanish—meaning the ridding of the anger.

I explained it all to him and asked for his permission to call a family meeting in order to straighten it all out. At first he was against my idea, but with a bit of gentle persuasion, he agreed.

We did indeed have the family meeting, at which time both his parents vehemently denied that there was ever going to be a divorce, and when he reminded them of their original argument that he had overheard, they both in unison expressed to him that it was just a fight and they were both angry and that in those kinds of circumstances people say things that serve the purpose of supporting the anger, but that the dispute evaporates even after a short while. And it was his father who was most vocal in explaining it all to him.

This boy reflexively looked at me, at which point I lifted my eyebrows as though to say, *Okay?* In short order I received a phone call from this boy, who happily and as though in wonder reported that the funny feelings lingered for a couple of days but somehow not in the same way. Then he said they were really gone and that everything was good. I asked him to come in for one more session so that we could review it all again and talk some more. He agreed and we had a good time at the end—talking and laughing.

It needs to be noted that what this boy was doing is understood psychoanalytically as being engaged in a repetition compulsion that repeats the magical act over and over again—the objective of which is to resolve the conflict. The magical act, of course, was placing certain kinds of bottles or containers under his father's side of the bed, which then keeps the real problem safely ensconced in his unconscious mine.

However, the conflict is never resolved as a result of the repetition behavior. Rather, this compulsion to repeat simply repeats itself but never cures anything. It's the need to identify the "who" as well as the anger toward that individual (at the bottom of it all) that will dissolve the symptom—no more stomach funny feelings.

6. He Wouldn't Unlock the Door

In another interesting situation, I received a phone call from a woman (out of state) who had heard that I was a specialist in symptom-cure. She told me her fourteen-year-old son had locked himself in the bathroom of the first floor of their private home and that she would need to deliver his food through the window of the bathroom located at the back of the house adjacent to their garden. Her son had been in the bathroom already for the second day. She and her husband had retained a cognitive-behavioral therapist who came to the house, but to no avail stood on the other side of the bathroom door trying to persuade her son to take one step at a time toward the door in the hope of reaching the door and opening it. This therapist spent a couple of hours trying to persuade the boy, but in my mind his attempts were doomed.

I asked the woman whether anyone in her family had made the boy angry. She immediately and with no hesitation whatsoever answered, "Yes, me. I made him angry." I then asked whether she regretted whatever it was she did, and again she immediately went into the story and confessed that it was all her fault and that she flew off the handle at him and at the wrong time. She then asked me what she should do. I suggested it might be helpful if she apologized to her son and asked him to forgive her. My objective was not to persuade him to open the door. Rather, my plan was for him to diminish his insistent anger at his mother; the point being that in any symptom there must be the presence of a "who"—a participant culprit, as well as an anger toward that culprit. And here we had both criteria in hand.

She thanked me and said she would let me know what happened. It didn't take long before the phone rang. She profusely thanked me and told me that after she apologized they then talked a bit through the window with her standing in the garden and with him in the bathroom. Before he closed the bathroom window he told her to wait in the garden. Apparently, in less than ten seconds her son was in the garden with her, where they sat on a two-person swing and were friends again.

What I briefly discussed with her was why her son was on such a hair trigger with his anger—was it because she had a habit of triggering him? She didn't answer me, but I told her that the question of why her son was on this hair trigger of anger was something that needed to be examined and that perhaps it was a family dynamic. And that was that.

Here again, I was drawn deeper into my new identity as a shrink and further and further away from a familiar *home*. In addition, sitting in my office and away from the world was an experience which, also in a way, helped me feel *anonymous* to the world—although not to this woman, this boy, or his family; and even further, but very importantly, I felt I had made a *contribution* to the promise of "Save or repair one life and you save or repair the world" ("tikkun olam" in Hebrew). I realize it's a bit exaggerated that something like that saves or repairs the world, but I do think the spirit of tikkun olam makes it quite relevant when you can give someone a bit of assistance—and, hopefully, some relief from torment.

There are a number of other signal episodes with patients that are striking in content, but these are too numerous to cite here. Some of these are described in my book *Curing Psychological Symptoms* (2020) and in other books of mine, including *Anatomy of Delusion* (2015), as well as in the book *There's No Handle on My Door: Stories of Patients in Mental Hospitals* (2016).

15

My Personality, Psychoanalytic Treatment, and Yiddish

Intersecting Structures

So to sum up my clinical career more fully, I was a psychology intern at Kings County Hospital, a staff member at Pilgrim State Hospital, and a senior psychologist at Middletown State Hospital, all in New York State. Along with this, my teaching positions as adjunct professor in the graduate doctoral programs at New York University and at the New School for Social Research University, as well as my faculty position at the Postgraduate Center for Mental Health's Psychoanalytic Institute, enabled me to launch courses in psychotherapy, dream interpretation, psychoanalytic process, and psychodiagnosis, as well as research in psychotherapy. All of it was exciting and interesting—and it seemed as though, with pleasure, I was always in a classroom.

Further, at the Postgraduate Center there were several important influences—individuals from whom I learned a great deal. For me, these were special individuals, including Dr. Lucille Blum and Dr. Max Geller, who were two of my outstanding supervisors—Lucille, who focused on developing consistency and in finding main themes, and Max, who focused on dreamwork and in developing an understanding of latent material with patients.

Both Dr. Harold Leopold and Ms. Deborah Hample were my control analysts with whom I spent countless hours examining my feelings and my psyche. These four individuals, along with Dr. Manny Schwartz, were phenomenal influences, who, I believe, contributed greatly to my emotional and psychological growth.

In addition, my five-year postdoctoral psychoanalytic training and my more than fifty-eight-year private practice, as well as my supervisory role, along with other of my professorial roles, finally fill in the entire landscape of my clinical career—of course, not including my prodigious efforts as a writer that over the period of half a century enabled me to present scores of clinical and theoretical papers at conferences, made it possible for me to publish a couple of dozen papers, and enabled me to write and edit forty-three books, including thirty-six original books along with seven edited books. Together, all of my published professional papers, along with my books, comprises a personal oeuvre—all of it listed at the end of this memoir.

But I had a problem. When one trains at a postdoctoral psychoanalytic institute, one of the first things you learn is not to impart your wishes onto the patient. Second, if the patient is less than enthusiastic about something that might be a good thing for him or her to do or pursue, but doesn't feel like doing, then the therapist should not push that patient toward it—even if the therapist's motive is based in good intentions. It feels to me that I didn't do very well in that class because I'm usually given to be on the side of value for the patient, and I can and sometimes do persuade myself to forgo the issue of therapist neutrality when it seems to me that for the patient to do something in that person's best interest is what that person should pursue. So I can be a little lilting that way, but only in the sense of "Let's talk it over." The point here is that such behavior on my part has occurred in several cases over the decades, and on only two or three of those occasions did things actually work out. Otherwise, it all was an abject failure on my part whenever I bucked the therapeutic trend of neutrality, which in shrink terms is stated as "Keeping the frame," as my colleague Dr. Stanley Teitelbaum has continued to enunciate.

Because of this rather bleak experience in some cases (although only a few), whatever grandiose sense I may have had about myself was certainly chastened. Despite this teeny-weeny failure index, nevertheless I'm always tempted to jump into the fray and create, may I say, the miracle of goodness—that is, *to bring good news*—and as Dorothy Martyn's brilliant book, *Beyond Deserving*, states (2007, p. xv), displaying the "powerful force of noncontingent, compassionate alliance with the essential personhood of the other." In a general sense, however, the spirit of my concern is conveyed (for the most part) as controlled and not expressed; yet I believe my motives and good intentions are experienced by patients, even though perhaps not verbalized or at the time never even discussed.

However, I also believe this focus of mine to help someone in their struggle, as well as my sense of empathy for such a person, was bred into me by a specific component of the Yiddish literature that I performed for more than two decades where I rendered such literature to interested like-minded Yiddish-speaking audiences. Surely, my sense of empathy, along with how I identified with the material I was performing, had an enormous influence on my psyche, one powerful enough to significantly influence my personality.

I'm particularly referring to two poems. One was titled "Shmooleek," written by Dora Teitelbaum. The title is a boy's name. It is a poem about a boy of seven who was the only remaining survivor of his family during the genocide of Jews during World War II. The other was a poem found after the war in one of the internment camps for Jews. This poem was titled: "The Poem of a Lonely Boy," or basically meaning: "The Poem of an Abandoned Boy." This poem was originally found discarded with other materials and missing any attribution of authorship.

Now, here, I will render each poem because as you the reader will see, these stories were what sent a wave of empathy over me starting at the age of seven and continuing for the remainder of my Yiddish performance career as well as being something that overwhelmed every fiber of my being. I'll begin with the first one which didn't force me to delete any of the stanzas or even a single sentence. It's translation was done from the Yiddish by Mr. Aaron Kramer, a noted Yiddish translator of poetry and prose. The second one (about the loneliness of a boy) was the one where I could not at all repeat to myself or to an audience what the lonely little boy thought and how he pleaded with his mother not to leave.

Here's the first one:

Shmooleek

Tvishn felder tvishn lunenn (*In the midst of fields and highways*)
Iz a kinder haym farannen, (*There's a home where orphans stay*)
Oon foon kinder haym a shpan (*And, close by, a locomotive*)
Fort farbye fartug a bann. (*Passes early every day.*)

Kukn kinderlalh durkh ludns (*Through the shutters little children*)
Oif dee shevndika shutns, (*Watch the shadows move, and wait,*)
Tsoo ess gayt a passajhier (*Hoping that some passenger*)
Du aher tsoo zeher teer. (*Will stop at last before their gate.*)

Oon zay kookn oon zay bettn, (*And they look and pray for mother*)
S'zoul a mammeh koomen glettn, (*To be coming on the train,*)
S'zoul a tatteh tsoo dem hoiz, (*For their father to return*)
Koomen haltn oifn shois. (*And hold them on his knee again.*)

Oon zay troimen oon zay hufn, (*And they dream and keep on hoping*)
Biz zay gayen vidder shlufn. (*Till once more the shadows fall.*)
Nur ayn Shmooleek blaipt vakh. (*But one Shmoolik guards the highway,*)
Nur ayn Shmooleek, heet dem shliakh. (*Does not go to sleep at all.*)

Vemen zookht er, vemen zet er, (*Who is it he seeks and finds there*)
In dee tsvaign in dee bletter, (*In the branches, in the leaves?*)
Vemen rooft er, vemen greast er, (*Who is it he calls and speaks to*)
Oon dee trehrn, vus fargeest er. (*Who—who is it that he grieves?*)

S'z oif shliakh a yeder shutn, (*Every shadow on the highway*)
In zine mammesheh geruttn. (*Has his mother's face and hair*)
Ver es gate nokh foon vugzal, (*Everyone who leaves the station*)
Trugt zine mammes shvartzn shaowl. (*Wears the shawl she used to wear.*)

Shmooleek, Shmooleek der klayner, (*One of the eight was little Shmoolik,*)
Iz foon akht farblibn ayner. (*None are left of all the others.*)
Foon dee shvester, foon dee breeder, (*Winds are wailing lamentations*)
Singn vintn troier leeder. (*For his sisters and brothers.*)

S'vet zine tahtn's ahlter neegn (*Never shall his father's light tune*)
Mer nit vartn oif dee shteegn (*Wait for him upon the stairs.*)
S'vet zine mammeh shoin nit mer (*Never shall his mother come here*)
Koommen glettn eem aher. (*To caress away his cares.*)

Er vult fargessn dem bageen, (*He could forget that dreadful morning*)
Oif dee vegn kine Loobleen, (*On the journey toward Lublin*)
Ven zee hut in tchemodan (*When she hurled him in a suitcase*)
Oroisgevarfn eem foon bann. (*From the car that they were in.*)

Er vult fargebn oon fargesn (*He could forgive them, and forget them*)
Alleh fintstereh mislesn (*All those black, black days—if now*)
Ven zee koomt itst tsoo zine bet, (*She would only come inside*)
Oon git eem khotch aiyn glet. (*And put her fingers on his brow.*)

Norr zee koomt nit foon Mydonik, (*But she comes not from Majdanek,*)
S'koomt dee zoon norr free tsoom ganik (*Early, though, the sun comes home;*)
Vile zee vayst, zee vayst mistameh, (*For it knows, it knows most likely*)
S'vet nisht koomen mer zine mammeh (*That his mother will not come.*)

Tvishn felder, tvishn lounnen, (*In the midst of fields and highways*)
Iz a kinder haym farannen (*There's a home where orphans stay,*)
Oon a kind foon zibn your, (*And a child of seven lives there*)
Mit a keple grouyeh hurr. (*With his little head all gray.*)

I could render this poem by Dora Teitelbaum without changing a word, primarily because it's about a little orphan boy but not done in first person throughout the story. But when the poem concerned a give-and-take between mother and child on a first-person basis, that's when I found it too difficult to use in my repertoire. The point about this is that I don't recite to an audience. Rather, I speak to them person to person whenever I'm rendering some piece of literature—prose or poem; that is, I'm having a conversation with the audience even when the words point me to be at an emotional high.

This reminds me of when I was in a stage play and my line was supposed to be that my mother had died. Of course I refused to say the line, and I put my entire participation in the play in jeopardy because I put it, so to speak, right on the line—and I was only nine years old. My stance was that I was not going to say that line and therefore, as I saw it, the choice was either to have the line changed or have me replaced. The director saw I was serious (and intractable), and he removed the line.

Now, in the following poem is when I couldn't even try to memorize the last part of the poem, when the child begs the mother not to leave him in strange hands and then he knows she plans to forever disappear. In this poem titled "Dus Leed foon ahn Elnt Kind" ("The Story of a Lonely [abandoned] Child"), the conversation between mother and child is here and there indeed in first person, and for audiences, I only conveyed the first half of the poem, in which a mother leaves this child with strangers, knowing she's headed for an extermination camp.

Dus Leed foon ahn Elnt Kind (*The Story of a Lonely Child*)

In a Litfish dehrfl vite, (*In a faraway Lithuanian hamlet*)
In a shteebl in a zite, (*Inside in the corner of a house*)
Doorkh ah fenster nisht a grois (*With narrow windows*)
Kookn kinderlakh arois. (*Are children looking through.*)

Eengelakh mit flaxn-kep (*Boys with blondish hair*)
Maydalekh mit blohndeh tsep. (*Little girls with blond ponytails*)
Oon tsuzamen dort mit zay (*And among them*)
Kookn shvartzeh oign tsvay. (*Are also present two dark eyes.*)

Shvartzeh oign fool mit khain (*Dark eyes full of charm*)
Oon a nezaleh a klaynce (*And a small little nose.*)
Lipalakh tzoo kooshn nour (*Lips designed to be kissed,*)
Oon shtark gelukteh horr. (*And strong curly hair.*)

Dee mammeh hut eem dou gebrakht (*His mother brought him here*)
Ayngeviklt shpayt bynakht (*Wrapped in a blanket late at night.*)
Gehoosht, gevaint, un geklugkt (*Kissed him, cried, and wailed*)
Oon shtilerhade tsoo eem gezukt: (*And quietly said to him,*)

Foon hynt mine kind iz do dine ort (*Here, my child, will be your place.*)
Gedenk dine mammess letzteh vort (*Remember your mother's last words:*)
Ess iz dine lebn in gefar (*Your life is in danger*)
Ikh bahalt dir dou defar (*And that's why I hide you here.*)

Mit dee kinder shpeel zikh fine (*Play well with the children*)
Doo zolst shtill, gehorkhsom zine (*Be quiet, courteous, and cooperative*)
Kine Eeddish vort, kine Eeddish leed, (*Not a Yiddish word, not a Yiddish song,*)
Foon hynt mine kind, bistoo kine Eed! (*From today, my child, you are not a Jew.*)

At this point in the poem I changed the last line to: "Uber gedenk mine kind, doo bist a Yid." ("But remember, my child, you are a Jew"). I did that because I was unable to establish that last line written in the poem as a reality that I could accept. It must be remembered that when I first learned this poem, I was only about eight years old. But here is the rest of the poem that I wouldn't read and wouldn't render in any performance.

Dus kind gebetn zeekh by eer: (*The child pleaded with her:*)
"**Eekh vill dukh mammeh, zine mit dir.** (*"But mama, I want to be with you.*)
Luz nit iber meekh alayn . . ." (*Don't leave me alone without you . . ."*)
Ess hut getsitert foon gevayn. (*He cried, shivering.*)

Zee hut eem tsugezugt a sakh, (*She promised him a lot,*)
S'hot nit gehulfn kine shoom sakh. (*But nothing helped.*)
Er hut geshreen: "Nayn, nayn (*He screamed: "No, no,*)
Khvil nit blybn do alayn." (*Don't leave me here alone."*)

Oif der hant genumen eem (*She took him in her arms*)
Oon mit a tsiderdickeh shtim (*And with a quivering voice,*)
Vee amoul in shtoob by zeekh (*The way it was at home,*)
Iyngeshlofert eem oif geekh. (*Quickly put him to sleep.*)

Mit roiteh oign foon gevain (*Crying with eyes of red*)
Gekooshed dus kepeleh dus klayn, (*She kissed his little head*)
Gekooshed, in hartzn fool mit shrrek (*Kissed, in her full heart with fear,*)
Alayn gelouzt oon iz avek. (*Left him—and left.*)

Ah kelt in droisn oon a vint, (*It's cold outside with a wind*)
Ah shtimeh hert zeekh: "Oy mine kind," (*A voice she hears: "Oh my child,*)
Alayn gelust oif fremdeh hent, (*I abandoned him to strange hands,*)
Undersh hub eekh nisht gekent. (*I could not do otherwise."*)

Es gate dee mammeh, mit zeekh zee redt, (*The mother goes and talks to herself,*)
Indroisn shreklekh kalt oon shpeyt, (*Outside horribly cold and late,*)
Es vaint in pounim ear a vint, (*A wind of pain cries in her ear,*)
"**Hub, Gut, rakhmoness oif mine kind**" (*"God, have pity on my child."*)

A fremdeh shtoob mit mentchn fool. (*A strange house with many people.*)
Er gate aroom fremd oon shtill. (*He mills around as a quiet stranger.*)
Redt nit, vaint nit, vill kine zakh, (*Speaks not, cries not, asks not.*)
Zeltn ven er git a lakh. (*Rarely does he laugh.*)

Zine kinder herrtzle shtark farklempt— (*His little heart very choked—*)
Vasil, zine nomen, is eem fremd. (*His name, Vasil, is strange to him.*)
Fremdeh shprakh, vus meh redt, (*Their language is unfamiliar*)
Khotch kayner zogt eem nit—aveck! (*Yet no one tells him—leave!*)

Dee mamme feelt es zayer goot, (*The mother feels it deeply,*)
Zee root nit ine kine ain minnoot. (*Not for a minute can she rest.*)
Zee feelt, dos hartz gate eer ois, (*She feels her heart is breaking,*)
Tsite Yoseleh iz foon shtoob arois. (*Since Yoseleh is no longer home.*)

Tsoo Moishes mammeh iz zee gleikh, (*She equates herself with Moses' mother*)
Azoi vee Moisheh oif dem tykh. (*Same as Moses on the river.*)
Elnt, aynzam, fool mit vind, (*Lonely, isolated, replete with pain,*)
Alayn gelozt eer aintsick kind. (*Alone, her only child she left.*)

The Shoes Are Strong

In fact, this is the first time since I was about eight or nine years old that I've actually read this part of the poem again without it choking me up. I believe that now, as an aging adult, my cynicism about the world has definitely hardened me. However, I gain a measure of resurgent strength when I shift to thinking about those marching shoes from the mountain—the mountain more sacred than Mount Sinai.

Yes, yes, far more sacred!

The reason for this resurgence of my strength is that the symbol of the army of marching shoes means that instead of marching singing kumbaya, they march in the sense of retribution—while simultaneously narrating who they were, and how and where they lived. Kumbaya is an African spiritual appealing to God to come and help. With respect to my angry inclination toward this alleged God, I say, "You never gave us help when we needed it, so we don't need or want your help now! And anyway, you're not even real. Given Jewish history, does anyone really believe that there is a God, or one protecting Jews? Get serious!"

So these shoes are not passive, cowardly, or weak. They are like the current Jews of Israel. Strong and able to defend themselves. My son Max has correctly said, in his interview with the Yiddish Book Center Oral Project, that the progressive left has mistakenly correlated strength with badness and nonviolence with goodness. He further stated that strength is important and good as in consciousness of protecting those in need or oppressed. And he's absolutely right! The marching shoes are *strong and good* and they are seeking the monsters! Thus, to protect others sometimes can mean that nonviolence is not the needed strategy.

Here they are again—the strength of this shoe army that lifts me out of my agony about all the children who were emotionally devastated by their "abandonment-rescue." So it is obvious to me, and probably to you, my reader, that my two-decade career immersed in such literature deeply affected me. Thus, I feel that on the one hand, never hurt anyone or anything that is helpless; but yes, make war on those who do—and do it hard!

Therefore, this literature also contributed to my neocon sense of being a hawk with respect to foreign policy, but still a leftist with respect to domestic policy. But now, what do the shoes say about who they were?

> **Hert ois, hert ois dus oisgemishteh tretn** (*Hear it. Here the march*)
> **Foon alleh gayng, foon Rebns shteevelietten**
> (*From all avenues of life, such as even boots that the rabbi wore*)
> **Oon shteevl prusteh oon gemain** (*As well as those shoes that were old and worn.*)
> **Foon prusteh Eeiddn, foon katzoveem, shinder**
> (*Shoes of simple Jewish people, of butchers and carpenters*)
> **Oon foon geshrtickeh shikhalekh foon kinder**
> (*And of the woven little children's shoes*)
> **Vus hoibn nor vus un tsoo gayn.** (*That they wore when they first began to walk.*)

> **Mit klangen allerlay, dee zoiln rashn** (*The shoes make all sorts of sounds,*)
> **Geshorkh foon khosens gemzeneh kamashn**
> (*Such as with the laced shoes of the groom's,*)
> **Der kahless letchelekh foon zide,** (*The bride's gown of lace—*)

Zay zynen tsoo der khuppeh nisht dergangen
  (*They never made it to the chuppah poles.*)
Itst yommern nokh zay dee khuppeh shtangen
  (*Now the only ones that miss them are these chuppah poles*)
Farluzn ergets in a zite. (*Discarded somewhere.*)

Meer sheekh foon Yas, Moonkatch, oon Atten,
  (*We shoes from Iași, Munkács, and Athens*)
Vus flegn gayn in mark oon tsoo varshtatn
  (*Who would frequent the marketplace and the workplace*)
Oon gain b'shulem oonzer veg (*And go these ways with peace in mind*)
In krum, in fabrik, in kindershool, in kheyder
  (*To the store, the factory, the children's school, the cheder*)
Itst gayen meer yeroosha foon a aydeh (*Now we go with inheritance of a hope*)
Vus iz foon oonz avek. (*That from us has disappeared.*)

In other words, whoever they were, whoever wore those shoes, from them, all was confiscated, *all was lost*. And in my not-so-humble opinion, not only did the world not help; rather, the so-called deplorables of this world actually participated in assisting in this catastrophe.

16

Sons and Books

Max, Sam, Harry, Jack

It is now in the year 2023. In these forty-nine years from the time I began writing that paper (which turned into part of my first book), as noted in total I've now (including this memoir) written and edited forty-three books. When I had more than twenty books published, one of my publishers asked me how many to that point I had already published. I actually didn't know precisely how many, but I said I thought it was perhaps twenty-two or twenty-three or even more. I went home and counted, and it was actually twenty-five. Since that time, I keep the count, and now the tally, also as noted, is: twenty-nine original single-authored books, seven coauthored books, two single-edited volumes, and five coedited volumes.

My five coedited volumes (with Robert Plutchik, Ph.D.) are focused on the clinical, biological, experiential, and academic scope of emotions, of which the title of this five-volume set is *Emotion: Theory, Research, and Experience*. It took us ten years to complete the publication of all five volumes (1980–1990). The volumes are titled:

Vol. 1. *Theories of Emotion*
Vol. 2. *Emotions in Early Development*
Vol. 3. *Biological Foundations of Emotion*
Vol. 4. *The Measurement of Emotion*
Vol. 5. *Emotion, Psychopathology, and Psychotherapy*

My solo-edited volumes are:
Group Cohesion: Theoretical and Clinical Perspectives
The Nightmare: Psychological and Biological Foundations

My six coauthored books with Anthony Burry, Ph.D., are:
Psychopathology and Differential Diagnosis
  Vol. 1. *History of Psychopathology*
  Vol. 2. *Diagnostic Primer*
Handbook of Psychodiagnostic Testing: Analysis of Personality in the Diagnostic Report
  (reissued in 2nd, 3rd, and 4th editions; translated into Japanese)

My one book with Raphael Osheroff, M.D., is:
Shackled, Beaten, and Starved: The Untold Story of One of the Most Shameful Scandals in American Psychiatric History (The Raphael Osheroff Story)

My twenty-nine solo-authored books are:
The Psychoanalysis of Symptoms
Dictionary of Psychopathology
Group Psychotherapy and Personality: Intersecting Structures
  (reissued with the subtitle *A Theoretical Model*)
Sleep Disorders: Insomnia and Narcolepsy
Curing Psychological Symptoms
  (translated into Romanian, Japanese, and Bulgarian; originally published as *The 4 Steps to Peace of Mind: The Simple Effective Way to Cure Our Emotional Symptoms*)
Love Is Not Enough: What It Takes to Make It Work
Greedy, Cowardly, and Weak: Hollywood's Jewish Stereotypes
Hollywood Movies on the Couch: A Psychoanalyst Examines 15 Famous Films
Haggadah: A Passover Seder for the Rest of Us
Personality: How It Forms
  (translated into Korean)

The Discovery of God: A Psychoevolutionary Perspective

A Consilience of Natural and Social Sciences: A Memoir of Original Contributions

Anatomy of Delusion

Psychoanalysis of Evil: Perspectives on Destructive Behavior

There's No Handle on My Door: Stories of Patients in Mental Hospitals

On the Nature of Nature

Psychotherapeutic Traction: Uncovering the Patient's Power-Theme and Basic-Wish

The Unconscious Domain

The Origin of Language

The 7 Keys to: Your Unconscious Mind

Injustice of the Predatory World: A Book of Essays

Covid—A Love Story: On the Psychology of the Virus

Acting-Out and Sin: Psychoanalytic and Theological Perspectives

The Psychoanalytic Codes: Encryption and Decryption

The Psychology of Diagnosis: What Your Diagnosis Is Saying to You

To Bring Good News: A Memoir

My Ghost trilogy of novels include:
1. *The Making of Ghosts*
    The theme underpinning this novel concerns the issue of unfairness as it relates to oppression of people.
2. *Ghosts of Dreams*
    The underpinning theme here concerns the issue as to whether morality is absolute or relative.
3. *The Ghost*
    The challenge here is to consider whether evil has a statute of limitations.

I worked for almost five years on my first book, and when it was published it was in the middle of the fifth year. When I finished writing that book (*Group Psychotherapy and Personality: Intersecting Structures*), incidentally in the year 1979 it was essentially the only science book in the group therapy literature. As noted earlier, at that time, there were fewer than thirty books published in the entire group therapy field. For the most part, all the other books in the field were "how-to" books, with a sprinkling of science here and there.

Having had no experience with book publishing, and not having had the motivation or even the inclination to seek an agent, I took matters into my own hands and thought that I would seek a publisher on the basis of proximity as to where I lived. Grune & Stratton was it.

I lived on lower Fifth Avenue in Manhattan, and Grune & Stratton, a subsidiary of the notable publishing company Harcourt Brace Jovanovich, was also located on Fifth Avenue, exactly seven blocks north, between Seventeenth and Eighteenth Streets. So I packed my double-spaced typed manuscript of 450 pages, took that walk seven blocks north, and strolled into the building and then into the Grune & Stratton offices.

I introduced myself to the secretary sitting at the entry desk, told her that I was a psychologist/psychoanalyst who had a book to show to an editor in psychology, and could she direct me to one? Surprisingly, she lifted the phone and spoke to my first love. I refer to Ms. Sharon Panulla as my first love because about two minutes later, she appeared. Then in about ten minutes of perusing my manuscript, she said she liked it, and sometime thereafter offered me a contract. It turned out that Ms. Panulla also published my next two books as well.

Sharon and I lost touch after that, and I, also because of my tendency to choose subjects to write about in a wide variety of psychological arenas, was then able to add many other publishers to my increasingly large tally of books that in the ongoing years I continued to write and publish. At this point I've now published books with fifteen different publishers. My special publishers/editors who published various of my books (twenty-three books combined) include Evander Lomke, of the American Mental Health Foundation; Don Peavy, Sr., of Prometheus Books; Inna Rozentsvit, of ORI Academic Press; Carole Stuart, of Barricade Books; and, of course, Sharon Panulla, now of Springer Science. On the negative side, I had a horrendous experience with the publisher of a press specializing in psychoanalytic books. It turned out that this publisher was not adhering to any contractual stipulations and was keeping a number of authors (including me) on an unending waitlist, along with going incommunicado. Under a legal threat, the publisher returned my contracts for two of my books that she had contracted to publish.

The reason she knew I was a serious and assertive person is that I had decided to drive to where this publisher was located and, unannounced, walked into her offices. I told the secretary who I was, and that I insisted on seeing this publisher immediately. I was then escorted into her office, where she visibly shuddered when she saw me. She instantly apologized for having gone incommunicado and promised that both books would be published forthwith. By that time she had kept these manuscripts then approaching two years, without even a notice or a reason for that highly unusual delay, and then why such silence about it.

Unfortunately, she was not to be trusted, because she then again sustained her nonresponse to all of us stranded writers. I had ascertained at the time there were at least four such writers, including me, so that my lawyer then pried loose my contracts from her. Then, like in Coppola's *The Godfather*, I thought, "I must call Sharon Panulla!" At the time Sharon was then a senior editor at Springer Science.

Sharon was happy to hear from me, and we spent time catching up. She said she had read about Sam and was very sorry to hear about it. After Sharon considered both books, I was then issued contracts for these books, which were then soon published.

My writing career more or less coincided with the birth of my sons. Max was born in 1973, Sam in 1974, Harry in 1977, and Jack in 1979. My first book was gestating in early 1974 when Sam was born, and it was published in 1979, one month shy of my forty-first birthday. Therefore, at that point, my life consisted of: family—wife and raising four children; conducting my private practice; directing a psychology internship program at Postgraduate Center; supervising therapists; writing books; teaching as an adjunct professor in the psychology graduate programs at New York University and the New School for Social Research; teaching the dream course at the Postgraduate Psychoanalytic Institute; and presenting papers at local, regional, and national conferences.

At times during my very productive career as an author, I've had the sense that my productivity had something to do with all the commotion around me, most of all concerning my commitments—especially those in a general sense involving my family relationships, meaning with my wife and children. I found it especially motivating to think through the books I was writing and things I was doing eventhough—or even because—I was in the middle of some turmoil, tumult, disorder, or maelstrom. The point is that conducting a family life with many kids (in this case, four boys) invariably takes the form of everything other than neat seams, or perfect compliance to rules, or to perfect order.

Yet, rather than creating in me a sense of doom or gloom or lassitude, or weariness, or general ennui, rather, it was instead energizing. I consciously felt I was up to the challenge, and furthermore I felt I was handling it as though I were a virtuoso juggler with endless balls whirling in the air, and that additionally it was cognitively, emotionally, and psychologically an undeniably challenging, no less privileged, experience.

Yes, the challenge was valuable, even cleansing—despite my joke that when I began it all I was six feet, four inches tall, and now a half century later I'm four feet, six inches short. However, all in all, I felt my productivity was in essence pollinating a nourishing *contributory* sensibility. Even the choice of material I used in my Yiddish performances, as well as later on with the subject matter and theories of the books I was writing, all of it concerned as a central objective, to underscore the importance of *contribution*.

What comes to mind about this maelstrom in which I found myself was that at times Linda would take care of the kids with the help of two mother's helpers, while we also had a housekeeper whose duties were scheduled for three alternate days per week. Because of this help, I was occasionally able to escape to our retreat apartment close to the eastern tip of Long Island (between Amagansett and Montauk), in a little community called Napeague. There we had a two-bedroom, two-bathroom duplex apartment directly on the dunes of the Atlantic Ocean.

My drive to our retreat apartment is interesting to me because it reminds me of a colleague I had at the time who was an expert with Emily Dickinson's work, and when she would drive to her retreat place in Connecticut, she would recite to herself a string of Dickinson's poems, so that when she awakened from this reverie while driving, she was already three-quarters of the way there and couldn't quite believe what had happened.

The same with me. On my drive to our retreat, I would find myself reciting my Yiddish repertoire of poems and prose, which I knew from memory. And that would also get me a considerable distance to my destination, which all told was a two-and-a-half-hour drive. But when I awoke from my reverie, I was also astounded as to how the time had gone. I once tried to remember the sequence of the poems I was reciting to myself (as well as saying audibly), and I realized I was having a dialogue between material that favored protest (and rebellion) versus material that favored peace and good family life.

Of course, the "mountain of shoes" poem was one of those I frequently recited to myself when I was driving to this Montauk retreat. In it was the reference to Majdanek (Mydonik)—an extermination concentration camp near Lublin, Poland. Then this poem describes how the shoes line up to their pairs and fall into rows and columns, and suddenly this army begins to march. The message to the world is a metaphor—letting the world know that they will never stop until the ones they're after fall and perish—but also to remind the world about never again repeating such a catastrophe with any group. As noted earlier, I love the lines that portrayed the mountain of shoes as holier than Mount Sinai, and that promoted vindication through action.

Yes, I especially liked those lines! But even more importantly, I vividly remember how I felt as an eleven-year-old thinking about those marching columns of shoes, and how impressed I was with what I felt was their determination to refute what had happened, and in contrast, to stand and march for redemption and justice—yes, and I believed it was also with the implication of revenge and retribution. I must admit, it wouldn't sit well with me in the absence of some form of getting back and getting even. Even that is not enough. It's got to be getting even exponentially.

Some years later, in my adulthood, I would still think about it, and I felt that getting even does not in any respect mean six million for six million. The reason is that six or seven million Jews killed was at least one-third to almost one-half of the Jewish population of the world. In that case, I figured that one-third to almost one-half of the German population would equal more than about forty million people or so. Even thinking about it that way was the only way I could feel satisfied with respect to justice, revenge, and retribution.

Thus, with respect to forgiveness, also as noted earlier, I could never be a true Christian. In contrast, Linda could, because she is ever peaceful and abhors violence of any kind. I sometimes think that because of such personality differences, perhaps something works, because at least in this respect, we complement one another.

Let's Go to Maryland

When it came time to marry, I asked Linda how she felt about a certain possible hierarchy of things in a marriage, and I listed them as: concern about aging parents, as well as, of course, concern about the children we would have. Then as to how I saw us, she would be next in line for rescue, and I would be last. She liked what I had to say, so I gave her a second test. I said that I loved the names Max, Sam, Harry, Jack, and how did she feel about those names? Because in my opinion, they were the coolest-sounding American Jewish names in the book. Linda laughed and agreed that they were great names. Then I knew we would be for life.

But then life went along, and we lived together for about four years when my blood brother Richie's parents (who as I've mentioned were Italian Catholics from the old country) retook their vows and married again in church (as is the custom in that culture at their fiftieth anniversary). Richie's father wore a tuxedo and his mother was dressed in an all-white wedding gown. Of course, Linda and I were invited, because I was considered an extended family member.

At the ceremony I saw all of Richie's family (his six siblings and any number of children and spouses of his siblings as well as a gaggle of grandchildren) gathered in a group for a family picture. One look at that assemblage and I knew I was getting married, and also motivated by and for Max, Sam, Harry, Jack, whom I hoped would quickly appear.

After the church ceremony, Richie's family threw a big shindig at a banquet hall. There and then I decided to rent a car on that immediate following Thursday night after work, park it in front of the house, go up to the apartment, and spring it on Linda about getting married. When I actually did that, and entered the apartment, Linda was standing on a ladder in a housecoat watering hanging plants at the window.

I said it to her, "Let's go on a trip."

She answered, "But Henry, we've been on two trips already this year."

"No," I said, "let's go to Maryland." I had already arranged lodging at the Holiday Inn in Rockville, Maryland. Maryland only had a forty-eight-hour residency requirement for marriage, while in New York State the requirement was a seven-day residency requirement and results of a blood test.

Linda said, "Maryland?" We looked at one another, she immediately climbed down from the ladder, we packed one bag, got into the car on that early Thursday evening at about 6 p.m.—and off we went. About three hours later, when we were more than halfway to Rockville, Maryland, I couldn't continue driving. I was wiped, and Linda didn't drive. By this time it was about 9 p.m. We checked into a motel and asked to be awakened at 4 a.m. We arrived in Rockville at about 8 a.m. and checked into the Holiday Inn. That enabled us to establish residency. We then hurried to the courthouse and were first in line to get a license. The only other people in line behind us was a couple who were there to get a fishing license.

We then spent a glorious weekend, including a visit to the National Zoo, to a movie, shopped for a wedding band, had a very special dinner in a great restaurant somewhere in the boondocks, and were married on a snowy Monday morning by a justice of the peace who was a youngish woman in a miniskirt and white boots.

Linda and me in our thirties and forties, and in 1988 in our late forties. I've dedicated several books to Linda. The last one, published in 2012, was the first of my Ghost novels. This first of the Ghost trilogy is titled *The Making of Ghosts*. My dedication was a simple: "For Linda." My first dedication to Linda (as part of the generational dedication of my first published book in 1979) was so unrestrained that I'm not going to quote it here. That dedication is in the book titled *Group Psychotherapy and Personality: Intersecting Structures*.

Then, a couple of months later, we had a grand party at Tavern on the Green in Central Park for two hundred people. The rest is history.

Our first son, Max, was from the start awake, active, and showed tremendous curiosity. Sam, our second son, was rather observant, but didn't speak early. Rather, when he started speaking, it was in complete sentences. Max and Sam were only fifteen months apart and so were referred to as "Irish twins." Max was a highly intelligent and tough-looking boy, while Sam was similarly but also and differently highly intelligent; he was simply as cute as can be. As an adult broadcaster, Max is clearly the handsomest man on TV—of course, in my mind without a doubt! He's also a concerned person regarding the broad issue of fairness—plus his debate skill is second to none, which he can back up with a depth of intelligence, great understanding, a firm social consciousness, and a high educational attainment.

Sam became an especially superb writer, and even by the ages of twenty to thirty had already established an oeuvre of a play he had written and had it mounted on an off-off-Broadway theater. He had also edited books for a publisher, had been in several TV commercials, and had written three screenplays. Sam, as his brothers will attest, was clearly a phenomenon.

Harry, our third son, was a scrawny preemie and weighed only five pounds, eleven ounces. However, from this sort of frailty he was soon indomitable, and extraordinarily observant. Ultimately, as an adult he turned into a six-foot, 175-pound Adonis whose looks and physical stature stopped traffic—in this respect similar to Sam. Harry became a writer, actor, and director, and with respect to his undergraduate stage-play work at Brown University, as well as his master's degree from Columbia University in film, had developed an uncanny understanding of dramatic structure. His first full feature film, which he wrote, produced, and directed, is called *Who Framed Tommy Callahan*. It was preceded by his two award-winning shorts, which he also wrote and directed: *Spidermen* and *The Little Gorilla*, both of which have won more than seventy-five film awards, nationally and internationally.

Jack, our fourth son, was almost a clone of Max. Therefore, as fate would have it, Max and Jack were similar in looks and overall appearance and were emotionally always somewhat strident and single-minded. As adults, they rivaled Sam and Harry in looks. Of course, Jack was both fortunate and unfortunate to be the youngest in this gang of four; fortunate in the sense that in addition to his considerable intelligence, he had the opportunity to internalize all sorts of qualities of his brother's; unfortunate because as the youngest he was not able to win fights with them. Along with this, Jack is a stalwart soldier standing guard at the family door, and has become in his maturity the glue of the family. Jack is also exceedingly creative, and started his own business (New York Clips) by generating an enormous catalogue of image content (still photos and video clips of material) that he then leases to interested parties such as corporate public relations people and Hollywood movie personnel. And along with all of it, Jack transformed himself from a skinny-malink kid (like I was) into a strapping young man. Jack is also a soldier at the gate of social consciousness, and is conceptually a deep thinker with a great command of language.

In contrast to Max and Jack, Sam and Harry were interested in conciliation and bringing peace to the world. In addition, with Max and Sam in the bullpen, Harry and Jack would inevitably become also quite assertive—although Jack, in this respect, didn't need all that help. In this sense, and as noted, the bookends Max and Jack were the warriors, and iron and steel on the outside but quite forgiving and loving on the inside. Sam and Harry, on the other hand, were quite the conciliators on the outside, but iron and steel on the inside. Go figure!

Once when they were kids, they were sitting in a circle on the carpet of our living room, and talking—actually having what among them had become defined as a conclave regarding what they would consider as something crucial in the family that needed to be worked out, and to that end, only among the brothers. At that point, I walked into the house, and to my surprise, they motioned for me to join them.

"Dad," one of them said, "we decided we don't want to be doctors or lawyers. Is that okay?"

I thought for a moment and answered, "Yes, that's okay. You can marry doctors or lawyers, but you don't have to be doctors or lawyers." I then had the thought that I might have been the only Jewish father who validated for his young children that they didn't have to be doctors or lawyers if they didn't want to be doctors or lawyers. I believe I was happy having the opportunity to shoo them away from these vaunted and important professions and instead was hopefully, even consciously wishing for them to become active in the humanities and arts, for example as writers, composers, actors, directors, painters, sculptors, or scholars of one thing or another.

That was the idea I had, as well as the feeling I had, that a life in the arts and the humanities was where, if I had my druthers, I'd want my children to be. The question is why? Well, I believe that society as a whole is, on the evolutionary scale, still quite primitive. That's why one of my favorite sayings is that society operates in this so-called oxymoronic modern-man world on a C-minus basis.

And to top it off, with this rating, as I've stated earlier, I'm being a bit lenient, thus exaggerating with my C-minus grade.

Therefore, I believe that at this stage of societal development, people need emotional and soulful nourishment. By soulful I mean something that nourishes one's spirit and hopefulness. Thus, I feel that contributing to the arts and humanities is the subject matter that can make a significant advance to the nourishment of emotional growth and substantive healing.

As it turned out, Max became a TV sportscaster and popular culture guru who, as I've indicated, has an incendiary social conscience. His verbal skill and overall command of language is simply sensational. He's also appeared in Sylvester Stallone's *Rocky* movies. Sam, at the age of thirty, was also about to become a TV personality when he was taken from us. Yet he had already been on TV in a number of commercials, and to boot was already an exceptional writer and had Linda's wonderful facility with language.

Harry turned into an award-winning actor, writer, director, and producer, and as stated, already in this year 2023, produced and directed his first feature film from an award-winning script that he wrote. Harry was at Brown University, where he was a star actor in a number of plays. Jack insists that Harry should also be in front of the camera and not solely behind it. Harry, like Max, had already been in a couple of feature films.

Jack's interests are wide-ranging, and after he graduated (also from Brown) it was medicine or media. One of his professors at Brown strongly suggested he should go to medical school, as did his personal internist. However, media triumphed, so that's that. Jack began a business of leasing film content which he himself had produced, and has nurtured it into a going enterprise. He has also become a genius of social commentary and he too, like Max, is able to see what's what in incontrovertible depth—especially regarding the social dynamics of injustice. His ability to communicate it all is also especially incisive.

I guess that neither medicine, law, nor engineering was ever in my mind in terms of what I wanted to do in life. However, as it turned out, I was especially interested in psychology and psychopathology as well as in the humanities and the arts, so it was natural for me not to be worried about my sons who asked me whether it was all right not to become doctors or lawyers.

As a parent, I discovered what all parents early on discover; that is, I started to worry about this or that regarding each of my sons. I knew that because they were boys, my message would always be, "I want to hear the bad news as soon as possible." And sure enough, there were times that events validated my tension about how boys can get into trouble. From my Claremont Parkway experiences growing up in the boogie-down Bronx, I knew how circumstance can win the day, and before you know it, trouble crystallizes. Notably, in one of Cormac McCarthy's books, a character makes the point that trouble is out there, and some of it is coming to your house!

As it turned out, all is copacetic, and as the co-CEO of this family Kellerman, I was very much on the case and supported my sons in every which way I possibly could. I made demands, but they were not outlandish. I just wanted them to know that life does not cooperate, and that in order to achieve things (and produce things), one must understand this issue concerning what life cannot do and therefore what the person must try to do as a solitary actor digging in and being persistent. I would always repeat the point that life does not cooperate, and therefore that *the only omnipotence is persistence.*

My ace in the hole was that I always knew they were intelligent and creative, so that correspondingly I always expected good stuff. Sam and Harry went to Stuyvesant High School. When Sam was a senior, he scored the only 800 perfect score on the verbal subsection of the SAT test—the only one in this genius school to do it, and it was announced through the loudspeaker in every classroom of the school. The entire school erupted in applause.

One of my favorite stories in which I was involved occurred at Stuyvesant, when Linda received a phone call saying she needed to be at the school for a meeting because Sam was being suspended. We agreed that I would go instead. I arrived at the school, where the meeting was held in one of the classrooms. I sat in a chair opposite to four of the leaders of the school, who sat behind a long rectangular table. Sam sat near to me on my right. Parenthetically, Sam was not one of these boys who wouldn't fight, although basically Sam's personality was such that his last resort was to fight because he hated violence; and therefore his first response, his first impulse, was to talk—to talk things out as a way of reducing any violent atmosphere into one of conciliation and even friendship.

I already knew what the circumstance was because Sam had told me the entire story at home. Apparently, there was a gang in the school composed of about five boys, and these boys would only pick on one particular group of boys who apparently would never fight back. I hated to hear that it was generally the Jewish boys who wouldn't fight back. This kills me because I do not believe in passive resistance. I leave that to Jesus, Gandhi, and King.

My feeling of fighting for justice is, in my sense of it all, quite a certainty. It reminds me of a rousing Yiddish poem that I rendered many times to a wide variety of audiences. The poem is by Arn Koorts (Aaron Kurtz) and is titled "Shtul oon Eyezn" (Steel and Iron; in the vernacular it actually should read Iron and Steel). Here are a few sample stanzas from this larger epic poem.

Eekh bin shtul oon eyezn. (*I am steel and iron.*)
Voonderlikh bin eekh (*I am wondrous*)
Vee dos lebn vunderlikh. (*Like the wondrousness of life.*)
Mine nomen iz grois vee dee velt. (*My name is as large as the world.*)

Meekh ken yeder teeran: Eekh zing arois foon zine
 (*Every tyrant knows me: I sing out from his*)
Bet oon foon zine trrun. Nitoh ah shprakh
 (*Bed, from his throne. There's no language*)
Vus hut mikh nit. Nitoh a hersher vus (*That can forbid me; no victor who*)
Farbut mikh nit (*Is able to forbid me*)
Nor kayner ken meer gornisht ton. (*So no one can do anything to me.*)
Eekh bin shtul oon eyezn. (*I am steel and iron.*)

Eekh bin a poushet vort—poushet oon grois.
 (*I'm an everyday word—simple and large.*)
Vee bloiz nokh ahn ayntsik vort: dos vort (*Although a single word: the word*)
Vus trugt altsding in zeekh: (*That carries everything in it:*)
Eekh bin fryhite, fryhite. (*I am freedom, freedom.*)
Eekh bit shtul oon eyezn. (*I am steel and iron.*)

Thus, the choice is passive resistance or fighting back! Given my entire repertoire of Yiddish intellectual left-leaning literature in prose, poetry, and stage plays, and given history's treatment of Jews, the choice is no choice at all.

17

Fight Back

Helplessness Is Not an Option

When it came to my sons, I was interested in conveying to them that ours is not a family of passive resistance, and so you cannot permit yourself to be bullied. In any event, the story was that on the subway station after school, Harry got into a minor scuffle with a member of the aforementioned gang on the platform. Harry was outnumbered, got sucker-punched, and decided on the spot that the math to retaliate was not in his favor. Harry went home and told Sam what had happened, and Sam then called Max, who was out of town.

Max told Sam that he couldn't get back soon enough and that Sam had to take care of it. As it turns out, Sam was a beautiful boxer, so that he and his two best friends, one an African American boy and the other an American Japanese boy, went to the school, sought out this gang, and Sam challenged the boy who had roughed up Harry to a fight after school and right on the block of the school. Sam's friends took a camera along to film it all, and of course made sure that Sam had backup. The truth is that all three of them, Sam, Zach, and Alex, were not afraid to fight. Sam, although pulling his punches, nevertheless won that fight, and the boy he fought survived the fight but was then not in good shape. I'm sure Sam felt bad about it because that's the way he was.

Now, as I've noted, it was the Jewish boys who would not fight. The Irish would, the Italians would, and the Hispanic and African Americans would—but apparently the Jewish boys wouldn't. So here we are sitting in this room, and of the four men sitting opposite to me, two were vice principals, another was the guidance counselor, and the fourth was the ombudsman of the school.

The first thing said was by one of the vice principals, who started, "Dr. Kellerman, we are suspending Sam for fighting."

I immediately cut him off and said, "Wait a minute, I have something to say first. See, let's talk turkey here. We are all Jewish in this room. I want to know how you four Jewish men feel about the fact that the only boys in this school that do not fight back are the Jewish boys—now only some more than fifty years after the Holocaust, where Jews couldn't fight because they were outnumbered and without weapons—and mostly poor." I continued, "Of course, Jews with weapons, like in Israel, that's another story. There, Jews fight back—and how! So tell me, how do you feel about the disgusting fact that in your school, Jewish boys are either afraid to fight, or don't know how to fight, or whatever. Did any one of you here tell your kids to fight back so that they would have the pride to stand up for themselves in a physical altercation?" By this time I was damn mad, and decided on the spot to juice up the challenge to them by saying, "I believe that you are right not to permit fighting on the block outside of the school, so that I have no argument with you about that. However, Sam did fight, did win, and on both counts I'm personally very happy about that. Second, if *I'm* going to suffer with this so-called suspension, then *everyone* in this room is also going to suffer. And I have the means to do it. I want to see how each of you men feel when presented with a subpoena to appear in court for undue discipline to a student."

The guidance counselor interrupted me as though I hadn't spoken and directed his attention to Sam. He asked Sam who had taught him how to fight. Sam answered him by simply stating that his brother Max had.

At that point I was feeling no pain, so I said, "We're all lucky that it was Sam that fought so that we can all visit that kid in the hospital, rather than Max fighting him and then we'd all have to visit the kid in the morgue!" And then I had extra ammunition and became even more inordinately obnoxious by saying, "You all know, of course, that of all the kids in the school, Sam had the only perfect 800 in the verbal section of the SAT, and everyone knows he's the best writer in the school. And this point is interesting because it's possible that I'm likely a decent writer, but I won't compare myself to the four of you. However, Sam is definitely a better writer than I. And the implication I'm suggesting here is that there's not a single person in this school—even teachers—that can write better than Sam. And on top of that *he fights back*! And you're suspending *him*?!"

At that remark there was silence for a moment or two. Immediately after this pause, the senior vice principal, without consulting the other three men, said, "Sam's not suspended. This meeting is adjourned."

At that we all rose and began filing out of the room. Sam went first, the other three as a group went second, and I was also about to leave when that senior vice principal who had called the whole thing off, and who was a taller, hefty man weighing about two hundred pounds, leans over my shoulder and shuts the door.

He looks down at me and says: "Dr. Kellerman, I just want you to know, I'm very proud of Sam."

I thanked him for saying that, and he and I then exited the room. I did very much appreciate his comment, so I used his surname as the name of the protagonist of the novel I was writing, naming the protagonist Glenn Kahn. I was going to send him a copy of the novel, but this great Mr. Kahn died a year before I finished the novel.

My participation in the meeting is one of the best things I ever did, and I didn't have a moment's hesitation: a) I didn't like the take on how the Jewish boys were handling themselves, and b) I would do anything to protect Sam—especially when I could see that he was right.

Anyone reading this I'm sure can understand how it was that I was dramatically confronting these men with language and images as a direct challenge to their masculine pride, and to their feeling about what happened historically to Jews. I didn't feel good putting them on the spot, but on the other hand I kind of acted on my sense of righteous indignation.

Given the context of the particular circumstance we were in, all in all, I felt justified. In addition, this was right up my alley because I'll never be able to tolerate some kind of leveling of aspersions toward Jews generally—especially when it's undeserved. That poem "Shtul oon Eyezn" (Iron and Steel) is in my blood.

The point is that my voice needed to be heard. It is this attitude that I'm sure influenced me since I was a child—while conveying these feelings of righteousness to audiences. As far as I was concerned, such an attitude was always gratifying to convey, and I always did it with an exclamation point when I performed the poem "Shtim foon Sholem" (Voice of Peace) by Khana Safran.

Dus harts kun nit shvygn (*The heart cannot remain mute.*)
Dee pen kun nit shtimen (*The pen must be audible,*)
Dee pen vus is tsapl foon harts (*The pen that derives from my heart.*)

Oon meygn dee vintn tseshturmenteh broomen
   (*And even though disturbing weather*)
Dershrekn, farshtikn dee shvakheh dee kroomeh
   (*Scare and choke the weak and disabled,*)
Dee pen vet nit zoogn meer: "Vart." (*The pen will not tell me: "Wait."*)

Oon, hynt is der tug oon hynt iz dee tsyt, (*Oh, today is the day and today is the time*)
Ven mekhtik mooz kleengen mine shtim! (*When my voice will strongly be heard!*)
Azoi hubn doiress foon nooent oon vite (*This is how generations now and past*)
Farkritst oon fartsaykhnt in teglekhn shrite (*Noted in daily memorializing*)
Foroisgang foon mentchlakhn meen, (*Related to human needs,*)
Oon hynt iz mine rye (*And today is my time*)
Oon dou is mine ourt (*And here is my place*)
Tsoo hoibn mine shtim oon zugn mine vort! (*To raise my voice and assert my say!*)

Although Sam's life lasted till he was thirty, the way he lived it and the experiences he had made the thirty equivalent to some uncommon age exponent. It is typically understood that the catastrophe of losing a child, a brother, a grandson is something one never gets over. And I can attest to the unalterable fact that that's true. However, people must get on with their lives, so that at the moment, more than a decade and a half later, only Max is married, and he and his wife have three beautiful daughters—my grandchildren who in the year 2023 Esther is fourteen, Sam is eleven, and Mira is eight—and as for Max's beautiful and wondrous wife Erin, anyone would give their right arm to have such a spouse raising their children; on top of it, she's beautiful and highly intelligent. I'm still wishing for Harry and Jack to also find an Erin. Yes, and the same for Sam.

Of course, life is unpredictable, so that relationships are always in the process of becoming (or "disbecoming"), and to my utter dismay, Max and Erin are now, after twenty-five years, separated. And this particular event is considered both by Linda and by me as a bona fide tribulation—especially when we think of Erin and the children. No question but that life scalds you. The Yiddish expression is "Klayneh kinder, klayneh tsooris; groiseh kinder, groiseh tsooris" (Little children, little problems; big children, big problems).

Our grandchildren are extremely interesting and bright. My name is Papa Henry. Linda is called Gara Linda—I guess because when the oldest, Esther, was

Max and Erin's children, my granddaughters: left to right, as of 2020, Sam is nine, Mira is six, and Esther is twelve. I dedicated the second novel of my Ghost trilogy to these wonderful children, titled *Ghosts of Dreams*. My dedication reads: "To my beautiful granddaughters Esther, Sam, Mira."

an infant, she couldn't easily say "Grandma," so that's where the Gara is derived. Esther is named after my mother. Esther is an excellent student, just as her mother was. She's also a fabulous dancer—really fabulous!

The same can be said of the other two. Sam is obviously named after Sam. She's a talented artist, very bright, beautiful, and like her namesake is a peaceful person. Like her uncle Harry, she's also a self-taught gymnast. Mira, the youngest, is named after my father's mother Miriam who, as noted earlier in this memoir, was shot and killed during the Holocaust. All three girls are also quite noticeably verbal.

At the moment, our son Sam is not visible—but he's very much with us. I had the greatest problem with sympathy cards and verbal statements regarding just how losing a child (in this case, an adult child) is the most painful of all pains. Sometimes comments were nonthinking, such as the mother of all nonthinking comments, to wit, "Oh, you'll never get over it," or some variant of this sentiment. The truth is that such sentiments by individuals are certainly meant as a condolence; that is, that such a particular sentiment of "never getting over it" really with respect to psychological arithmetic means that such a person can't see how *they* would ever get over it. I've never gotten viscerally angry about it, although I'm possibly repressing or avoiding such anger, because I believe it's a natural reaction to avoid the inevitable pain that those making the comment are relieved that this is not going to interfere in their lives. The truth is that no one wants it. However, we got what we never asked for.

So what, with regard to Sam, did we get? What we got was the ecstasy and the agony. That's what we got. The ecstasy with Sam was ecstatic and the agony gave as agony gives.

The Yiddish poem "Aybik" (Forever), by H. Layvik, says it all for me. Here's the first stanza:

Dee velt nempt meekh aroom mit shtekhikeh hent,
   (*The world embraces me with thorny hands,*)
Oon trugt meekh tsum fyer, oon trugt meekh tsum shyter.
   (*And transports me into the fire, and carries me to the pyre.*)
Eekh bren oon eekh bren, oon eekh verr nit farbrent.
   (*I burn and I burn but I am not consumed.*)
Eekh hoib zeekh oif vidder, oon shpan avek vyter.
   (*I rise up again, and stride away further [in the sense of being steadfast].*)

And in this same spirit, the Yiddish poet Shika Dreez also put it beautifully. Here are a couple of stanzas of Dreez's poem, entitled "Ah Hoikher Boim, ah Shayner Boim, ah Shtarker Boim" (A Tall Tree, a Beautiful Tree, a Strong Tree).

Khotch meh hut ah halbeh velt (*Even though half the world*)
Mit mine bloot fargusn, (*Spilled my blood,*)
Hundert mull geharget meekh (*A hundred times they killed me*)
Oon toizent mull geshusn— (*And a thousand times they shot me.*)
Dukh hut nit genoomen meekh (*But no fire and no sword*)
Kine fire oon kine shverd. (*Was able to defeat me,*)
Oon ut-ouh, vee ear zet meekh, (*And as you see me now,*)
Vacks eekh aff der erd— (*I am generative on this earth as*)
Ah hoikher boim, (*A tall tree,*)
Ah shayner boim, (*A beautiful tree,*)
Ah shtarker boim! (*A strong tree.*)

A Disappearance

So, I had an out. I had a way out. Yes I did. You see, one of my friends suggested we join a bereavement group. I instantly and reflexively rejected the suggestion. It was then that I realized that I was not accepting the reality of Sam's disappearance, and that's why I had that reflexive reaction to my friend's suggestion. That's what and when I began calling this catastrophe a "disappearance." That was my way out. Therefore, perhaps as a disappearance there is no reason for any bereavement. It's only a figurative death. And now, more than a decade and a half later, I still feel that way. In fact, I speak to Sam all the time. One of my colleagues supports the process of bereavement and of mourning as essential to psychological and emotional growth. I wouldn't argue the point except to say that in most things there are exceptions, although I'm not sure I agree with the assumption of the relation of mourning to inevitable emotional growth.

Sometimes, when I finish the day at the office, I begin thinking what I would say to Sam regarding why I chose to say something to a particular patient, and I imagine my explanation nourishes his considerable interest and his unusual intelligence. You see, Sam was a very literate and creative person. He was also an athlete. He won a "best" something (I don't remember what it was) on his baseball team. As my wife and I along with his brothers will attest, Sam was, especially, and for his age, arguably the best writer anyone could imagine. And with regard to his SAT, the late and very notable Pulitzer Prize–winning English teacher at his high school, Frank McCourt, inscribed his own Pulitzer Prize book *Angela's Ashes* to Sam with the personal note, "To Sam Kellerman, may the muse stand always by your side."

When in about fourth grade, he was one of a large nationwide sample of fourth graders who was given some sort of test that purported to measure maturity, cognitive power, and creative thinking. Linda and I were called by the director of the project to come in for a talk about how Sam did on the test. At first I was a bit concerned, but Linda said, "Relax, it's about Sam." Of course she meant that if it's about Sam, then it couldn't possibly be bad. I've also had that thought on a number of occasions, to wit: If it's about Sam or about Yiddish, then how bad could it be? Of course, historically speaking, the answer is in both cases: pretty bad! And this reminds me about a great story regarding Max and Erin.

They both went to that extraordinarily high-level high school Hunter College High School, and eventually, like Linda and I—who also went to the same high school, Music & Art, and were in the same grade—they too married. When they first started going together, they both realized that they had something in common, and at the same time not. What this meant was that they were both called to the principal's office on a number of occasions. The amusing part is that Erin would always think, "I wonder what award they're giving me now?" but Max would think, "Uh-oh, now what have I done?"

I digressed. Back to Sam. At that meeting with the director of this nationwide project, she said she was happy to tell us that in this nationwide sample of fourth graders, Sam came out with the highest score of anyone. I remember it was a cold, wintery day, and as we left the school, Linda turned to me and said, "We'd better listen to everything he says!"

To continue with the art projects that Sam did independently—some of which I began to describe earlier—at the age of nineteen, Sam wrote for ABC TV, he wrote a sitcom for European syndication, he was a book editor and edited a half dozen books. When he was fifteen he wrote the screenplay *Cove of the Ghoul*. Then after he turned twenty he also wrote two original screenplays, *Infinity King of All Everything Man* and *Ha, Ha, Stick 'Em*. He and Max also recorded an EP (extended play record) for Sony Music that was also produced. It was written by Sam and is titled *Young Man Rumble*. The week we lost him was the same week that his agent had scheduled for Sam to sign a contract to do a half-hour TV talk show for one of the edgiest channels on television, MTV2. Then, before we lost him, Sam had completed writing a book entitled *Conversations with Zeida*. "Zeida" is Yiddish for "grandfather." Here's how he started it:

> Zeida was my grandfather and best friend; he lived to 95, at which time I was 25. We talked about everything, from the dependability of condoms to the Russian Revolution to the Yankees to Yiddish to rap music to the Holocaust. Our conversations document the intersection of two very different worlds—the Eastern European Jewish shtetl at the beginning of the 20th century, and downtown Manhattan in the hip-hop '90s. This book contains enough Jewish history to merit inclusion in college syllabi, and enough sex and violence to entertain Tarantino fans.

Sam's prodigious efforts started young and included his off-off-Broadway productions of three plays he produced by the Bardalotry Theatre—a title Sam coined. One of his plays was based on Shakespeare's *Troilus and Cressida* and was performed in Washington Square Park in Manhattan in the center of the park at the fountain. Sam had invited Professor Stephen Jay Gould, the paleontologist from Harvard whom he had befriended while taking a special course at Harvard, as well as Marisa Tomei, whom he also had known because our family was friends with Marisa's family. These two notable individuals introduced the program at the park.

In addition, he also produced and directed two other plays that were performed at off-off-Broadway theaters and literally to packed audiences—as well as writing the play *The Man Who Hated Shakespeare* (based on the true story of Robert Greene) that was also performed at an off-off-Broadway theater. And speaking of Shakespeare, Sam could quote from close to all of Shakespeare's plays. He made a special project of learning them all. It took him more than two years of a prodigious effort to do it. At another point when Sam was participating in a film program at UCLA, he won awards for best director and best film. In addition, the New York State Olympic Committee was in competition for filming New York as the potential site of the 2012 Olympics. Sam was the star of the film.

When he was about five years old, I was at my desk working on a chapter for a book I was writing. Sam climbed up on the chair behind me, draped himself over me with his head on my shoulder, and for about ten minutes or so, just kept watching what I was doing—just watching me write. Then he slid down, pulled up a chair at the side of the desk, and started writing his book. And we both worked like that for about a half hour. Then he finished his book and asked me to staple it and tape on a spine to the book so that it would contain the title of the book and his name as author. He actually used the term "spine," and he was only about five.

One year later, in 1980, I had a book reception for the publication of my first book. Sam was six. As I began to speak to the assembled, Sam burst forth from the crowd and plopped himself right down at my feet, holding on to my pant leg for the entire time I was speaking. Years later he told me that he just knew that what I had done—writing a book—was important. He said he had been watching me work on that book since he was two and so he knew, really knew, that books were crucial, and furthermore, that he was very proud of me.

When Sam was about eight, he accompanied me to an art opening of an internationally known painter at one of the finest galleries in New York City. While in the gallery, he started tugging at my arm. I leaned down, and in hip-hop language he whispered, "Dad, Mom's stuff rocks this." He was comparing the art in the gallery to his mother's art (Linda's art), which is what he cut his teeth on. I've always loved that memory.

Sam was also the person in the family that kept us laughing. Max, Harry, and Jack were always hilariously laughing with what he said. So was I. With Sam's disappearance, with all the tears and cumulative crying that we all did, and with my personal psychoanalytic insight of what crying and mourning means, it, the crying, and crying specifically, all boils down to an attempt *to retrieve the lost object*—to retrieve the person who disappeared, the one we lost, the one who was killed in a way that was most ironic notwithstanding its awesome cruelty: he was fatally smashed on the top of his head. Yes, the target was Sam's exceptional CPU (his exceptional brain, his central processing unit)—a phrase I learned from Max.

When Sam was on a special program at Harvard, he walked into Harvard's famed paleontologist professor's office to meet Professor Stephen Jay Gould. He wanted to meet Gould in person because when Sam was a sophomore in Stuyvesant High School, he read a book written by Gould and loved it. He also noted that Gould mentioned Joe DiMaggio as someone Gould loved. Sam wrote Gould and told him how much he had liked Gould's book. Then he received a copy of Gould's book in the mail with an inscription thanking Sam for Sam's comment. So when Sam was told by Gould's secretary that the earliest Gould could see him would be in a month, Sam was sorely disappointed and he returned to his dorm room.

In his dorm room, Sam wrote a note to Gould reminding him that Sam was the one to whom Gould, three or four years earlier, had sent the book and, in addition, told Gould that the way Gould felt about DiMaggio, Sam felt about him. So, Sam then went back to Gould's office and asked the secretary to give Gould the note. Then Sam returned to his room.

When he got there, there was a message waiting for him on his answering machine. Sure enough, it was Gould in person, asking Sam for lunch the very next day. They became friends, and Sam was periodically invited to Gould's home for dinner with Gould and Gould's family.

It was about 1 or 2 a.m. and Linda and I were asleep. We were awakened by Harry and Jack who were standing at the foot of the bed.

Harry said, "The worst has happened."

I suddenly and reflexively answered, "Sam is dead."

Harry said, "Yes."

At the time, Sam was living in Hollywood and we hadn't heard from him in a few days. I had a funny feeling.

Linda and I just stared at them and they stared back at us. I got out of bed, made many phone calls to cancel my entire patient schedule for the week. Max came over and we all entered into this new, terrible reality together. It was now the five of us, not the six of us. The next few days were of course also terrible, and I kept having the repetitive thought, *Oh Sam my Sam*. My second thought was, *This family is destroyed*. I was wrong. We were not destroyed, and my answer to a friend who asked, "Are you and Linda getting divorced?" was a simple "No!" But that many couples do separate or divorce after such a tragedy is the circumstance that was not ever going to happen to us. Nevertheless, and for sure, we were all devastated.

And by the way, the typical phrase of "You'll never get over this" is not quite accurate. The point is that time is a healer, and as in our case, the memory of such a catastrophic event is etched and therefore sustained, yet gradually, inch by inch and step by step, the agony dissipates; that is, the emotion attached to the memory also detaches from the memory, and it too (the emotion of agony) almost, but not quite entirely, recedes.

What remains is event related, insofar as whenever Sam enters consciousness, a momentary assaultive feeling sears through me (one of ineluctable certitude of what actually happened), so that in an urgent moment of attempting to distract myself (gratefully and in a usually successful manner), the horrific feeling attached to the memory again fades.

But I do remember how he looked in certain clothes and even in his shoes. And the moment I think of Sam's shoes I also think of Shulshtayn's mountain poem, where he continues from noting that the shoes were the last evidence of those who wore them:

Meer sheekh vus flaygn gayn in parrk shpatseern
(We shoes who would take walks in the park)
Oon khosn kalleh tsoo der khooppa feern.
(And also escort bride and groom to the chuppah.)
Oon gayn azoi door ois, door ayn.
(And do this sort of thing generation after generation—)
Oif simkhess, khasseness, oon gayn tsoom kimpet
(At celebrations, weddings, and also attending childbirths)
Oon oikh a tantz gayn fool mit rahsh oon impet
(Along with dancing with spirit and joy—)
Oon rooeek oif leveyess gayn. *(As well as quietly attending funerals.)*

Despite that Sam's funeral called forth more than a thousand people so that it concretizes it all, still, how I feel about Sam's shall I say decampment is that I feel it is temporary. Yes: how I feel about Sam is that he is ongoing—partly in a sense of reality, and partly in the sense of his shoes marching with Shulshtayn's sacred army.

On this note, I must report two other situations that drew me into projects that in certain essential ways correspond to the entire catastrophic event that we all faced with the disappearance of Sam. In all of these events, the underpinning theme is the one that always gets me—down to the core. This theme that hits me is the one of oppression and the terrible unfairnesses of life; that is, that life does not give a hoot about individuals, cultures, or societies.

But, again to detour for a moment, I believe that part of the devastation I felt about losing Sam may have been based upon the sense I had that Sam was originally the glue of the family, and that he was the one who not just swallowed the Kool-Aid but that his brothers did as well, which became a symbol of what our family was like. The Kool-Aid was the imperative that ours was a family of "one for all and all for one." It was Sam, seemingly as the point man reflecting and representing this idea of family unity, who embodied it for us all, even though we all also strongly felt it. Yet, ultimately it was actually Jack, as I've said, who was the one to keep this symbol alive and vital—even to this day, in the year 2023—and it is my loving Jack who I've also said is the soldier standing at the family door, and who remembers how when they were growing up, that these brothers were always there for one another—along with the exceptions of fighting and arguing.

When in 2019 Linda needed spinal fusion surgery, Harry jumped in with Jack and they both made sure that Linda was well taken care of. Jack took the reins pre-surgery, and Harry took over in his inimitable way during the recovery period and did an impossible-to-believe supervisory role over every detail of Linda's recovery. Max also provided a brilliant insight.

With Sam, I must say that what is equally agonizing is my belief that I should have been more on the case with Sam. The point is that how I was with Sam reminds me very much of how my parents were with me; that is, they thought I was special enough that they didn't need to be overly supervisory, so that their belief led them to feel that I would be able to handle everything needing to be handled. They were wrong, and about Sam, I too feel I was wrong. Sam's experience with girls and women was also very similar to mine, and to some extent was made possible by the absence of sufficient and parental supervision.

So, I know that Sam was living a very exciting life. He was productive, creative, but in a very big hurry, so that his schoolwork suffered despite the fact that he was a standout student. An interesting and revealing thing occurred in Sam's honors English class. His teacher originally kicked him out of the class because Sam was not handing in his homework assignments. Then when the news was announced on the loudspeaker in each classroom that Sam was the only student to have cracked the perfect 800 on the English part of the SAT, his honors English teacher came into Sam's homeroom class and asked if he could make an announcement regarding Sam. Sam's teacher consented and Sam was asked to stand. His honors English teacher then publicly apologized to Sam for banning him from the honors English class. Sam quickly answered him by stating that the teacher was right about banning him because it was clear Sam was disregarding the assignments. They then embraced and the class applauded.

The question is: Why did I not know about his delinquency in class? English was his forte and he could have easily been an A+ student. Where was I in all of this, and the searing question is: If I had been specifically on the case with Sam, would his trajectory from that point on have sent him off in a different direction rather than wandering around the way he wanted, a bit like the nomad I was? And second, wouldn't that have prevented what ultimately happened? My answer is a resounding yes; that is, had I been on the case in the way I should have been, Sam would surely still be with us in an extant condition and not as an "if only."

18

Mitch, Lenny, Ray, Sam

Mitch and Lenny

This example at the end of the last chapter regarding how I take the onus of Sam's situation onto myself is quite different than when I'm on the case. This kind of what I'm referring to as a "situation" is related to the theme of resisting oppression and injustice; a theme that, as I repeat, hits me to the very core. The first such event that drew me into this thematic strand of my life concerned a soldier's death. This soldier was posthumously nominated for, and ultimately won, the Congressional Medal of Honor for his valor in the Korean War. His name was Leonard Kravitz. He was the uncle of the modern extant award-winning virtuosic music man Lenny Kravitz.

The story begins with my college roommate Arty Libman. When we were rooming together, Arty would occasionally mention that his brother Mitch was involved in some kind of mission to right a wrong. It was about Mitch's best friend, Lenny Kravitz, who, rather than going to college, joined the army at the beginning of the Korean War in the early 1950s. Lenny was killed while single-handedly rescuing his entire platoon of about forty men. The award itself listed what Lenny did.

Platoon Leader Telke writes:

```
    Pfc. Leonard M. Kravitz, RA12322776, Co. M,
  5th Regimental Combat Team. "L" Co. 2d Platoon,
        U.S. Army 24th Infantry Division
        Killed in action, March 7, 1951,
```

```
                    Yongpyong, Korea.
                     Recommended:
              Congressional Medal of Honor
      For uncommon bravery in the face of certain death.
                Initiating recommendation:
            Reconnaissance Officer, Company M
                       Approved:
         Commanding Officer, 5th Inf. Regt, APO 301
```

What Lenny did was to take over the machine gunner's position after the machine gunner had been killed. At that point communist Chinese forces joined the conflict by supporting the communist North Koreans and en masse lodged an assault on Lenny's platoon's position. Lenny refused the order to retreat and rather unloaded a barrage of machine-gun fire on the oncoming Chinese regulars. There was no significant response by the enemy to Lenny's incessant machine-gun chatter, so that after taking a terrible beating, the Chinese regulars retreated. However, they returned with reinforcements, toward whom Lenny responded with firepower equivalent to that which he had originally delivered. By this time, Lenny's entire platoon had evacuated, minus any fatalities.

The following morning, when the platoon returned to the battle site to look for Lenny, they saw that the wounded and dead on the battlefield had been removed through the night so that only two of the Chinese regulars were found dead in the ditch near to Lenny, who had also been killed—lying splayed over his machine-gun.

The problem that literally propelled Mitchell (Mitch) Libman into this scenario was that even though Lenny was recommended for the Medal of Honor (essentially by doing the same thing Audie Murphy did in the Second World War, for which Murphy was easily awarded the Medal of Honor, and had been then the most decorated veteran in U.S. history), in Lenny's case the recommendation was denied and Lenny was instead awarded the Distinguished Service Cross (the second-highest award for bravery).

Mitch didn't like it. He said it stunk to high heaven and he was going to do something about it. And he did a lot about it. It took him an incredible, unbelievable sixty-three years to get it done. He said that doing it was the most important thing of his life, and to boot, Mitch's effort probably validates the aphorism that *persistence is the only omnipotence.*

What Mitch ultimately did was that he kept digging into all sorts of records as well as contacting untold individuals and organizations, until after a couple of decades (yes, decades), Mitch had accumulated enough data and indefensible evidence that revealed the Defense Department of the United States of America to have an institutional bias against African Americans, Asians, Hispanics, and Jews.

Mitch had recovered the data of 138 men, including those of World War II, Korea, and Vietnam, who were discriminated against in this manner. It felt to Mitch that lurking in the underlying muck of institutional bias was what actually characterized attitudes—at least in the U.S. Defense Department. As I said, Mitch didn't like it. Something wasn't fair and this American, Mitchell Libman, insisted that America must be fair!

So, Mitch spent these decades writing and speaking to senators, congress-people, and even presidents in order to have this issue gain valuable and visible support. In the end Mitch had most of Congress (Senate as well as the House of Representatives) on board, and this included President Barack Obama. But he also invited on board, and the invitation was accepted by, the Clintons and the Bushes.

As such, the Lenny Kravitz law was proposed mandating the Defense Department to "re-vet" these 138 veterans of the three wars (World War II, the Korean War, and the war in Vietnam) who were nominated and subsequently denied the Medal of Honor. The proposed name of this congressional mandate act became the Leonard Kravitz Jewish War Veterans Act of 2001. This proposed name of the Veterans Act was ultimately changed. Nevertheless, the Defense Department was ordered to investigate the entire situation. It took the Defense Department another decade to accomplish the task of re-vetting all 138 candidates noted by Libman, who, by the way, had collected complete files on each of these men, and because of it, 24 of the 138 actually received the Medal of Honor. At that point it had been sixty-three years since Mitch, when he started his investigation, was twenty. And then, finally, in 2014, when Mitch was eighty-three, he received a phone call from President Obama.

"Mitch," Obama said, "it's President Obama."

Mitch then instantly said, "It must be good news, otherwise I doubt whether I would have the pleasure of this phone call."

Obama instantly told Mitch that Lenny had gotten the Medal of Honor. However, Obama also quickly added, "You know, Mitch, we can't really set up the ceremony tomorrow."

Mitch, in his quick-witted style, answered, "Okay, how about next week?" They both had a good laugh.

The ceremony took place soon thereafter, in March 2014, and it can be seen in its entirety on YouTube (including the assembled who represented the twenty-four who got the medal), all witnessing the thank-you by Obama to Mitch, followed by the standing ovation given to that incandescent spirit—Mitchell Libman.

Sometime thereafter, when Arty, Mitch, and I were together, I suggested that the story had all the hallmarks of a screenplay, if not a novel—for which then Mitch assigned the job to me. In addition, he told me that he's been keeping notes over this more-than-a-half-century period on everything he'd done on the project. Excitedly, we then went directly to his house and Mitch produced a ream of paper totaling a bit more than eight hundred pages of notes, copies of letters he'd written and received from a myriad of sources, and all sorts of other notations regarding Lenny and the story of bias in the military.

Mitch gave me this treasure trove of material and I produced a screenplay (yet awaiting an angel for it to be produced as perhaps a feature docudrama, tentatively titled *Looking for Lenny*).

As I saw it, and in summary, this is the story of another death and its redeeming end about which I was the one able to escort the project to such an end point. I also loved the idea that Mitch refused to relent and repeatedly insisted that America must be fair. At the ceremony, he got the attention of a nation.

Ray

The second project that invited me in was about a man whose life was essentially ruined by several people and several circumstances. I tried resisting this project for a period of about a decade, but with considerable persuasion by the protagonist of the story—also an amazing true story—I was no longer able to resist entering the fray. And the issue that again got me was incredible unfairness and oppression—perpetrated on one person.

The backstory started as follows.

Dr. Raphael Osheroff and I were classmates at the High School of Music & Art. During that time, although we were not best friends, we were instead casual and friendly acquaintances. However, as is the case after graduation, people fly off in any number of directions, so that Ray and I were no longer in touch until our fortieth high school reunion.

I had been asked to chair the reunion committee of nineteen members. Our entire senior class consisted of 486 students. The formal reunion was held on a Sunday at the LaGuardia High School of Music & Art and Performing Arts. During the Koch administration in New York City, Mayor Koch was the one who decided to merge both schools: the High School of Music & Art (specializing in music and art) with the High School of Performing Arts (with majors in drama and dance). I believe it was the first one-hundred-million-dollar high school.

The latter school (Performing Arts) was eventually known as the "*Fame* school," where a large percentage of graduates went on to professional careers in performance fields. The High School of Music & Art was the school where almost all of the students went on to college as well as a large percentage also pursuing graduate school, doctoral degrees, and degrees in a wide variety of specialties.

Raphael (Ray) Osheroff become a nephrologist (kidneys). He was highly successful and was an originating partner in a series of nephrology clinics within the Washington, D.C., and Virginia/Maryland/Delaware region. In summary, Ray had become depressed and his wife (they had two children), as well as his physician/business partner, convinced him to check himself into Chestnut Lodge in Rockville, Maryland—the internationally reputed mental hospital that was the site of the highly successful novel *I Never Promised You a Rose Garden*, written by Joanne Greenberg under the pen name Hannah Green.

Ray's admittance to Chestnut Lodge turned out for him to be an incarcerated tyrannical internment. The lodge itself was run by orthodox Freudian psychoanalysts who were seemingly in a psychoanalytic delusional trance regarding treating people strictly without the aid of any medication. In this sense, Ray (having eventually obtained his records) saw that his doctors at the lodge were planning on him having a five-year therapy plan or even a ten-year plan so that they could, in essence (and in retrospect to their discredit, as well as to their delusional, deranged, and even corrupt conception of what constitutes a true psychoanalytic objective), felt they could rather break Dr. Osheroff even down to zero and then build him back up as a normal person.

Parenthetically, this seems to me to be similar to that Cambodian communist narrative whereby these communist goons aimed at bringing the Cambodian populace down to zero in order to build everything back up so that it could be perfect—which in essence is a bunch of unadulterated nonsense, characteristic of these Cambodian communists ending their plan in the Killing Fields of Cambodia!

The fact was that Ray was always, and without any doubt, a normal person who unfortunately became depressed, largely because his marriage was falling apart. In fact, his wife eventually divorced him, and with the children relocated to Europe. Ray accused his partner in their clinics of pilfering all the patients so that when Ray was, after eight months of unbelievable mishandling, busted out of Chestnut Lodge by his stepfather, he was then transferred to the Silver Hill Hospital in New Canaan, Connecticut. There at Silver Hill he was immediately given medication and in about three weeks released from the hospital—fully recovered.

After discovering what had happened to him professionally, Ray sued Chestnut Lodge and won the case. Because of this case, Chestnut Lodge was closed—shut down! Furthermore, in any modern "history of psychiatry" book, the Raphael Osheroff/Chestnut Lodge case is described as a benchmark case, meaning that any psychiatrist refusing to prescribe medication to a depressed patient was now, because of the Raphael Osheroff case, liable to a malpractice suit.

But Ray wasn't finished. He formed a symposium of a large number of panelists composed of respected psychiatrists from all over the country to discuss the ins and outs of his experience at Chestnut Lodge. The conference was held in San Francisco and sponsored by the American Psychiatric Association. The title of the conference was "The Patient's Right to Effective Treatment." It was at the American Psychiatric Association (APA) San Francisco 1989 annual meeting, and it was organized by Dr. Osheroff himself. The conference was attended by more than *two thousand psychiatrists*, and it was filmed.

Ray's story was one replete, through and through, with a transparent theme of injustice. For me it instantly brought to mind a poem I occasionally performed to audiences of immigrant Jews who were all too familiar with injustice and their oppression by others. The poem was written by the noted Yiddish writer I. Buvshahver, and in the following I will offer a gist of the poem. Literally, the title is "Lift Up Your Eyes My People," meaning "Be Conscious My People"—open your eyes and see what's really happening.

Hoib Oif Dieneh Oign Uh Folk (*Be Conscious My People*)

Hoib oif dieneh oign mine folk (*Be conscious my people*)
Vus doo bist azoi elnt oon ourem. (*That you are so alone and poor.*)
Oon zay dee gezamlteh oitzress, (*And see the accumulated treasures,*)

Oon zay foon dine arbet dee pairess, *(And see the result of your efforts,)*
Oon zay dem geblibenem rykhtoom, *(And see the rich result,)*
Foon freehr gevezeneh doiress. *(Of prior generations.)*

Hoib oif dieneh oign mine folk. *(Be conscious my people.)*
Gay arois foon dee fintztereh khvorem. *(Free yourself of your travails.)*
Oon nem foon dine arbet dee pairess.
   (And take what you've earned by the dint of your efforts.)

The essence of the message here is to not endure exploitation and oppression. Rather, the natural choice is to rebel and to insist on fairness. Thus, what happened to Ray Osheroff eventually opened his eyes to the possibility of gaining rectification. And to this end, I eventually could not refuse his plea for me to assist him in putting together the material of his story, and to write the book.

So this was the situation with which Ray approached me at our fortieth reunion. He arrived with Paula F., a classmate of ours at Music & Art. Paula and I had been good friends in high school, and we were happy to see one another again. Then Ray took me aside and told me that he had been following my career and knew that I had published many books. He asked me to let him give me a rundown of this bizarre history of the Lodge as well as other things of his personal life regarding his former wife and former partner.

The main point of our discussion was that Ray made it clear he was sure I could translate his voluminous store of notes into a book, and that he was also confident that then the story would be rendered faithfully. He knew the proposed project was challenging, but said that nevertheless he strongly felt that I would be the one to tackle his 150 single-spaced typewritten pages comprising his diary of the entire hair-raising and disgusting scenario of his recent life—by then in the year 2005.

I agreed to listen to him, and we arranged to meet that week for lunch. He presented me with this tome of single-spaced typed material, and over our three-hour lunch also kept summarizing it all for me in an attempt to keep it all cohered. The truth is that Ray was a superb writer—a true literary virtuoso. He lamented that he was unable to organize the material and put it together in a way that rendered the story accurately and in the right *key* (a musical reference). Incidentally, Ray was also a trumpet player and well educated in musical theory.

At the time of this lunch, I told Ray that I was in the middle of writing my own book, and despite my full empathy for what he had gone through, I didn't think I was in a position at that point to take on his project. He then offered me a 50 percent commission on all sales. My answer was that I could not accept his generous offer of that high commission, and wondered whether he was always giving away the store. Nevertheless, I devoted the following week to carefully reading all of Ray's notes as well as reviewing a host of magazine articles on his case, and finally I researched the case in a couple of history of psychiatry textbooks, such as in Edward Shorter's 1997 book *A History of Psychiatry: From the Era of the Asylum to the Age of Prozac*, in which the essence of Ray's story is noted.

The question is: Why couldn't I accept his offer the way Ray presented it?

The "why" of it is that after I indeed read his notes and all the other material, as well as listening to his story of failed marriages and the loss of his practice, I again told him I still was unable to undertake the project. However, a decade later, after we had had our fiftieth high school reunion, I agreed to do it.

During that ensuing decade, we had met intermittently though continuously. When finally I decided to do the project, the first thing I did was to coin the ultimate suggested title of this book that I felt was the only title possible given his detailed and corroborated vile treatment at Chestnut Lodge. In addition, one of the other initial steps I took to understand how to keep the book cohered was to coin chapter titles that could keep the narrative of the story from disintegrating based upon the sea of data I now had. I did all of that after chronologically sequencing all of his material with respect to Ray's notes—which he had not originally done—and that in itself took me about a month to do. But that was the initial prep step.

My proposed title to Ray's book was actually a sentence, and with respect to how much writing and work I actually put into it, I eventually agreed to authoring it.

Here is the title: *Shackled, Beaten, and Starved: The Untold Story of One of the Most Shameful Scandals in American Psychiatric History (The Raphael Osheroff Story)*, by Henry Kellerman, Ph.D. (with Raphael Osheroff, M.D.).

I soon realized that Ray, in all of his important personal relationships, usually, as mentioned, gave away the store; he was uniformly and consistently a self-abnegated player, meaning that he was exceedingly sacrificial to others, which then was equivalent to appeasement behavior—so that those appeased would ultimately exploit him (as would usually be expected in response to any appeasement act). Of course he was that way with his medical practice also, and I daresay with his marriages as well. I was not going to participate in that kind of so-called assassination plan of which Ray was undeniably, and unconsciously, the architect; and I told him so.

Therefore, historically, at least for the following decade (from our fortieth high school reunion to our fiftieth), we had become good friends and often met for lunches and dinners, when he would always and predictably discuss the unfortunate vicissitudes and losses of his life. So by this time he had worn me out and consequently won me over. His win was that I accepted the challenge of writing the book. During that decade, I had written four other books, so that I felt free enough and inspired enough to do what Ray had asked, in an uninterrupted and gentle albeit relentless approach, essentially persuading me to write.

I accepted a 15 percent commission to Ray's original offer of 50 percent because I refused to be party to anything resembling Ray's tendency to appease. In addition, as it was with Mitch and the Lenny Medal, it was encouraging for me to know that Ray had these copious notes because it meant that he too was memorializing his entire experience in this abundance of notes.

Then it literally took me another couple of months to further sort it all out (especially in consultation with Ray) concerning time elements, chronologies, as well as fleshing out personality characteristics of those who played important parts in his life—negative and positive. My job from that point (as it revealed itself to me) was to create interstitial connective tissue and to essentially write the book.

In Ray's acknowledgments section, he included his appreciation for my participation and also expressed his appreciation to exactly thirty-four others who had importantly helped him along the way. I finished the manuscript in 2005 (Kellerman, 2005b). Ray said about me:

And getting this work to be a book means a very special thank you to:

Henry Kellerman, Ph.D., Clinical Psychologist/Psychoanalyst/Author. This memoir would have been but a loosely conjoined pile of recorded nightmares had it not been for the editing expertise and perseverance of my esteemed "High School Of Music and Art" classmate who, separating the wheat from the chaff, helped me render a complex and Byzantine narrative comprehensible to the reader. There were, at each point of my life critical individuals who pointed the way and re-meeting Henry after we had reached maturity is proof positive that indeed, you *can* go home again.

With respect to the searing injustice of losing Sam, of telling Mitch's story about his loss of his friend Lenny (along with its special heroic circumstance), and of assisting Ray in his wish to have his story told (perhaps as an attempt to regain a measure of self-respect as well as a sense of empowerment)—in all of these, I was inexorably pulled in by issues of corruption, unfairness, and injustice. I guess I felt it an honor to be involved in things that could possibly redeem bad news and have it transformed in some way that brought some relief, that brought some justice, *that brought some good news.* And I readily felt that my immersion in Yiddish literary works regarding Jewish history especially as it related to injustice made me a person who was particularly suited to be able to do this job for Ray and in a way that understood the implicit injustice of the evil that embraced his life.

I also felt that my work on this project made me the last witness to Ray's agony, insofar as I would be the one to open this entire story of justice and redemption to a general readership. And Shulshtayn also mentioned in his "mountain of shoes" poem the importance of last witnesses, where in a hopeful fantasy, the shoes marched to the end point of gaining the ascendancy, and in this hopeful fantasy, victoriously ended forever unfairness and injustice.

I will quote from this Shulshtayn's last stanza when we come to the end of this memoir.

At the very least, apologies are important. President Clinton's apology to African Americans and President Obama's apology to Native Americans count, as does Germany's apology to Jews. In contrast, the Turkish refusal to apologize to Armenians for the Turkish genocide against their Armenian citizens is shameful and full of the dissolute character flaw of hubris—especially perhaps because the genocide against the Armenians was, in essence, an attack also on Christianity—since the Armenians were the first Christians as well as being the minority in Turkey, as Jews were the minority in Europe.

I believe the Yiddish poetry and prose that I performed for audiences always contained in my presentation the sense to me that I was also on a machine gun protecting the Jews of Europe from the onslaught of the degenerate Nazi. My son Sam said it best. He noted that even though Hitler's objective of erasing Jews from the world was thwarted, nevertheless he was successful in essentially erasing Yiddish by a significant and critical factor.

Sam

And Sam was right—so that at the moment, in year 2023, despite the resurgence of Yiddish in what might be considered a token renaissance, Yiddish is now below the critical mass necessary for it to flourish as a national language—especially as a national language of the home.

Therefore, during the years of my anointment as the person carrying the torch for Yiddish—especially on the Yiddish radical left—I believe I always felt during that period of my life that speaking it, speaking Yiddish, bringing Yiddish to the masses, was, as Sam correctly stated (and for all intents and purposes), a refutation of its demise and therefore a profound corresponding refutation of the Nazi ideological criminal mentality. In addition, understanding this enabled me to see that my strong inclination, in my performance litany, was to select content material of "protest to injustice"—rather than the kind of poetry that focused on the reverence of beautiful sunsets and fields of flowers.

It all was implicitly as a result of what I refer to as "the Sam principle" regarding the importance of Yiddish and what it means in the larger conceptual framework of justice/injustice. Of course, this conceptual framework corresponds to and reflects the pain that people do indeed suffer at the hands of injustice.

Along with this kind of thinking—especially about injustice—I believe that to make gut-wrenching attempts to do something valuable for oneself is one of the only dignities. It can lead one to also fundamentally care about others, even to the extent, and in the worst of circumstances, to do something equivalent of walking out of a nightmare.

It is in such a sense that I actually did such a thing (walk out of a nightmare) when I read a sentence from some account that was written about the value of what I personally define as *persistence*. For example, I've usually confirmed for certain patients, who by dint of their own efforts have obtained for themselves the important "something" they had hoped for, that in the end this is probably best considered as that which can be thought of as really *the only omnipotence*; that is—one's personal struggle.

After we lost Sam, whatever omnipotence I might have always felt about myself seemed very, very wanting. In my boogie-down Bronx Claremont Parkway neighborhood of my formative years (until I was seventeen), this kind of attitude was called "die-hard." This meant you don't stop trying until you get what you want—even by a series of successive, slowly agonizing and approximating steps.

And by the way, being a die-hard or dying hard can usually be found in the culture of poverty, where people living this culture really have nothing that gives power except persisting in whatever it is they want. The point is that without the privilege of affluence, the only thing left is trying hard—is to be a die-hard—which, without a doubt, I am.

And then one day I was reading an article, the theme of which escapes me, but I believe it was at the conclusion of the article that the author ended with the biblical reference "Seek and ye shall find"; that is, something can be found if it is looked for—which is both an adage and possibly a reference to an omen (in the positive sense) of some miraculous "find." That phrase of "seek and ye shall find" hit me squarely, as though the bullet went directly into my forehead and then, somehow, to my heart. It electrified me—I, this stone-cold Jewish atheist.

Looking for Sam

I then immediately made plans to fly to Los Angeles, where Sam had been living. I had once visited him there for a three-day weekend and we spent all of our time together. He showed me around, to a variety of places he had frequented. One was an interesting restaurant, one was a fair in San Diego that was about two or three blocks long and permanently closed to traffic, while another was a park near his house where people played chess as they do in Washington Square Park in the Gold Coast of New York City, south of Fourteenth Street at the northern tip of Greenwich Village. And coincidentally, here I was, becoming a prospector looking for gold.

My son Harry made the plane reservation for me while never asking me why I was doing this, but of course sensing that such a trip, at that time, was important for me to do, especially since I was without a doubt doing it. Max and Jack never said a word to me about it, and neither did Linda. Everyone understood who I was and that I was serious about making that trip. They all knew what gold I went looking for.

I arrived in LA about noon West Coast time, checked into a hotel, and immediately started seeking. I went directly to Sam's house and walked around his block. I went to that restaurant as well as to other places we had visited, and I spent the rest of the day walking until I even found the park where people were milling around a chessboard watching the chess game.

Sam wasn't there.

That night in my room at the hotel I continued reading Dostoyevsky's *Crime and Punishment*, which I had started reading on the plane. The confluence of events here concerned my reading of this, what has been considered a classic novel, when I was nineteen years old and in college. I remember not liking it in college and thinking that either it's not really a great novel or that I was too young to appreciate it. Therefore, I decided that if I was still extant in fifty years, I would read it again. At that point I would be sixty-nine years old.

So here I was at sixty-nine when we lost Sam to a violent end, and the confluence is that I'm reading *Crime and Punishment* as a way of respecting my promise to myself that I made fifty years earlier. I finished the novel on the plane home. I still didn't like it and didn't think it was valid to consider it a classic. I thought the ending was too abrupt and that Dostoyevsky's understanding of Rozkolnikov's personality was a bit scattered, incomplete, and never with the feeling of validity regarding tying Rozkolnikov's formative years to his brutal behavior as an adult. I was also terribly upset by the reference of Rozkolnikov's bashing in someone's head.

I also spent one full day at that San Diego fair to which Sam had taken me. I sat in a chair at an outdoor café and monitored the people walking up and down that main street. I would glance at a newspaper, or have a cup of tea and some pastry, but I would not miss any of the visitors who were passing by walking up and down the street. That night I went to a couple of nightspots which Sam had also shown me, but—no. In the middle of the third day I again walked the block where Sam lived, and then a few hours later I was on a plane to New York.

Knowing full well that I was on a failed mission even from the moment I read about "seeking and finding," nevertheless, doing it was for me a singular catharsis and it helped me kind of, again, practice the walk in and then out of a nightmare. Kind of, but not entirely. However, I think it was my way of being with Sam and also helping him when I couldn't because I wasn't then there to help him, but surely would have prevented it all had I actually been there.

In 2008, four years after we lost him, I published my book *The Psychoanalysis of Symptoms*. My dedication reads: "To our extraordinary Sam Kellerman." However, speaking of one's presence, as I've mentioned earlier, not only do I briefly think of Sam after my last patient leaves the office, but in addition, as I leave the office I keep the office door open a touch longer to allow Sam to leave with me. Then I keep the waiting room door a bit open as well, so that Sam and I can both together enter the waiting room, leading to another two doors to the street, so that I also keep those other two doors open a bit longer as well, thus allowing both of us to be on the street together. My office has a professional entrance so that one enters the office from the street. Keeping him extant like that neutralizes my pain.

I love you, Sam.

P.S. So you see, I'm still that smiling innocent two-and-a-half- or three-year-old in that photo of me in chapter 2 who surmises and even expects (or even insists) that the world is a good place, insofar as only good things should happen to people, and that that's the way it should be. In this sense, I never accepted that so-called fate is irrevocable. And therefore, I'm always fighting to get back what was taken from people by others who perpetrate catastrophic events—and that's why I'm in the retrieval business. I want to retrieve Yaruga so as to prevent pogroms and I want to refute Sam's disappearance and so I still think of him in my office. I want him back. There is not a chance in the world that I would attend a bereavement group. And that's why the title of this memoir is *To Bring Good News*. Nevertheless, it has occurred to me that in addition, the emphasis in my life of the effects of the Holocaust (given my identification with it all) leads me to think I suffer with a bit of PTSD (post-traumatic stress disorder) as though I, myself, also experienced it. Despite having a strong ego, I also experience a bit of "remove" in my personality containing some anger—perhaps as well with respect to the death of my son, Sam.

Thinking of myself this way feels as though it might be difficult for anyone to live with me given my ironclad stubbornness in contention with the past. The past be damned.

But then thinking about Mitch, Lenny, Ray, and Sam, Shulshtayn again comes to mind, when he talks about funerals.

> **Biz ayn mull in a trouyer tsoog a langgn**
>   (*Once then, in an unending funeral procession*)
> **Oif aybiker levahya shtill gegangen** (*To our own funeral we slowly marched.*)
> **Tseshayt mit gang foon alt oon yoong**
>   (*Our sounds were the mixture of old and young*)

Ven lebn iz avek foon oonz farbourgn (*When life left us on our borrowed time*)
S'hot nit bavizn oonz aryntsookhapn
Der tlion in zine roiber zahk. (*The hangman never had a chance to snatch us into his*)
Itst gayn meer tsoo eem s'zol yeder herhn (*Sack of loot—but now we go to him.*)
Dee treet vus gayen vee der floos foon trern
　(*Let everyone hear the steps, which flow like tears*)
Dee treet vus clappn ois dem psaak. (*The steps that measure out the judgment.*)

As noted earlier, the last measure to this poem will be presented at the end of this memoir.

PART 2
INFRASTRUCTURE
Home, Anonymity, Contribution

19

Power-Themes

Introduction

The premise of this memoir, or the definition of a memoir generally, is seen here as an attempt to identify fundamental themes of a person's life. The assumption made is that together, these themes form the template that decodes the entire trajectory, objectives, and highly probable decisions a person makes at the early stages of life, and then throughout life. In contrast, this view of mine of the memoir herein is understood somewhat differently than the overview of "memoir" that Professor Alex Zwerdling makes in his review volume of the nature of the memoir (*The Rise of the Memoir*, 2017). Professor Zwerdling (p. 2) states:

> This kind of writing is personal; it is not the anonymous story, nor the public record, but rather the idiosyncratic, private, anomalous version of an individual history, itself often inconsistent and full of unpredictable turns.

Yes, each person's story is idiosyncratic and private but probably, I submit, not anomalous nor necessarily inconsistent. If one digs deeper into the infrastructural bowels of memoir, I believe we will see a rather fairly consistent reflection of the person's life. In this sense, it is and will be proposed (and considered throughout this book) that the memoir is really a philosophy of the person's entire life. Further, the important point here is that "entire life" will also be seen as fundamentally governed by two or three thematic strands that together form the basis of all of what Professor Zwerdling seems to consider to be a cluster of issues involving "inconsistency" and "unpredictability." I consider this all in Afterword II, at the end of this book (which was my original first preface of the first draft of this present memoir).

However, a focus on those thematic strands that presumably govern a person's life—this cluster—with respect to feeling, thinking, and doing, gradually begins to dissolve the ideas of "inconsistency" as well as the notion of "unpredictability." In this regard, I believe that whatever is the longitude and latitude of a person's experience (and behavior) can actually be seen as such a life being fairly rather consistent as well as fairly predictable, or if not predictable, then certainly consistent in the sense of being understandable.

It may be that such an assumed truth regarding fundamental themes of a person's life (also stated in the premise and preface of this book) transforms the memoir to philosophy—to something different than simply the chronology of events of a person's life that at times may even seem scattered. "Something different" really means that we are interested here in the introspective nature of the person as well as derivatives of these fundamental themes—the two or three themes that combine to cohere some greater understanding to the meaning of a person's life especially with respect to such a person's feelings, thinking, and behavior—the doing of it.

This means that—as far-fetched as this may sound—what a person feels, thinks, and does may not be at all random; rather, such feeling, thinking, and doing may again also have an underlying economy as well as an engineering to it, both supporting the notion that all of it is perhaps actually deterministic—meaning that no one's life is a conjoined mixed-up mass of accidents in its sequence and/or experience in what the person feels, thinks, and does. This also means that one's life, in a certain way, contains a lifelong stream of consciousness. This is, again, in contrast to Professor Zwerdling's (p. 5) statement that the memoir is "a flexible form without a predictable terminus . . . in a life that shapes us rather than is ours to shape." Zwerdling says it well. However, how a life shapes up is largely based upon given experiences (in fact, possibly *with* a predictable terminus), and this shaped-up life is an example of what I'm here proposing. With respect to this present memoir, therefore, I needed to identify that which comprised what can be the unearthed steering mechanics of my own history with respect to the two or three themes that seem to have determined it all—no less, with a high probability.

In my case, I see three themes. These are: *home, anonymity, contribution.*

1. The Theme of *Home*

As noted earlier in this memoir, the *unthought-known* is a concept coined by Christopher Bolas (1987) which means one knows something, but as it turns out, what this "something" specifically means is unconscious. In other words, the "something" had been felt consciously but in the absence of a specific thought. However, the particular "something" is now repressed and/or perhaps even acted out. The idea is that the unthought-known is an unconscious construct but then again, possibly *not* acted out. If the "something" *is* acted out—meaning that the person *does* something in *behavior* that represents the unthought-known—then the *doing* of it is in place of the *knowing* it. In other words, again, this is "something" that one knows but without a conscious particular or specific thought. It is, in a conscious sense, possibly an intuition.

In my case, I believe I was there halfway between feeling something was wrong but not knowing what it was except that I was, whenever possible, and on a regular basis, noticing my interest in apartments in buildings in the early evening when it was dusk as in the stage of twilight time, just before getting dark, and the apartment was nicely lit and the surround was beautifully composed and everything was peaceful.

I could never resist gazing at this kind of setting and feeling something that said, "At last!" I think this feeling of "at last" was my sense that at last I was *home*. And I believe this meant "safety," and very importantly, the successful escape from something chaotic—but then again, mostly as meaning peacefulness. In thinking and trying to understand it more in depth, it occurred to me that the sense of "safety" and "the successful escape from harm" meant that in some way achieving this kind of nirvana must have had a corresponding notion equivalent to the act of rescue; that is, once the sense of rescue hit me, it brought to mind the history I had always heard with respect to my parents' growing-up years in Yaruga.

Thus, the unthought-known seemed to have brought me back to that same feeling of rescue regarding what I'd always heard about pogroms that occurred in Yaruga and how the denizens, the Jewish ghetto inhabitants of Yaruga, managed to get through these traumas. In my stream of consciousness, I also connected my first appearance in kindergarten at age four, where I checked out the situation, turned to my mother who was at the door watching me, and waved her away. The question is, Why did I wave her away? I still remember that feeling of mastery in sort of telling her, by waving her away, that I could take care of it all myself; perhaps meaning I was *home* and that I didn't need to be rescued. The good feeling I had (and that I can now sense) is that I could see the other children crying and so it may have occurred to me (or that I instinctively felt) that I could (*would*) rescue them, and then everything would be all right.

But Yaruga I believe was it—*at the core of my epic search for home.* Yes, where I lived on Claremont Parkway in the Bronx was also home, but I was still unconsciously living in Yaruga. My son Jack, I think, said it best. He once said that my address was 493 Claremont Parkway, Bronx, New York, Apartment Yaruga. He then added that I was flooded with the sense of Yaruga that occupied my feeling that that's really where I was. And I believe Jack was right—as usual. Yet, in the sense of the arc of my life, it was by and large an American life.

Actually, Yuri Suhl, the well-known Yiddish writer, wrote a story entitled "Dee Finif Vus Zynen Avek" (The Five Who Went Away). It's a charming story of the Yiddish alphabet in which five of the letters decide that they're tired of hanging out with the same old other letters of the alphabet as well as with all that punctuation stuff, and they've decided to split. Despite pleas from the others, these five do it. They leave and begin to travel the world seeking adventure.

The remaining letters of the Yiddish alphabet feel chaotically disrupted, so that whatever they said made no sense. Without those five letters, it all became gibberish. Meanwhile the five who had gone all went here and there, and even in different directions—but they too couldn't talk. Then by chance, they happened to all meet in a place where there was a Yiddish school. They were happy to see it and quickly entered the school. They saw the teacher at the blackboard, who was unfortunately unable to write any sentence because those five letters were missing. The five letters were happy to then see all of their friends. At that, the five letters who were now reunited with the rest of their Yiddish alphabet friends were feeling so happy to be back home in the alphabet that they hopped onto the blackboard. And, in a moment of insight, the entire alphabet decided to form themselves into three good words which they now could form with the letters who had returned. They wanted to proclaim something important, so they made the words:

PEACE, BREAD, FREEDOM.

The teacher and the students laughed and laughed and were so happy.

I loved this story and for many reasons. It readily confirmed for me that which I always knew: that being at a place you can call home is something to celebrate.

In many of my life's venues, I don't think I was really at home. I did all sorts of things, went to all sorts of places, had a lot of fun, but I was never sure if any of it really felt like home—perhaps yes, here and there for a few of these places: Claremont Parkway, Hofstra College, Kinderland, Yiddish school, and, of course, Linda with the boys. But for sure, also Yaruga.

In fact, I was always hearing my parents talk about Yaruga, and after a while I could name several individuals and families from Yaruga and also knew what they did and what characteristics of this panorama shone through the ages into my mind and into my heart. Further, in order to see and feel Yaruga as my home, I simultaneously needed to imagine it as no longer a victimized klayn shtaytaleh (little hamlet). Thus, when I began to feel home was Yaruga, I also felt that I was at one with both my mother's and father's families, who would now be living there in some existence of safety and in peace—and with bread!

This fantasy life of mine—apparently just below the line of consciousness—was, I believe, always urging me to think about where I really belonged. My wandering life into outlying environments had little resemblance to my family environment, or to my fundamental political orientation, or to Yiddish, or actually to this otherworldly Yaruga. This perplexity related also to my so-called romantic liaisons; that is, all of it was taking me far afield of home. Not that it wasn't interesting or enlightening. But something was, in a sense, perhaps feeling wrong. Something seemed always to be inexact or amiss. What was missing perhaps was not being able to rescue my family in Yaruga. It could be that my wanderlust was an attempt even to find Yaruga. I was always looking for Yaruga—even though unconsciously perhaps I was already living there—ergo, perhaps I am suffering with a bit of PTSD.

I never told Richie about it because I felt that he, as an American Italian Catholic, wasn't part of this situation, nor would I want to involve his family in any difficulty. The happy ending was that the Nazis never came, the pogrom never happened, and we never needed to get my bubba over any fence. This was the United States of America! Yet, it was never lost on me that for African Americans, it had always been absolutely necessary to get Granny over that fence.

The point here is that my immersion in Jewish history, family history, political dynamics; my immersion and performance of the Yiddish oppression literature of protest and resistance to unfairness (along with the need for retribution); as well as my knowledge of the history in Yaruga, had all pervaded and infused itself into my very being. All of it, then, pertains to this thematic strand of my life involving the issue of home; that is, where do I think is "home"? In this sense, this immersion in Yaruga and its apparent vicissitude as "home" is to me somewhat analogous to Goodheart's smothering demand to only be productive in his schoolwork as the overwhelming mandate of his life and its hypothetical connection to his later agonizing asthmatic condition; that is, that one's experience of one's formative years connects very directly to nuclear issues of their adult lives. In my case, perhaps, was my need for closure—the sense of finding, at least with a touch of verisimilitude, Yaruga—my home? And of course, a need for closure is always a need for empowerment.

Pogroms in Yaruga

Of all the stories about Yaruga that I've memorialized on paper and that are etched in my brain, six are most vivid. First was when the townspeople were alerted that a band of sixty or so armed men on horseback were approaching the town and a pogrom was about to unfold; that is, an onslaught against Jews. My father's brother Zonia was co-leader of the resistance. At the time Zonia was about eighteen and my father was thirteen.

The small army of men entered the town and began to loot and kill. Then, after a few hours, they rode off—except for one straggler. Zonia and the others pulled him off his horse and disarmed him. My father, who was witness to it all, told me the straggler had blood on his clothes and was carrying stolen goods. Zonia and the other men dragged him to the river (the Dniestr River, on whose banks was located the Jewish sector). It was the dead of winter and so these Jewish resistance fighters, led by Zonia, cut a hole in the ice of the frozen river and shoved the straggler in. They covered up the hole and the straggler drowned.

I was about fourteen years old when I again heard this story. It was the third time since I was about eight or nine years old when I first heard it. But now, at fourteen, I was about the same age as my father when he witnessed it all. This time I asked my father whether he could have done what Zonia did. He said no. I believe my father was remembering it through the eyes of his thirteen-year-old self. But I'm rather positive that had it happened when he was Zonia's age or somewhat older, the answer would have been a definite yes. He could have and would have done it, and I don't think I'm projecting it as though it's what I would have wanted him to do, or what I would or wouldn't do.

The second story is connected to this first one. Before this little army arrived in town, it was a chance to get the girls all hidden. Different families had different methods of doing so. In my mother's house, both she and my Aunt Bessie (my mother's sister) were walled up in a false chimney—bricked up for the entire day, standing silently at attention within their vertical tomb.

The third story is about another pogrom in Yaruga. There, the leader of that band of killers decided to utilize my grandfather's house (my paternal grandfather) as their temporary headquarters and ordered all to leave the house—except for my grandmother. He wanted her to remain. My father protested but nevertheless was ordered out. However, he remained on the side of the house, and in a few minutes could not take the agony he was feeling. He ran back in.

The leader, in a moment of outrage, ordered him out by shouting at him. My father wouldn't leave. Suddenly this leader unsheathed his sword and raised it as if to come down on my father with it. My father said that in a reflexive moment, he grabbed the sword, but the leader pulled it out of his hand, and that's how he got the scar across the palm of his hand. Apparently because he was so young and so brave—along with his bleeding all over the place—this leader walked out. And that was a perfect example of my father's natural sense of fairness, justice, and assertion, which at that moment was in stark evidence. Even as a child I always knew this about my father, and in all ways I always admired him and wanted to emulate him. What I loved about these stories was that in each case a collective unified urgency of the community took place and everyone did anything they could to protect themselves as well as the entire community.

The fourth story is also about that same pogrom. These cowards entered the humble abode of an old Jewish man. This man slept on a straw cot. After tying him to the cot, the bandits lit it up. My father said that when they pulled the dead gent out of the house he was charcoal and his skeletal feet were visible as they buried him.

The fifth story is about my father's best pal. His name was Max. At this time my dad was about eighteen and already living with Zonia in Bucharest, Romania. He and Max and others of their friends hung out at a popular café. One day a man rushed up to my dad and gave him a note. The note was for Max, but instead, the man gave it to my father. The note informed Max that rumor had it his father was killed in a pogrom. My father consulted with the other guys and they decided not to tell Max, but that my father would need to sneak back into that town and get the lowdown firsthand. They chose my father because it would be necessary to swim the width of the Dniestr (about less than half the width of the Hudson). It was known that my father was the strongest swimmer of all the guys, in addition to the fact that he was the best horseman.

My father got the deed done, and the truth was that Max's father was indeed shot and killed and his body tossed into the Dniestr. Then they told Max about it. Incidentally, my oldest son, Max, is named after Max, my dad's best pal.

The sixth story is about my father's best pal during his formative years. This friend was Dovid Kohnor. He was not a good swimmer, so that my father would help Dovid swim to the little island in the middle of the Dniestr River where my father and his friends would hang out. Dovid became a teacher, but my father and he still kept in touch even though they were no longer in that growing-up foxhole, the same kind of foxhole as it was with Richie and me.

After the war, my father received a letter from an eyewitness noting that Dovid and his wife were summarily shot down by a Nazi contingent. My father was devastated by the news and always repeated to me over the years how Dovid was "such a nice guy." He also said that Richie and I growing up together reminded him of how he and Dovid were such great friends. By mentioning Dovid Kohnor here, I kind of bring him safely to America. That's really how I feel.

Coming from the tough Bronx, I couldn't avoid thinking of what would have happened to this army of bandits if it all happened in my Claremont Parkway neighborhood; here in the Bronx, these Ukrainian bandits would be losing many men. But of course, these fantasies were just my way of neutralizing my anger, my need for victory, and my need for revenge. Revenge for what? Revenge for what they did to my people, to my home in Yaruga? Yes, this is the hint; that is, what these men did "to *my* home in Yaruga." You see, I refer to it as "my home." And so I can now see that when I wrote the prescript to my Passover Seder book titled *Haggadah: A Passover Seder for the Rest of Us* (2005), I was implicitly and even explicitly stating it—referring to my grandparents' Seders as though I was there. Yes, in fact I did feel that I was there. In fact, in our dining room, we have all of our relatives from the old country set on the walls of the room and so when we celebrate with our Haggadah the Passover Seder, all of them join us in this essence of family.

In the introduction of my Haggadah, I stated:

In all my growing up years I never attended a full traditional Passover Seder. All I remember is my mother telling me about how her father would conduct the Seder, beginning in the early evening and going through the night. The children would be fast asleep by morning.

I always pictured this scene in that little shtetl called Yaruga on the Dniestr River in Ukraine. I could hear my grandfather, Kchaim, who I never knew but after whom I'm named, telling the Passover story, and I could almost hear everyone singing in this Chagall strawroofed little abode.

A few mud filled streets away lived my father's family; his father, my grandfather Meyer, after whom I'm also named, and who was conducting their Seder. The same Seder. For me, this history, these almost-memories, were compelling. After our second son, Sam, was born, I realized that Max, our first, was reaching a point where he would soon be able to participate in a modified Seder—one for young children.

Soon thereafter when Harry and then Jack completed our family, my wife and I decided that it was necessary to celebrate Passover with our children in a way that would convey the entire spectrum of meaning in the Seder ritual. I also wanted to capture the spirit and fervor of my grandfathers' Seders in Yaruga—these Seders that I carried in my memory as though I was there.

In the postscript to the Seder, I stated:

So this, *Haggadah: A Passover Seder for the Rest of Us,* hopefully has helped us further understand and appreciate who we are and what it was that shaped our values and identity. In this spirit I would like to think that my grandfathers Kchaim and Meyer, and of course also my grandmothers, Pessie and Miriam, perhaps would have approved of this Haggadah and considered it praiseworthy—a further contribution to Jewish continuity, albeit in a secular voice.

So, yes, *home* for me looks like it was Yaruga. In that case it was Yaruga that I had been seeking—and probably also felt that it was seeking me. It is presumably the place for which I've been searching whenever I see a quiet place—one that is all peaceful. I think it means that I'm in a dreamscape in which there are no more pogroms and everything is copacetic, so that my closure on this point is that everyone is safe in my favorite place. This obtains especially when I see a serenely lit beautiful home setting. It's Yaruga, where I guess, in fantasy, I feel almost as the place where I spent my childhood.

It's interesting that because of this overwhelming issue of where *home* might be located and for what purpose had it become so important to me, that I also hit upon these two other issues, all three of which seem to account for the greatest variance (taking up most of the space) of my life—insofar as these three issues become in my opinion the pivotal plot points of my life; that is, the indelible issues of *home, anonymity,* and *contribution.*

2. The Theme of *Anonymity*

At a certain point in my life I began to notice that I would seek not to be in the limelight. As mentioned earlier, this was and remains true, despite that as also mentioned earlier in this memoir, I had already gained a certain measure of celebrity—albeit in a small corner of the world; that is, in the left-wing progressive Yiddish culture mostly composed of about less than a million Jewish immigrants living all over America. My celebrity was also true among Jewish Zionists—also all here in America—and also despite the fact that I had not ever expressed a particular zeal nor felt especially deeply about Zionism—although I knew that I felt strongly about supporting the State of Israel. And I need to say the following to whoever is interested:

I don't like anyone messing with Jews. Enough is enough.

I'll say it more simply so that I'm sure everyone will see what I mean. And this message is for individuals as well as for countries, because if you mess with Jews, you'll get it back—in spades. Here is what I really want to say, and in no uncertain Bronx terms:

Don't fuck with Jews!

Did I say something that wasn't clear? Now back to *anonymity*. When thinking of Eugene Goodheart's memoir, I could see (or at least speculate) that his power-theme perhaps concerned the issue of autonomy. Whether Gene may have known it or not, I believe his fight was for greater degrees of freedom so that he would no longer be controlled by superego constraints directly emanating from his father and implicitly, I'm sure, supported by his mother. Superego essentially means one's conscience based upon demands that have been internalized—that is, mandated self-imposed stresses.

Therefore, Gene's superego intensity was, I believe, presumably internalized directly from the supreme value of education held by his parents—especially heard by his father's powerful, resonant, and audible voice, along with his mother's quiet congruity although not in bombast or specific words, but in her obvious love of literature which consistently was visible by her wonderful reading appetite. If Gene could have succeeded in attaining this alleged wish for greater or even maximum autonomy, my prediction is that his debilitating adult asthmatic onset would never have had the strength to ignite. Gene called me after his mother died and we had an interesting conversation. I was shocked, as noted earlier, when in 2021, I found Gene's obituary in *The New York Times*. He died at the age of eighty-eight.

For me, and in contrast to how I understand Gene's particular organization of personality (especially with respect to my guess that he had this wish for *autonomy*), I believe autonomy was already a mature characteristic existing in every fiber of my being. My need to avoid being conspicuous is of course oxymoronic given that I typically found myself at the center of dance contests, standing out, so to speak, chromatically, while other dancers were frequently so to speak relatively monochromatic. My psychoanalytic take of my seeking anonymity may be a result of finding myself below the operant level needed to feel entitled. This means perhaps that to feel entitled was, for me, from a political point of view, too elite.

However, I was rather quite conspicuous during my performance career in the Yiddish progressive cultural movement. It was not that I didn't relish what I was doing in this career. Yet at the same time I think I was simultaneously searching for greater invisibility despite this typical center-stage position in which I found myself.

The point here is that I also stood out by measure of winning all the dance contests I entered—all fourteen of them—from the age of fifteen till my early forties. And in an unselfconscious way I was comfortable in the limelight when I was performing—kind of like how my father was in his unselfconscious manner. But even at parties, I am not given to what I consider small talk. The reason for this I'm embarrassed to say is: Could it be that I'm a bit tongue-tied if the conversation I might be having is not about me? The contradiction I live with is that I'm probably not a good listener except when I'm in my office listening to patients. There, in my office, nothing is small talk and nothing is manifestly about me, although all of it is in its latent psychoanalytic context about the two of us—the patient *and* me. Further, I also think that this difference between talking and listening at a party versus the talking and listening at my office is that at a party, it all seems equivalent to the planning aspect of rehearsals, which for me was typically tedious, cold, and uninteresting. These were difficult for me to endure. Yet in my office it feels like the real thing, and not at all related to small talk. I know that even at parties, if the conversation concerns political or philosophical or therapeutic issues, I easily swim, and these are generally not at all about me, although they might concern my underlying focus on what constitutes justice.

Is the Past Really Past?

So, the issue becomes the elements that defined my *anonymity*. For one, I believe I suffer with the idea that the past *is* the past, or in my wishes, *might* be the past—along with what Faulkner said: "The past is never dead. It's not even past" (1951); and here's the important point—the past can't be changed, can't be transformed from unfairnesses that had actually occurred to the condition of fairness, or from "injustice to justice." And as a parenthesis here, it may be that my little oedipal idea referred to earlier, regarding my mother's full-time work in the store with my father, can bring us full circle as well to the business of "injustice to justice." Thus, my impossible wish may be, in essence, an attempt to challenge fate, to transform unfairness to fairness, and injustice to justice, and—to change the past and save the world. It's a matter of defying so-called "fate" and disclaiming destiny. And I think the perfect example of it all is that:

I want Sam back!

We lost him to a madman who did him in after Sam had tried to help this person. This person was raised in a deprived, poverty-stricken, urban ghettoed population culture, so that anyone (especially boys) who grow up in such desperate situations (Black, Hispanic, or white) are likely to be, in this sense, desperate—especially if one is also a bit mentally challenged.

In the case of Sam, implicit in the socio-politics of our family was the idea of providing aid to such people (whoever they are). Nevertheless, what was absent from our philosophical idealizations was that you should also be aware that someone who grows up on the streets of such ghettoed deprived neighborhoods—specifically if such a person is also desperate as well as being a bit deranged—that such a person could be definitely violent. I missed reminding Sam of this affect. I missed it. I had been *over*-inoculated against thinking those things.

So I say to my progressive friends, please be aware that when one crosses cultural lines, one needs also to be aware of the vicissitudes of that neighboring culture. Had I oriented Sam more about this facet of life, he very well might still be with us. Of this I am achingly certain.

Of course I couldn't help what this reminded me of with respect to my performance material. And such audiences needed to hear that despite all the desperation and tribulations of Jewish history, Jews still manage to endure, contribute to society, and even flourish. In history with Jews, they were usually out-and-out killed, but there are other ways in which people are, so to speak, killed—like the tribulation of the auction block where, in American Black history, families and relationships were so fractured that even to this day it becomes a fantastic struggle in America for Black people to gain a consistent ascendancy—notwithstanding, of course, the incessant racism and caste system still infecting America. Pulitzer Prize winner Professor Isabel Wilkerson's masterful work *Caste* is one that reveals this underlying caste system here in the USA (Wilkerson, 2020).

A poem written by Yuri Suhl, titled "Moisheleh's Kholem" (Little Moishie's Dream) immediately comes to mind. Moishie's dream recapitulates the entire Passover drama. The following is the last part to the story in which Moishie falls asleep at the Passover Seder while his grandfather is telling the story of the tribulations in Egypt. Then Moishie awakens from a dream and the story ends with a nod to the overcoming of tyranny.

Oon du hut zikh Moisheh plootzloong tsevekt (*And Moishie suddenly awakened*)
Der tish iz vee freeher noukh geven gedekt
   (*The table was still beautifully prepared as before*)
Der zaydeh geheelt inem kittle dem vysn
   (*The grandfather still dressed in his finery*)
Hut vyter geshpoonen dee oor alteh myseh: (*Was still weaving the very old story:*)
Dos Eedisheh folk hut a sakh shoin gelittn
   (*"The Jewish people have already suffered a lot*)
S'hobn nyeh Pahress dee alteh farbittn (*New tyrants have replaced older ones.*)

Affileh nukh hynt farahn zynnen Pahress (*Even today such tyrants exist*)
Men met zay fartrybn dee finstereh khmaress.
(But we will drive out these evil people that they are.)
Meer veln dus ahlts noukh dertsalyn in fraydn,
(We will continue to tell this story with a joyous ending.")
Oon azoi hut farendict der zayda dee mynseh.
(And that's how the grandfather ended the story.)

But in my case, the story is not in the least ended. In the following chapter, the theme of *contribution* shall be considered.

20

The Power-Theme of *Contribution*

Introduction

In my case, I believe my ego was quite strong and nothing, including even something catastrophic in life, could threaten the general state of my cohered being. So in a way, I didn't need to adhere to dependency conditions, which in a way explains why I didn't cry the first day of kindergarten, and in fact waved my mother away. This was also true when I never felt a need to write home from camp and needed to be reminded to do so by the director of the camp. It could also be because there may be even a bit more than merely a smidgeon of isolation in my personality—also not unusual in an only child (even one who is loved).

Therefore, the need for *anonymity* can at best be considered as a defense against superego demands—meaning a defense *against* needing always to do something required. In my case, any demands were probably internalized as implicit demands of my parents, which became manifest and directed as related to my Yiddish performance career. In this sense, although the parental demands by Gene Goodheart's parents were similar to the implicit probable demands of my parents (to do well and to contribute), yet these respective demands certainly were not congruent with respect to subject matter—although the efforts of both sets of parents, it seems to me, might have been quite similar; that is, Gene's direction was a focus on school, and mine was a focus on my particular performance objective. It could also be asked whether *anonymity* essentially refers to separateness. Apparently, for me, it seems the answer is yes; that is, it is possible to be "connected" along with needing anonymity.

In any event, my third power-theme, that of *contribution*, in addition to the first two respectively of *home* and *anonymity* (expressed in the previous chapter), now follows.

3. The Theme of *Contribution*

Whether it was playing ball incessantly on the streets of the Bronx; or spending twenty-six years in educational institutions starting at four years of age and ending with postdoctoral certificates in psychoanalysis and family dynamics at age thirty-two; or dancing into the wee hours in nightclubs, community centers, colleges, and vacation spots (and winning all those dance contests); or whether it was performing as an actor in Yiddish stage plays or interpreting poetry in individual recitations for over a two-decade career (ages seven through twenty-seven); or whether it was an uninterrupted seemingly extravagant sybaritic life (up and until Linda and I were together); or whether it was my full life of best pal-ships; or whether it was my life devotion to my family (parents, wife, and four sons); or in my compelling love of creating a body of work and spelling it out in published books (all in all, forty-three books sporting a variety of themes); or teaching in universities and postdoctoral institutes; or working in several mental hospitals—all of it could be characterized using the adjective "fullness": all done in the most non-dilettantish manner, and some possibly done even, may I putatively say, in a virtuosic manner.

The question I ask myself is: Why this orientation to be involved in such a variety of things, and in such a deep way? Why all this productivity, this systematic excitation of life? The answer, I believe, and in this case, is related more to identifying with my mother. As described earlier, my mother was very talented. She danced beautifully, sang with that arresting smoky alto, she could sew anything and cook anything, she could speak in at least four languages, and generally she was a joyous person who loved life, and in all of it she was unselfconscious. Her buoyant and joyful self told me that to be productive was in itself joyous and implicitly she also conveyed that not to be productive was more or less an empty life.

In Yiddish this kind of empty life is referred to as "going around empty" (the Yiddish word for "empty" is "laydik"). It's an extremely evocative sentence when said in Yiddish: "Er gate aroom laydik," literally meaning "He goes around empty" but figuratively meaning "The person's doing nothing"—that is, essentially, the person has no purpose in life or even that the person is empty-headed. In legalese the word would be "nugatory"—meaning useless or even that the person is invalid.

Thus, in the sense of Yiddish colloquialisms, having nothing to do or being "laydik" is to not have worth. In a way, "not having worth" is the equivalent to being in a position (with respect to the overall importance of *contribution*) to not at all being able to repair or save the world. In Jewish culture generally, the Hebrew phrase "tikkun olam" means helping those who are at a disadvantage, so that as also mentioned earlier, repairing or saving even one person essentially means repairing or saving the world. And by the way, Yiddish and Hebrew are two distinctly different languages.

From the time when I was two years old and my mother went to work with my father in that little hole-in-the-wall luncheonette they opened, and without quite knowing it, I became a bit concerned about how hard they needed to work. Maybe it was not that I only felt "concerned," or even more than "a bit concerned," about what looked like their enslavement in that store, but that really it was a twelve-hour day, six days per week, with both of them in constant motion. Nor was it that I was particularly traumatized by it—maybe a little.

However, it was that I became a bit alarmed about how this would end. Despite how hard they worked, it was still touch and go each week and each month—as to making the bills and meeting their financial obligations for rent and so forth. So I believe I became angry about it and made some implicit promise to myself that as the only child, I was the one to rescue them.

There was no other choice, nor did I want any other choice. Hence, tikkun olam was in my blood, and it was this kind of rescue blood that nourished my motivation to do it and to do it as fast as possible. I believe it may have been another reason that I didn't follow the path into the dramatic arts. I probably realized that such a path was too risky as to ultimately bring the kind of success that would mean being able to care for my parents as well as for the family I would eventually be making.

In fact, once when I overheard them wondering how they'd be able to pay the rent that month (both for the apartment plus the store), I reflexively jumped into the fray. I flashed to a decapitated bicycle on a pile of rubbish in the junkyard located a few blocks from my house. It was missing handlebars and a seat. The next morning, on a Saturday, the junkyard guy told me I could have it but the handlebars and seat (which were strewn nearby) would cost me two dollars each.

At the time I was twelve years old. I ran home and fished out four dollars from my stash of the ten dollars I had. Then I bought a two-dollar can of black paint, leaving me with four dollars. I reconstructed the bike, painted it, and put a little sign in the lower-right window of the store: "Bike for sale." About two or three hours later, it sold for twenty dollars. I gave the twenty to my father, who in turn gave me a long look of disbelief. He had seen me working on the bike. I did the same thing a few days later with another damaged bike. This time Richie paid half the cost. We fixed it up, and that one also sold for twenty dollars. We split it, ten bucks each. The thirty-dollar total saved the month and gave my parents a chance to breathe. Then I retired from my burgeoning business of bicycle resurrections. I was happily almost stone-cold broke.

In this sense, I also went through school in a flash. I did college in three years, and graduate school with a double master's and Ph.D. degrees in six more years. Then, my full postdoctoral education was accomplished in five years more, which was a course that required six years. However, after college I worked full-time during the day and went to school at night. At the same time that I was a student in the graduate psychology evening programs, I was also working full-time in mental hospitals, and then in private practice.

Therefore, I began making a decent living at the age of about twenty-two, when I also worked in a motivational/marketing research firm. But at the age of twenty, when I got my first professional position at Pilgrim State Hospital in New York, was when I began subsidizing my parents. I gave them more than half my salary, and that began to save the day.

As reported herein earlier, when I was twenty-two, I became a bit affluent as field project director of the Kennedy presidential poll for Furst Survey Research Center, subcontracted by the Simulmatics Corp., and was paid handsomely for it. At that point, with my help, my parents could then again consistently breathe more easily. Of course, when I was in private practice is when I financially took over completely. By that time my parents had sold the store for seven hundred dollars. It was a store they had built and slaved in for twenty-five years. Also at that point, the dream I had of saying something particular to my mother materialized, so that after the store was gone I was able to say it. This something I said satisfied my longtime deep need. I said:

"Mom, you're never going to work another day in your life. I'm now going to take care of everything."

Then I said to my father that we both knew he needed to work. He agreed, and they both laughed.

At that time, I had accumulated a little nest egg, and by the year 1965, when I was twenty-seven years old, I bought my parents a lovely apartment on lower Fifth Avenue in a luxury co-op building with full-time doormen and concierge. In those years the apartment I purchased for them was sold to me for thirty thousand dollars. And guess what? My nest egg that I had accumulated amounted also exactly to thirty thousand dollars. So I was broke again, but the purchase for them was one of the absolute highlights of my life. It was another thing I had dreamed about.

At this point I think it's important to remember that my salient themes other than *home* are those of *anonymity* and *contribution*. What I'm discussing here is the theme of *productivity*, into which is contained the deeper theme of *contribution*. In the preceding sections of earlier chapters, the issue of *home* was unearthed as to its genesis, which was hypothesized as my being wedded historically to my parents' home in Yaruga. The question now asked is, Where does this thing of *contribution* relate historically to some important variable of my life? The answer of course is that it's in my identification with my mother, Esther Kellerman. In a word, the term "productivity" is surely defined in any dictionary as "Esther Pellis Kellerman." Yes, she was inordinately productive and in the most unselfconscious and *contributory* manner. And without a doubt it is where I get it from.

A couple of vignettes:

In the 1950s, when I was a student in the Yiddish equivalent of high school (held on Saturdays), an international weekend conference of Yiddish progressive schools represented by people around the world was held at the Manhattan Center in New York City—a mammoth assembly hall that with standing room could accommodate 3,500 people. And at this particular conference, the hall was at capacity. I was fourteen years old at the time.

On that first day, the Saturday of the conference, the director of the Yiddish school was called by the director of the conference to immediately deliver Henry Kellerman to the conference to perform some relevant Yiddish literature to the attendees. Thus, I was rushed from the Bronx, where the shula was located, to the Manhattan Center in Manhattan.

I was immediately placed on the program, and from memory delivered about fifteen minutes of poems and prose. The next day, on Sunday, my parents attended the conference. As they walked in, my mother was almost accosted by a friend of hers. These bosom buddies had not seen one another in about four decades. Sonia was her name, and she had emigrated from Yaruga to Mexico City and raised her Yiddish-speaking family in Spanish-speaking Mexico.

They embraced and kissed and cried. Then my father told me that after they more or less finished catching up (just standing there and talking), suddenly Sonia said in Yiddish, "Feeritchka" (Feera is apparently a nickname for Esther in Russian and adding the -itchka makes it, figuratively, "Esther, darling"), "you should have heard this boy yesterday. I've never heard anything like it. And he performed it all in Yiddish."

My father said that as Sonia was raving about what I had done, my mother kept silently pointing to herself, until Sonia said, "Yours?"

My mother answered by nodding yes. Sonia then again embraced my mother, and they uproariously laughed and hugged.

Another vignette:

When I performed as a solo presenter I wore a suit—even when I started performing at the age of seven. When I was ten years old, I had grown out of whatever I was previously wearing, so that I needed a new suit. My mother took me to Klein's, then located on Fourteenth Street and Union Square. I tried on many different suits and wound up needing to make a choice between two of them. One was herringbone blue, the other herringbone brown. On sale, each sold for about fifteen dollars.

I told my mother that either one was okay with me, so that she should make the choice. But she wanted me to decide. I repeated what I said to her, and she stood there and thought for a moment or two. Then she said, "Nem baydeh." Translated from the Yiddish, "Nem baydeh" means "Take both." But knowing how shortchanged we always were, I couldn't do it. So that's what I said to her. But again she repeated, "Nem baydeh." And that's what happened, because she insisted I take both.

Then thirty or thirty-five years elapsed, and never had we reminisced about that day when she bought both suits for me. One day after this more than three-decade interval, my mother called me and said she needed a coat, and was I free to go shopping with her? Even had I not been free, I would have made myself free, so I told her to meet me in front of my building. She only lived two blocks south of me on lower Fifth Avenue, so she agreed, and within about fifteen minutes we met in front of my building and then both of us walked another ten blocks north on Fifth Avenue to Rothman's—a clothing shopping center where I had known that Rothman's carried women's coats.

My mother tried on many coats and wound up with two that she liked. She asked me to make the choice, but I told her I liked both and that she should make the choice. She then said she couldn't, and that whichever I liked was the one she would take. With a straight face I said, "Nem baydeh." At that moment, and as I said it, we both started really laughing, because obviously neither of us had forgotten the origin of how I came to say "Nem baydeh." We did take both. When I went to the counter to pay for the purchase, the total was $1,200. The two suits she had bought for me some thirty-five or some years earlier cost, combined, thirty dollars.

It was the best $1,200 I ever spent!—of course, not counting the apartment I had purchased for them. All of these events somehow touch on the issue of *contribution*, because my mother was all about *contribution* and my issue with this value is, as I understand it, certainly based on identification with her.

My sense of private practice was in tune with my need for *anonymity* because I guess I needed to be alone in a room with a patient or alone with a group of patients (as in group psychotherapy), and to ply my trade extemporaneously, creatively, and within the frame (the framework) of the psychoanalytic thinking, emotion-centered, and interpretive psychoanalytic process. In addition, such work gave me the feeling that I was doing it offstage, so that my expertise and my art in doing it was essentially an act of *anonymity*, in a place that felt like what I thought *home* should feel like, in this sense of something that *home* meant to me.

To this point, as mentioned earlier, I furnished my office to be somewhat more formal than a living room but less formal than an office, and importantly, all of it in the absence of clutter, which is not what my original nuclear family home felt like—cluttered and beat-up.

In contrast, my office was art-filled and, for the first number of years, without a single diploma in sight. I guess I thought diplomas would be a distraction as well as some kind of artificial verification of expertise. It was only later on in my career (perhaps twenty years later) that I strung a number of my diplomas in several visible places of the office, but kept the office as a nifty, orderly environment, and entirely uncluttered. I consciously considered that this sensibility would also be a model that could possibly help those I was seeing. Further, in doing this therapeutic psychoanalytic work, I could be assured that I was making a *contribution*.

The upshot of it all was that I was leading myself intuitively to a place where my intelligence, cognitive style, and empathetic sensibility could embrace a feeling of *home*, a sense of *anonymity*—and, very importantly, to an uninterrupted process of *contribution*.

In this sense, my *anonymity* is equivalent to being a Scarlet Pimpernel, the literary character who was a person able to assume disguises and therefore be kind of invisible so that correspondingly he would be able to construct conditions to help people escape potential danger (Orczy, 1905). It must be therefore that in my wildest, deepest unconscious I see myself as a savior or see myself with an intense wish to change the past, and in some kind of grandiose notion containing also a belief along with the wish that wouldn't it be great if that were true—that perhaps I could be a savior. This kind of sense of it all (though if actually existing in my unconscious) is the kind of unthought-known that, I think I could say, heals me—again, meaning it's possibly a conscious sense of it although in the absence of any specific actual thought, despite the unalterable fact that I'm now conceptualizing it right here and now.

It also occurs to me (although as a psychoanalytic possibility) that underneath it all I identify with the victim, so that perhaps I personalize this victimization effect as though it's true of me, and so unconsciously it's possible that I always feel so-called Yaruga-threatened. I don't consciously feel this, but as a thinking shrink, I can see that this kind of what's known as a *projective identification* is a distinct possibility. This metapsychological concept means that I intuit this savior thing as residing in my unconscious mind but somehow disavow it in my consciousness.

To further develop this idea, it could mean that, although not as a crystallized thought, but rather as a repressed one, it then becomes hypothetically revealed as some other phenomenon—as for example in the feeling to protest any injustice.

In this sense, the protest impulse exists in place of a victimization fear. In fact, it was that kind of repressed thought that enabled me to feel the pull of strong wishes—apparently so much so that, as I've mentioned earlier, my son Max once told me that he could see that my wishes were so strong that no one in the world could persuade me otherwise. In fact I believe that my unthought-known (that which exists as a repressed issue) also contained the issue of my need for *anonymity*. As a Scarlet Pimpernel—that so-called invisible presence—I could then challenge fate and, for example, defend those in Yaruga who were under the yoke of pogroms.

I think I must have had a deep unconscious fantasy signifying that I was in a thrall of living an alternate life. The wish was so strong of rescuing my parents in the here and now (in America) that not only was I focused on how very hard they were working and how close we were to always being penniless, but that with respect to this fantasy, my rescue-wish also morphed into some kind of rescue war story. Parenthetically, in our immigrant working-class neighborhood, anyone who owned a store, a business, was seen as affluent. What a joke! I believe it was not that Max was referring to my strong wish-system as a neutral comment. Rather, I felt his comment to be pejorative and particularly accusatory, especially because we were in a heated debate about something. He said it so definitively that the thought lingered, and I think eventually I agreed with him. So with respect to belief, I think my wish for Sam to be with us is so strong that it's the reason I never would attend a bereavement group. My wish is for Sam not to have disappeared, and I'm just never going to accept it—in the hope that he will reappear (or that I'll get him to reappear).

"Seek and Ye Shall Find."

And here is my exception to never believing in supernatural nonsense; in never believing in ghosts, gods, or ghouls—and in agreeing that natural events such as death can never be changed. Of course it's about Sam. As mentioned, I wouldn't join a bereavement group because in essence I wouldn't accept the fact. It's not actually that I denied it, because I knew what I knew. Yet, I wouldn't accept it even to this day, almost two decades after the fact. So what do I do about it? How do I keep him extant? It's really simple. It's what I said earlier about embracing him when I'm about to leave the office.

So, folks, that's what Max meant about how resolute I am, and it resonates with me as having the ring of truth. The tikkun olam is also defined as retrieving an advantage that was disadvantaged, and that's where I think I live—in the world of *anonymity* as the Scarlet Pimpernel—in a fantasy that has pervaded my unconscious and propelled me into some sort of grandiose mysticism—which in itself is ridiculous because I have no belief whatsoever in so-called mystical experience. Precisely, I mean that of course people can have mystical experiences, but the scientific proof is that it's never mystical. What it is, is a brain event stimulating, as well as therefore simulating, such so-called mystical experience.

Once when Richie and I were hanging out on the roof of our building on Claremont, I even remember having this particular rescue fantasy about changing the past by rescuing my parents in Yaruga. I believe I had equated my Claremont

Parkway working-class ethnic neighborhood with Yaruga while accounting for the "pogromshchiks" as the other America—the affluent America, the racist America, and the America (like all other countries) that contains populations who are without any real culture or democratic anchorings.

Even with the characteristic partition of various environments of my life, it all gave me the sense that I was simultaneously living a life of *anonymity*. And it seems that perhaps this kind of partitioned *anonymity* made it better for me in the sense of giving me peace of mind because the grandiose fantasy of rectitude is apparently mandated by my wish for a gratifying ending. In the case of Sam's wished-for reappearance, the conclusion of the wish is to right the wrong—the wrong of course that desperately needs righting—but which I know is not possible.

My craziness is also in view even when there is no wrong that needs rectifying; even when the idea is just to bring joy, or happiness, or satisfaction to someone—especially someone who truly deserves it. For example, here is more detail to the story I related a few pages ago. It was in that case that I was fortunate enough to have had a strong wish materialize. To wit: It was when my parents came to visit Linda and me at our new apartment on lower Fifth Avenue sometime in the early 1970s. They walked up Fifth Avenue from the subway station located below Washington Square Park. As they passed a certain building with a front circular driveway, my father said to my mother in Yiddish,

"Zayst, Esther, in azah meen platz vult ikh amoul gevult voinen—ayder eekh'll shtarbn." ("You see Esther, in such a place I would like to live before I die.")

My mother told me this, and I filed it in the recesses of my mind. I knew that sooner or later I was going to get an apartment for them in that particular building. Several years later, my mother called me and said that the excellent building I had moved them into some years before, on the grand Grand Concourse in the Bronx, had transformed into a welfare building, and it was no longer safe to live there because violent episodes were then frequently happening. I hadn't known that, because my parents always traveled to Manhattan to visit us and never told us about it because they never wanted us to worry. I told my mother I would call her back within a half hour. Now it was time to get my father what he had dreamed about—an apartment in that building in which he wanted to live before he died.

I immediately ran down to my father's dream building and spoke to the concierge, asking whether any apartments were for sale. He said yes, and I asked him to ring the apartment to see whether I could meet with the owners. Before you knew it, the owner of the apartment met me in the lobby and escorted me to his little gem. I immediately saw that my parents would love this apartment (as did I). I bought it by writing a check for a down payment.

I called my folks and asked my mother for her and my father to meet me at that building. I gave her the address and told her it was the building my father loved, and also told her not to tell him. When they arrived, my father said to her,

"Esther, gib a keek, dus is dee building vos ikh hub deer oongevizn." ("Esther, look. This is the building I pointed out to you.")

My father was ecstatic, as was my mother. They loved it. It was a concierge doorman building with that circular driveway in front. It was a three-and-a-half-room, one-bathroom apartment, and the space was beautifully designed. It was then that I told my father that from that day on I was paying all the bills, including maintenance and for everything else.

Again, it was one of the happiest days of my life. It was a moment in time when I got them safely away from any possible pogrom in Yaruga, and also when I got them (and my bubba) over the fence of the Central Railroad depot leading from Grand Central Station to our station (below Park Avenue in the Bronx) and then further north to Canada. It was the time when I had the thought that if the Nazis would attack, they would start their attack from Crotona Park and Fulton Avenue down to Claremont Parkway, precisely where Richie and I were sitting on our stoop, and that then we could possibly get to that train heading for Canada.

Yes, I got my parents that apartment in a full-service building—to safety! For me that was an example of *home*, of *contribution*, but not of *anonymity*; we all know who did what.

Here's my one regret. It's about my mother. I did everything I could for each of them, including escorting each in life as far as was possible. The one thing I didn't get around to doing was for my mother. She loved musicals with singing and dancing. When *A Chorus Line* first was released as a movie, I knew she would have loved it. So I planned to take her to see it, but I never did! I just never got around to it. Damn it! My mother died at age eighty-two of heart failure. My father died at ninety-five of lung cancer. Both of them retained all cognitive functioning to the end.

With respect to my father, who had glaucoma, he needed medication to control it. His maternal aunt also had it, and because of the absence of any treatment for it, she was blind for the last number of years of her life. She died at 102. In my father's case, one of the eye drops he was taking created terrible bloodshot eyes. Not understanding the importance of such medication, my mother told him to stop using the drops. She didn't realize they needed to be replaced with some equivalent. So my father's next appointment with his ophthalmologist was an alarming visit because his eye pressure was dangerously high. He called me about it, and I escorted him immediately to his pharmacy with the prescription for a different eye drop that his doctor ordered. The prescription was filled and as I was leaving to get back to my office, my father turned to me and said, "Henry, thank you."

Thank you?! What the hell did that mean? Of course, I understood what it meant, but then again I didn't understand what it meant. I would have done anything for him, so I didn't get it. The thank-yous were, I felt, always implicit. But in a moment of a typical interaction I had with Max when he was a kid, I would always say to Max as I was leaving, "I love you, Max." Then he would say, "I love you too, Dad." And then I would typically say, "Thank you, Max." On one of those occasions, Max then said, "Dad, why are you thanking me?" I didn't know how to answer him. So the question becomes: Why didn't I understand why my father was thanking me, and why I was thanking Max? A probable answer is that in certain ways I had become my father. I had always wanted to be like him. However, the real answer for this kind of reflexive comment from my father of "Thank you, Henry," and from me, "Thank you, Max," is, I believe, about how my father and I both grew up. He in poverty in a place where there was frequently no certainty, and me in a place where certainty was assured but in my mind it was not assured because I was, in my unconscious, living in Yaruga.

However, from a deeper psychoanalytic perspective it could be that when my parents opened that little luncheonette is when I may have experienced it as an abandonment, despite the obvious fact that my mother was indeed very loving. Nevertheless I may have experienced it as her need for my father more than for me. Thus, it becomes a logical psychological jump to wonder whether therefore I felt I didn't deserve to be loved. Hence, perhaps I would always thank someone for saying, "I love you too," with the reflex of my feeling grateful to be loved.

Therefore, under such daunting circumstances, one may express appreciation to any thoughtful gesture by someone—even if that someone is a loved and loving member of your family. I don't quite remember whether or not I then refrained from thanking Sam, Harry, and Jack for expressing their love for me. At the moment I can't ask Sam, but I am going to ask Harry and Jack—except—wait a moment, I *am* going to ask Sam!

So from thinking about Sam, I'm now thinking about Linda. My stream of consciousness has a mind of its own. Linda's father died of heart failure at the age of eighty-two, but starting at age seventy-seven he developed memory symptoms. Then at the same age of seventy-seven, Linda's mother also began noticing that her memory was similarly failing—along with some confusion. And along with this sort of family drama, Linda's brother, Albert (Al), died at age eighty-four, but his memory issue showed itself when he was about seventy-seven.

With Linda, I started noticing memory symptoms, yes, when she turned seventy-seven. The truth is that even in high school, Linda would frequently be visiting the lost and found to retrieve a lost pen, or book, or whatever. Now, at eighty-four, her cognitive situation is still wanting—especially with respect to her memory. Along with this, about three years ago Linda took a bad fall and popped two spinal discs. It became so bad that in August of 2019 she underwent a four-hour spinal surgery. At this point, in 2023, Linda is improved, although her apprehension of collisions still obtains, so that it interferes with her walking confidence. I call it a work in progress.

Our sons have been instrumental in guiding her recovery. On top of it all, Linda lived through a dental implant procedure, and with that, she becomes as beautiful as ever.

21
Original Professional Contributions

In the Natural and Social Sciences

In my book *A Consilience of Natural and Social Sciences: A Memoir of Original Contributions*, published a decade ago in 2011, I presented a series of original theories formulated over my more than fifty years first as psychologist and then as psychoanalyst. These theories, reflecting phenomena both in the natural and social sciences, are foundational theories—some of which have practical clinical treatment value, and some that are solely based in a scientific context but not necessarily designed or targeted for general clinical objectives.

Of course, in order to make possible the success of the key issue of *contribution* in my life, it was necessary always to be highly and consistently productive. This issue of productivity has been a signal, and a natural ineluctable evocation whereby I was always active in all sorts of projects, literally all of my life.

And I never felt this kind of love of projects as burdensome. I would start projects only if they interested me—lit me up—and unlike many people I've known who start things but never finish them, I had an unnatural, sky-high so to speak "finishing index" when it came to closing with the third act.

I've used this idea of the third act with patients I've seen who start things but never finish them, by explaining that dramatic structure in literature concerns beginnings, middles, and ends, and when the third act is missing, the dramatic structure disassembles, and finally disappears. My ability for third-act closures, therefore, has always been significant to me; that is, for example, I've always finished whatever book I was working on—all forty-three of them.

In this sense, all of my life has been devoted in one way or another to high productivity, out of which grows any number of contributions I've made in a number of arenas. In my professional life these venues included my practice of psychotherapy and psychoanalysis, as well as my career as a writer.

I've also had the idea of the level at which I would consider whatever contribution I've made to meet a standard that I could personally respect. For example, I determined that such contributions to the clinical and scientific literature should be governed by the principle that whatever the theory, it should be able to cohere various facets of its domain in a way that reveals truths and connections that then promotes greater insight to the subject matter at hand, and in addition motivates future investigation.

From a personal point of view, formulating such material was an endless source of joy. Thinking through and synthesizing a fund of knowledge from disparate academic and research arenas, and having feedback from colleagues and also from clinical and university publishers who consented to publish the material I was working on, simply put, has always been confirming and inspiring. I felt myself moving through it all smoothly and seriously, with convinced anticipation and with gusto. As follows, I will briefly list nine of these contributions.

1. A Theory of Basic Nightmare Themes:
Its Relation to the Structure of Personality

I created a mnemonic device (a blueprint utilized to cohere or remember phenomena, such as with respect to levels of personality) which was the first time in the psychological literature that an image was created of each major facet of personality in the form of a similarity structure then related to corresponding emotions. This insight gradually unfolded, leading to a book I wrote entitled *The Psychoanalytic Codes: Encryption and Decryption* (2023). In it, I utilized the nightmare as the pivotal underpinning in which to consider the consistency of personality organization as it is all encrypted in the unconscious. In this sense, the seemingly chaotic facets of personality, rather than endlessly seeming so random, numerous, and in frantic disarray, translates into a consistent, correlational, encrypted matrix that reflects this discovery—that elements of the nightmare could be the pivotal phenomenon correlating emotion, personality, defenses, diagnosis, psychophysiological (psychosomatic), and cognitive categories as unified connective categories. This encrypted personality matrix is then presented in its deciphered and decrypted form both in a visual correlational matrix as well as seen in a chart format.

2. A Theory of the Basic Small-Group Structure as a Parallel to a Proposed Shape of the Physical Universe

This particular contribution was an attempt to question the actual shape of a small group (as in a basic therapy group). The point is that because the visible shape of such a group is determined on its optics—because everyone sits in a circle—therefore the question becomes: Does this obvious circular shape of the group truly reflect the group's actual shape? My answer is that such optic verification of the circular shape of the group may be obvious, but that the true shape of the group was *not* circular, and even *could not be circular*.

Because the conflict-value measure of each person (of a group) who is sitting in a circle reflects different diagnoses, then "different" means different. Such difference implies that the circle is only an apparent shape and requires some method to seek the actual shape (of the group), which would be a transformation of this *apparent* circular shape into its *actual* shape. Again, this transformation, therefore, would be based upon these differing conflict measures of the different diagnoses of the various members who are sitting in this circle.

All of it led to hypotheses regarding the shape of equivalent large physical forms, such as that of the physical universe—perhaps at first typically visualized as something round like a circle. In any event, the result of this work was that after I implemented several methods to obtain these more proposed relevant data, it became possible to locate each member of the group in the entire space of the room. Therefore, after such a transformation of the *apparent* circular shape to one that was not circular, the *actual* shape of the group was putatively then revealed.

When I plotted the location of each member of such a standardized small therapy group of eight members on a three-dimensional graph (representing a square room entirely both vertically and horizontally), it could be seen that based upon emotion/personality diagnoses, one person was sitting on the far side of the room near the ceiling, another person was sitting on the other side of the room near to the floor, while others were scattered here and there in the overall space of the room.

The new shape reflected the three-dimensional form of a *hyperbolic-paraboloidal* saddle shape. This meant that it is the hyperbolic-paraboloidal structure that is at least, again, putatively equivalent to a so-called circular-to-the-eye group boundary condition—one that permits (or facilitates) the dynamic interplay of forces characteristic of such an interactional environment.

Several other implications become then relevant—especially that of suggesting the possible presumptive actual shape of the physical universe as a saddle shape of the hyperbolic-paraboloid. Astoundingly, this same assumed shape of a physical universe was also predicted by the Nobelian physicist Sir Roger Penrose and reported in *The New York Times* (Dreifus, 1999).

3. Remembering My Hospital Work

Here's another exciting project. I wrote a book titled *There's No Handle on My Door: Stories of Patients in Mental Hospitals* (2016). The question is: How did I decide on the title of the book? Well, the story begins more than sixty years ago in 1958 when I graduated college, and when my friend Adrian Applebaum and I applied for staff positions at the Pilgrim State Hospital in West Brentwood, New York, located in Suffolk County.

Adrian and I were accepted, and on the first day of orientation we were given a tour of the admissions ward. As we were walking through the ward, we passed two adjacent isolation rooms (in colloquial language referred to as "rubber rooms"). At that point, we heard one of the patients shouting: "Gladys, Gladys, help, help." Gladys, the occupant of the other isolation room, shouted back: "Shirley, Shirley, I can't, I can't. *There's no handle on my door.*" The moment I heard Gladys, who in no uncertain terms shouted her answer to Shirley, I filed it in my memory bank under the heading "possible title of a book." I felt that should I ever write a book about my experiences in mental hospitals, the phrase "There's no handle on my door" would be a perfect title. Fifty-seven years later in 2015, I did write that book, which was published a year later in 2016 (fifty-eight years from the time I first heard the phrase). It was published by the American Health Foundation Books—and of course entitled *There's No Handle on My Door: Stories of Patients in Mental Hospitals.*

It was an encounter like this one that definitely satisfied my need to be near the deep human nature of pathology. In addition to this story of "no handle on my door," in 1961, I also had the privilege of interning as psychologist at Kings County Hospital in Brooklyn, New York.

One of the stories I related in my book of "no handle on my door" concerned three patients, each occupying one of the three adjacent cells on the prison ward of Kings County Hospital. In the first cell was George Metesky, who was dubbed "the Mad Bomber of New York" and who had planted bombs in the city during the 1940s and 1950s. Several people were injured in these explosions. Metesky was finally apprehended and landed exactly where I was working as intern psychologist in the hospital.

In the adjacent cell was Burton Pugach, the man who hired thugs to throw acid in his girlfriend's face. It worked, and she was, for all intents and purposes, blinded. Years later when Pugach was finally released from prison, she married him.

In the third cell was someone whose name I could not locate even after an extensive search in current media organs, as well as a futile hope of searching in former hospital records because unfortunately those records had been destroyed by Hurricane Sandy's flooding of the Bellevue Hospital basement (in New York City), where such old records had been stored. This John Doe had, in a fit of rage, eye-gouged his wife. He was a large six-foot, six-inch, 260-pound man.

I believe my attraction to these execrable, heinous acts that I reported in my book had as an unconscious source the undeniable fact that for me the motive of justice was at the bottom of it all. I further believe that:

Perhaps I translate the feeling of equating retribution as the psychological equivalent of a triumph over fate.

In this way and unconsciously I could triumph and overturn fate, and therefore, I guess, protect those injured by Metesky, protect Pugach's future wife, and the same for the big guy's wife. It pretty much all seems to mean that all those persecuted people who, again, were killed in Yaruga might be rescued, as well as also ultimately saving my parents from any edge of disaster in Yaruga or anywhere else.

I don't think this fantastical implication is a far-fetched explanation of my inner life; that is, in the most basic sense, ultimately trying to open doors and bring good news but also stubborn about needing to overturn injustice. Thinking about this probable dynamic of my personality implies that the entire operation of this justice/retribution issue is for me to manage my underlying anger by becoming the Scarlet Pimpernel and thereby doing all of this wish for justice—and, for good measure, also to be accomplished with Pimpernel invisibility, so that all rescue is done anonymously.

At bottom it all means things such as retribution, reprisal, and retrieval. Of course, the retrieval part relieves me in the sense of retrieving Sam. Then Sam would no longer be, as I've considered him to be, "disappeared." I guess I can be a little crazy. It also seems that the unconscious can be considered a wild arena, although I also see that this unconscious arena has a deeper underlying organizational mandate. Perhaps the crazy thing here is that this issue regarding Sam sends me back to the Yiddish poem by Martin Birenboim about the story of Purim in which Queen Esther through Mordecai saves the Jews. A stanza goes like this:

> **Oon gelaynt hut der maylikh** (*And the King declared*)
> **Ahz Mortkhah der Eed** (*That Mordecai the Jew*)
> **Hut amoul foon gefar** (*Once saved him from*)
> **Eem dos lebn farheet.** (*Making a terrible mistake.*)

I'm certain that my association to this poem—especially this fragment of it—gave me pause because, of course, I've always wished that I could have rescued Sam. Yet, notwithstanding this interlude of my hypothetically based ruminations, there are other of my original theories that were published in my book *A Consilience of Natural and Social Sciences: A Memoir of Original Contributions* (2011), plus one other in a book currently in press and targeted to appear in 2023, entitled *Covid—A Love Story: On the Psychology of the Virus.*

4. The Basic Emotions Inherent in DNA Structure

In relating basic emotions to the basic constituents of DNA (deoxyribonucleic acid), I first had this heady, sky-high and perhaps outlandish notion about the possible connection between DNA and basic emotions. This flight of fancy of mine occurred when I read James Watson's book *The Double Helix*, first published in 1968 (the other best book I'd ever read in addition to *Day of the Jackal*).

I especially liked the term "genetic code" because I also had derived a code I referred to as a "symptom-code" designed to unravel psychological symptoms. I immersed myself in research on Watson and Crick's work into the double helix and I followed every lead in order to understand which basic emotion possibly corresponded to which basic constituent of the DNA structure. I thought that once I had that possible connection between these basic constituents of DNA structure with basic emotions, I would then also see how basic emotions themselves, in the sense of a geometric shape, form into perhaps a double helix.

Given my theoretical formulations and empirical research over several decades concerned with the *eight* basic emotions (four pairs) and their relation to facets of personality structure, it was irresistible to not investigate the possible connection between the four pairs of bases of the DNA nucleotide and the four polar pairs of *eight* emotions.

What I noticed first was the idea that all of the base pairs are attached to the sugar/phosphate backbone of the double helix in the specific form of each base attached to a sugar and each sugar to a phosphate. Since each base is connected to a sugar, the simple and admittedly thin assumption became one in which sugar can (or should) be associated with an *id impulse nature* (the need to express impulse), while then by inference it also could be speculated that the phosphate would naturally relate to a *superego* or *control nature*.

With the considerable amount of research I did, plus the thinking through of it all, my objective was to see if any connections could be hypothesized regarding the basic four id emotions and the basic four superego emotions as, again, they may correlate to the DNA four pairs of bases. I've since made perhaps a bit of a dent into such correlations regarding what I consider to be this fantastic imagined psychobiological drama of ultimately seeing bases and emotions as theoretically related. My ultimate focus will be trying to understand how it all applies in the clinical arena of behavior, disease, and treatment.

To this point, it seems that the *id emotions* of joy, expectation, anger, and acceptance are connected to the sugar base pairs of the DNA molecule, while the opposite *superego emotions* of sorrow, surprise, fear, and disgust are then related to a superego or control nature related to the phosphate of the phosphate/sugar backbone, and theoretically related to environmental triggers for their expression—known as triggers of epigenetic phenomena. Id and superego emotions are detailed in chart format in my book *The Nightmare: Psychological and Biological Foundations* (1987, p. 334), which also charts the hypothetical structural arrangement of the forces of personality.

The next step (as in "becoming") is to perhaps see if the emotions appear together with the bases on the actual structural double helix of DNA—admittedly a bit of a grandiose idea.

5. The Code to Unravel Psychological Symptoms

In my books *The Psychoanalysis of Symptoms* (2008) and *Curing Psychological Symptoms* (2020), I present a detailed method of understanding the entire infrastructure of how psychological symptoms are formed and how they can be unraveled. I said in the preface of *The Psychoanalysis of Symptoms*:

Prevailing wisdom in the clinical arena claimed that each psychological symptom is really a separate lock requiring its corresponding unique key. Thus it was thought with respect to symptoms, that there are an infinite number of locks along with an infinite number of keys.

Never was it proposed in the broad psychological literature that only one key could unlock all the locks germane to each symptom. Since I had been working with patients over several decades, it was a dozen years ago, in 2008, that I first published the formulation of this possible *single key*. The following was my so-called proclamation:

> The psychoanalytic sense of it was that each symptom needed to be assessed, analyzed, and approached with reference to the unique experience of individuals along with compiling the person's history . . . With only a few qualifiers my discovery and conceptualization concerned a single universal code that would unlock any and all specifically defined psychological symptoms. Examples such as phobias, panic attacks, obsessions and compulsions would then for the first time now be under specific attack. I then presented the system and procedure—a blueprint with which to do it. *One key!*

I developed a four-step approach to the curing of such symptoms, and I listed these steps in both books referred to above, which I then applied to clinical cases of actual symptom cure. Particularly, my book *Curing Psychological Symptoms* has been translated into several languages and is utilized by clinicians in America, Asia, and Europe.

Oh symptom-code, my symptom-code, how I love you.

6. Penetrating a Dilemma of Parkinson's Disease

My encounter with the issue of Parkinson's disease began with something I had noticed. I never had any family or close personal friends who had this disease, so that I had not ever been focused on Parkinson's. What I noticed were the interaction of three separate couples whom I only casually knew. In all three cases, the wives were streak talkers and the husbands were more or less normal and calm talkers or not at all particularly talkative. In addition, the three husbands had symptoms of Parkinson's and were so diagnosed. In one case the husband was somewhat frozen in his movements, which indicated apparently that he was in an early phase of Parkinson's. In another case, the husband also had a frozen symptom as well as having some trouble walking. In the third case, the husband was walking with two canes and was visibly displaying tremors—a sign that he was in a more advanced stage of the disease.

The coincidence or the stark contrast between the verbal output of husband and wife of each of these couples felt to me less a coincidence and more of some kind of possible phenomenon. Some time later I came across another couple with exactly the same contrast between husband and wife, with the wife as a manic talker and the husband as a rather quiet person. Since then, I have compiled a total of twenty-eight such couples where the wife is a compulsive talker and the husband significantly less so, and even more, a rather quiet person. The only exception was with one couple (the twenty-seventh), where the husband was a torrential talker and the wife quite a sedate person. In this case the wife had Parkinson's.

Thus, I thought that this kind of discrepancy between husband and wife and its seeming correlation to Parkinson's disease might not be a random occurrence. I decided then to research literature on Parkinson's disease, and I also began to formulate the "why" of why when one of the partners is clinically talking a blue streak, but the other remains verbally significantly more quiet, that this might constitute some interesting connection to perhaps some form of Parkinson's.

I've also been able to predict which one of a couple has Parkinson's the moment I see the one who is a nonstop talker. Once at a wedding my wife and I attended, we were seated at a very large round table for five couples. Seated on the opposite side of the table from us was a woman who was talking a blue streak. Her husband's chair was unoccupied.

The groom's father, who was a close yet erstwhile friend, and who was going around greeting people at the other tables, pulled up a chair and sat next to me. I asked him whether the woman who was compulsively talking on the other side of the table had a husband with Parkinson's disease. He said to me either as a question or as a declaration, "Oh, you know them? I didn't know you knew them." He told me her husband was a neurologist who indeed had Parkinson's. At that precise moment, this man walked over to our table with the aid of two canes—obviously in a later stage of the disease.

In another situation, the exact scenario was played out in a taxicab. Here, my wife and I were sharing a cab with a woman after we all had attended a professional dinner and party sponsored by the psychoanalytic institute. Driving along, this woman began telling a story about another woman who she described as an uncompromising compulsive talker. At that point I interrupted and asked, "Does her husband have Parkinson's disease?" She was surprised by my question and said, "Oh, you know her? I didn't know you both knew her." I had two other similar experiences, and when I told these experiences and my theory to another friend of mine who is a hematologist (blood), he responded by telling me that he knew a couple like that also where the wife was a compulsive talker and the husband a quiet man who had Parkinson's.

Thus, with this sort of confrontation of coincidence versus perhaps cause and effect (or at least correlational relationships), again I felt that the so-called correlation was too compelling to ignore. Therefore, I began even more serious research on Parkinson's.

Basically, there are only a few considered causes of Parkinson's. One is identified as *hereditary Parkinsonism*, the second is identified as *multiple-system degeneration* (Parkinson's plus syndromes), and the third is identified as *acquired* (secondary). The fourth is identified as *idiopathic* (primary), where there is no external identifying cause.

Most of the symptoms of the disease are a function of reduced activity of dopamine-secreting cells in turn caused by cell death in a region identified as the *pars compacta* of the *substantia nigra*. Dopamine is one of the brain's neurotransmitters. It is a chemical that transports information between neurons. Dopamine helps regulate movement, attention, emotional responses, and learning.

The first thing that occurred to me was that any treatment intervention into Parkinson's disease could only be successful with a result whereby the dopamine amount in the system increases. But my sense of one of the original symptoms of Parkinson's was frequently cited as the frozen state where those beginning to suffer with the disease seem to be, over time, bit by greater bit, gradually more frozen in their movements. This beginning frozen symptom as a possible indication of Parkinson's is also frequently accompanied by tremors of the hand.

I quickly made a connection between how the person with Parkinson's was somewhat of a low-index talker, so that a notion of evolutionary mechanisms came to mind. The evolutionary issue involved the principle that evolution favors adopting adaptational mechanisms that can fulfill more than just one function—

in contrast to selecting some functional adaptation that would only address, with respect to survival, a single such adaptational challenge.

This led me to the sudden insight that vocal quietude does not vibrate within the body cavities to the necessary amount of vibratory health normally required. If this were true, I thought, then such lesser vibration possibly might be externalized as a compensatory vibratory phenomenon to the outside of the body—and perhaps is what causes hand tremors as well as the frozen condition as one of the first symptoms of Parkinson's—in a sense indicating a factor that further reinforces or defines an *idiopathic* context as one of the causes of Parkinson's.

After doing extensive research in the literature on Parkinson's, and with the tool of tremendous inspiration that I felt upon entering this perplexing domain, it seems I was able to cobble together at least enough minimal support of my contention regarding the relationship of dopamine decrease to the physics of insufficient vocal vibration on the cavities of the body.

I am at the point now of preparing a program to assess my theory regarding vibration as a key factor in the Parkinsonian research arena, and about which I am predicting that increasing vibration to the body cavities will have a stimulating effect on the production of dopamine, which will then hypothetically decrease such symptoms and perhaps eliminate this type of idiopathic Parkinsonian disease altogether. Other researchers (Darling and Huber, 2011; and Sapir et al., 2007) in the arena of Parkinson's are now experimenting with magnitude of sound (loudness). I think it's wrong. Vibration to the body's cavities is it—not volume (Kellerman, 2011, p. 210).

7. Dolphins

In the early 1960s I began reading the work of John Lilly, M.D. (Lilly, 1960). I became both skeptical as well as fascinated with Lilly's contention that interspecies communication could possibly be achieved—especially with dolphins (*Tursiops truncates*). The Communication Research Institute in Miami, Florida, and at Lilly's sister lab in Saint Thomas, Virgin Islands, USA, was where Lilly was studying this possible verbal communicational relationship between dolphins and humans.

After reading the research in the scientific literature of dolphin studies, I soon realized that results of these studies suggested the need for an overall look at dolphin emotional behavior utilizing a system that might be able to identify emotional social behavior in a parsimonious fashion. Then it occurred to me that since I had been for many years involved in the theory and research on emotions, I might be able to convert the Emotions Profile Index (EPI)—a test of emotion and personality that Robert Plutchik and I had constructed, and had in the early 1960s already administered to a number of varied populations. The actual EPI index and manual was published in 1974 by Western Psychological Services. It is translated into several languages.

Swimming with dolphins. In the summer of 1965 I was a senior scientist at the Communication Research Institute in Coconut Grove, Florida, and at the lab in Saint Thomas, Virgin Islands. I had transposed the Emotions Profile Index—a paper-and-pencil test by Robert Plutchik and me designed to assess primary emotions—to be applied in the observation of dolphin behavior (*Tursiops truncatus*).

The thought that I might be able to convert this index as a standard measurement of dolphin behavior got a grip on me because this idea of interspecies communication (also on the basis of emotional interaction of dolphins), in turn, might offer an advantage in providing a tool to assess such behavior. To this end, I wrote to Lilly and described what I had in mind. He immediately responded favorably and invited me to his lab in Miami with the designation of "visiting senior scientist." This was for the month of August 1965 when I spent half the time at the Miami lab (in Coconut Grove) and the other half at the lab in Saint Thomas, Virgin Islands. I swam with dolphins and ultimately by the following year published the study I did at the labs (Kellerman, 1966).

It was in these labs that for the first time the Emotions Profile Index had a dolphin form, which I successfully fashioned and which started to be used by raters almost immediately. Results were used to assess almost all of the behavior observed in dolphins both as individuals and in the interpersonal relationships of dolphins sharing the lab's mini-ocean space at shore. Then such assessments were used at both the Miami and Saint Thomas Virgin Islands labs.

The final dolphin form of the Emotions Profile Index refers to the entire emotion spectrum of dolphin behavior and not only to one or two general states. For example, the analysis had to be useful in the evaluation of sexual as well as learning behavior, dolphin-dolphin as well as dolphin-human interaction, social as well as sleeping behavior, eating behavior as well as patterns of vocalizations.

Basically, two major patterns on the profile indicate that *seeking pleasure* is the dominant motivating force in the dolphin's behavioral repertoire, while anxiety or caution serves to control the instrumental activity in seeking this gratification. In addition, anger and disgust appear to be insignificant in the total emotional expression of the average dolphin.

It is even possible to characterize dolphin behavior as classically hedonistic. Paradoxically, even though the dolphin (in this case *Tursiops truncatus*, the dolphin used as Flipper in the TV series) has a brain and cerebral development almost equivalent to a human's brain, nevertheless, its hedonistic nature makes it difficult to imagine such a dolphin reaching a point of complex communication with humans.

To this point, the dolphin can speak what is known as Delphenise, composed of quacks and whistles and other such sounds. In communicating with people it tries to form words, and each word, although understandable, sounds like Donald

Duck speaking. Yet, to think that a dolphin could be taught, for example, to recite a Yiddish poem (no less to understand it) seems rather far-fetched.

Such communication with humans is formed through the dolphin's blow-hole on the dolphin's melon (the dolphin's head). However, when dolphins are "talking" to dolphins, they frequently can be face-to-face and not respond until about five such quacks and whistle or blat sounds have been emitted. At that point, the other dolphin will respond. Such behavior makes it appear that conversational communication is actually occurring.

At the Communication Research Institute the greatest number of words that one of the dolphins could repeat (and use well with respect to meaning) was about a touch over one hundred words. In itself this is quite miraculous, but in my opinion did not at all constitute any probable achievement of a communicational common linguistic structure with people. Yet, results also showed that the dolphin does in fact lean in the direction of enjoying human contact.

My work with dolphins and my contribution to the scientific literature regarding this work was published in 1966. My paper was titled "The Emotional Behavior of Dolphins—*Tursiops Truncatus*: Implications for Psychoanalysis."

8. Is Language Innate?

In one of my latest books, *The Origin of Language* (2021), I present a Chomskyan idea (Chomsky, 2005), that language is innate. My contribution is to show that the primary emotions we are born with are inhered or subsumed with a latent language—all determined by each emotion's DNA mandate. I then enumerate what each of the primary emotions "say."

9. Covid—A Love Story: On the Psychology of the Virus

In the latest (2022) idea I had regarding the possible psychology of the virus, it became clear to me that the problem was the mutational process that kept the virus quite persistent in its objective. The question possibly became: What is its objective? The answer that popped into my mind concerned a ubiquitous organismic characteristic—to seek attachment.

It was in this sense that I had the realization that the virus (considered scientifically to be only half alive and half not) actually may have had a motive to be fully alive (just like the host is, onto which the virus attaches itself).

Therefore, my approach was to name the entire process as a so-called wishful love story. I then understood that it was in the RNA of the virus where work needed to be scientifically done to undermine the virus's repetitive nature with respect to its unending process in the appearance of mutational variants. And in the book I wrote (2023), I proposed the only *psychological* approach to date regarding a possible curative method of finally ending the virus's mutational process—and, therefore, finally ending the virus.

This *psychological* approach is then added to the complement of other theory and research categories in the literature that included the *microbiology* of the virus, the *genomics* of the virus, the *structural biology* of the virus, the *architecture* of the virus, the *paleo/archeology* of the virus (past history—even prehistory), the *physical virology* of it (even perhaps the *physics* and *chemistry* of the virus)—none of which has yet led to a cure.

I'm asking whether the *psychology* of the virus might offer another understanding leading to, or revealing, a curative path.

Looking back at all of my meanderings, I feel that my entire professional experience (both clinical as well as in research) was extraordinarily interesting. Professionally, in the therapy room, I'm still the actor I was as a little boy growing up in Yiddish theater, but the roles are real, and there are no scripts to memorize. In this way, I think I may have taken the easy way out; this means that day in and day out in my office, my involvement in all sorts of dramas (and dramatic structure) requires me to use my science artfully as it interacts with the patient's historical as well as existential life—notwithstanding how it all also relates to the vicissitudes of my own historic/existential life.

Thus, I believe that I may have taken the easy way out by canceling out the interactional and collaborative complex busyness of an actor's life—preferring the quietude of strictly a two-person adventure happening all the time, and of course, in the absence of rehearsals. And this is true also in the therapy work with groups. And at the office I'm comfortable being recognized.

And it's all, thank goodness, unrehearsed.

Epilogue

All in all, my decision to go into this field of endeavor, despite my occasional uncertainty and perhaps even a sense of loss of any other potential career I may have had as an actor, was in the long run for me a good decision. I became educated in a number of arenas and contributed as much as I could, while enjoying it immensely, also finding it ever interesting and intellectually stimulating, and so never feeling tired or that it was tedious. Along with this I could satisfy the three components of the longitude and latitude of my life: *home, anonymity, contribution*; that is, my office felt like home, where I could sustain a certain measure of anonymity, and in addition, I could contribute.

I managed to find a *home* for the family that Linda and I made, that was then populated with my sons whom I loved and love, along with our cats, Mr. Goldstein and Gaffy (named, respectively, for Max's fifth-grade teacher and for the farm we would frequent for several summers (Golden Acres Farm and Ranch, or GAFAR) where we found these newly born cats.

Our family apartment was physically beautifully designed, along with being embraced by a gallery of Linda's paintings. I've always felt, with Linda and the boys, that I was living in a painting. Linda and I have continued to occupy this apartment, this gallery of paintings, for more than fifty years, in a Beaux Arts building on the Gold Coast of lower Fifth Avenue, in a ten-room, palatial living space with rococo carvings and ten-and-a-half-foot ceilings. This was not Claremont Parkway, which, by the way, I had also loved for any number of reasons—yet it had been a time of tension with respect to the struggle my parents needed to make to keep us going; touch and go all the way. But here in my professional life, I became quickly affluent, and the unforeseen suddenness of it was a bit bewildering—though welcomed.

Our family cats. Photo taken in 1989 when Jack was ten, Harry twelve, Sam fourteen, and Max sixteen. The male, Mr. Goldstein, is named after Max's fifth-grade teacher. The female, Gaffy, is named after our vacation spot where we adopted them—Golden Acres Farm and Ranch (GAFAR). They loved our ten-room and ten-and-a-half-foot-ceilinged palatial apartment in a Beaux Arts building on lower Fifth Avenue (at the northern tip of the so-called Gold Coast of Greenwich Village). In this apartment I have my own library where I do my scholarly work, and Linda has her own artist's studio. Linda is a painter. We both attended the High School of Music & Art; I in music, Linda in art. We were students of the same graduating class, 1955. Our cats, Gaffy and Goldstein, really reign the domain.

And again, by the way, in my twenties, in the summers, when every once in a while I would visit my parents at the store (the store door was always open in summertime), I would pull up in my car at the curb, open the door, and the store cat (named C'mon) would absolutely know it was the sound of the door to my car. She would then come out from under the counter at the back of the kitchen, all the way in the back of the store, and peer out to the street, double-checking her sense that it was, in fact, my car. She would then make a mad dash to the front of the store and look both ways up and down the street, so that when the coast was clear (no dogs) she would dash out and leap into the car, and roll over on the seat next to me so that I could give her a loving and good scratching on her neck. Then she would get up, lean on the dashboard with her front legs while her hind legs were on the seat as her anchor, and after I leaned over and closed the door, we would go for a ride around the block. When we returned, I would open the door and she would leap out of the car and make a mad dash into the store and to the back of the kitchen to her place under the counter. Then again she would peer out when my visit was over until I drove away.

In our so-called modest abode on lower Fifth Avenue, I didn't need *anonymity*, and it was where I worked on my books in my library—containing almost two thousand books, including my original twelve-volume Yiddish performance archive as well as about one hundred books written in Yiddish by Yiddish writers. In this sanctuary I was productive, generating what I considered to be a *contribution* to literature, to the greater understanding of dynamic psychology, and specifically to that of psychoanalysis.

I've also noticed that in important ways, I'm not a competitive person; that is, in my contribution as a performer/contributor to the Yiddish word, I only cared about the virtuosity of it all, and I had no interest whatsoever in comparing myself to whatever someone else did. The same has always been true about my working on books. I never cared whether someone was writing more than I, or I more than they. All I care about is the extraordinary privilege I feel about being able to construct a piece of literature, whether in the sciences or in fictional work, and how beautiful is the process of working it all out—until I hold the actual published book in my hands. As noted earlier, I have a bit of remove in me, so that sitting for hours at the computer, writing and thinking, is for me as though I'm having the best meal at a banquet.

In doing so, while I'm working it all out, I feel at *home*, I'm *anonymous*, and certainly doing something *contributory*.

To add to these themes of *home*, *anonymity*, and *contribution*, which was intended to be the skeletal structure of this memoir, Linda's and my initial promise to one another to be able to house any surviving parent was achieved; that is, for example, Linda's mother, Mildred, lived with us toward the end of her life. I need also to mention that Mildred (Grandma) would each year prepare the best Thanksgivings ever, and that Linda's father, Irving (Grandpa), was a great storyteller and regaled the kids with all sorts of interesting stories, and that Grandpa was cognizant always to include their names in the stories. Both Mildred and Irving were highly intelligent individuals, with Mildred a can-do person who was multitalented, and with Irving a man who for a short period of time attended law school.

The six of us (Linda, the children, and I) spent many weekends and vacations at Mildred and Irving's home in Bethel, Connecticut, where Mildred prepared all those fabulous Thanksgiving dinners. After Mildred passed, some years later, my father lived with us for the last four or five years of his life. It was a joy for us to be able to do this, especially with the great experiences my father had with our sons and they with him. When I was a kid I could never get my father interested in baseball. He was a soccer fan and would take Richie and me to soccer games that he attended. But with my sons, my father became a faithful Yankee fan. He and the boys would all pile into his room and watch the games. It was the most wonderful thing to see the guys educating my father about baseball.

The boys adored my father, who they could see was the human template for honesty and decency, and certainly my mother, who was some kind of magical and mystical (as Max put it) Yoda-like figure. When my father lived with us, Linda cooked his special foods in addition to making dinner for the boys and for me. When my father tried cooking those special Jewish dishes that my mother cooked, he would first phone Maria Goodheart, Eugene Goodheart's mother, and she would instruct him as to the ingredients to use and how to compose it all.

All seven of us (including my father) had dinner together each evening. When my father was at his last breath, we all took turns at his hospital bedside twenty-four hours per day. Each of us had a shift sitting next to him. He was never alone. In his early nineties, when he was still healthy, Sam became his escort to whatever events he attended. When two of my sons would be in a dispute and one of them said "Zayda," (the Yiddish for "grandfather"—a reference to my father) it was equivalent to asserting "honesty," so that then the dispute ended. When I asked them why they didn't say "Bubba" (Yiddish for "grandmother"), the answer was, "Too sacred." When I think about my parents—especially the way my sons think about them in this sacred manner, it always reminds me of the poem by the poet Morris Rozenfeld, noted as the Jewish Yiddish-speaking sweatshop poet. A sample one or two stanzas tells the story:

Dee Historisheh Pecklakh (*The Historical Packages [suitcases]*)

In tooml foon gahsn derzhen hub eekh greeneh.
  (*In the chaos of the street I saw greenhorns [immigrants],*)
Gekumen foon epess ah vyter medineh (*Arrived from some faraway domain.*)
Batrakhtndik zayerh turbess oon pecklakh
  (*Thinking about what they were carrying—*)
Dee orehmeh shvartzeh farlattetthe zeklakh,
  (*Regarding these poor threadbare packages,*)

Hut plootzloong ah frahggeh basheftikt mine zinnen.
(Suddenly a question occurred to me.)
Dee peklakh, vus kun dort leegn derinen?
(These threadbare suitcases, what could they possibly contain?)
Uh zugt meer eer alteh historisheh peklakh
(Oh tell me, you ancient historical packages)
Eer Eedisheh torrbess, eear Eedisheh zeklakh.
(You Yiddisheh bundles, you Yiddisheh bags.)
Oh zugt meer eer klumkess, mine hartz vert tserrisn
(Oh tell me please, my heart breaks)
Vos lickt dort in aykh bin eekh gerrn tsoo vissn?
(I'm eager to know what you have there?)
Ah folk vus vandert doorkh nekht oon doorkh kvoreem
(A people who wandered through dark nights and tribulations)
Doorkh shreck oon doorkh toit *(Through terror and death)*
Oon doorkh helleshn fire *(And through the fire of Hell)*
Ou haylickeh pecklakh, leeblikheh shayneh *(Oh you sacred, marvelous bundles,)*
In aykh lickt mine fun foon mine folk, *(You contain the flag of my people,)*
Mineh breeder *(Of my brothers)*
Doorkh aykh vet mine folk noukh oiflatern vider.
(Through you will my flag again flourish.)

And that's precisely how I felt about my parents—who came through the pogroms, whose family perished in the Holocaust, and who, with their threadbare bundles, miraculously made it to Claremont Parkway, in the Bronx, New York—in America!

And here, in America, we were able to give the boys Bar Mitzvahs—our way; that is, these Bar Mitzvahs were secular. In these Bar Mitzvahs I presided as the prophet equivalent (not the rabbi). According to biblical lore, God gave the people two authorities—the rabbis, who were responsible to guide the people solely in their devotion, and the prophets, who instructed the people in their secular life. Thus, I took it upon myself to occupy the secular authority role of prophet in each of these four Bar Mitzvah ceremonies in which I examined in my speech to the audience at each of the Bar Mitzvahs a single characteristic of each of four Gods: the *intervening* God, the *impartial* God, the *irrelevant* God, and finally, the *inexistent* God.

Parenthetically, I've always thought that during biblical eras, the prophets of the Old Testament were agitating for evolution and revolution. Because of such radical thinking, the kings and authoritarianists suppressed them. The prophets then languished in their suppression until in modernity when they resurfaced as revolutionaries, social workers, philosophers, sociologists, political scientists, and, of course, doctors of every stripe, including psychologists, psychiatrists, and psychoanalysts—of which I am one. My afterthought is that they also surfaced as novelists, literary critics, playwrights, directors, and actors—that is, prophets of the New World—scientists and speechifiers of justice and fairness reflecting to humanity its humanity.

At these Bar Mitzvahs we had this sort of thing in mind so that our sons would experience these affairs as important benchmarks in their lives—but not with respect to any godly devotion. Rather, we wanted them to be embraced by important social thinking. Agendas for the Bar Mitzvahs were divided into my initial comments, and Linda's singing of a song with a lyric she composed relevant to the character of each of the boys (which she sang and played on her guitar). In addition, each of the boys needed to find a theme that they felt reflected who they were. They then read their respective speech to the audience, in which each of them at the end of their talk also rendered a Yiddish poem.

Max's theme was that he didn't like to turn the other cheek. Sam's theme was that he never understood why the second part of the phrase "do unto others as they would do unto you" was necessary. He said it's sufficient just to do good things. Harry noted that he felt he was a "bridge builder" because, as an example, when a new kid who was a foreigner came into his class, he would be the one to greet and welcome him. He told me he then noticed he was like a bridge builder. I believe that Jack said that to find his theme was easy; it was his brothers. Yet, Jack insists it was I who suggested the theme. It's not the way I remember it, but he's sure of it. I guess I'll defer to him.

These Bar Mitzvahs were great, and before the ceremony began we had a dance band and people danced (I sure did)—along with a full lunch for the two hundred guests. Each of the boys lit thirteen candles for people and/or causes that they thought were important to them, and explained to the audience what each candle meant.

We were fortunate to be an intergenerational family, whereby our sons knew all their grandparents. Linda was a second- and third-generation Jewish American. Her mother was a first-generation American and her father a second-generation American. I would kid Linda by saying that her family came over on the Mayflower. I, of course am a first-generation Jewish American with parents from Ukraine—notwithstanding that because of Richie, I'm also an adopted Italian American Catholic.

Therefore, taking everything into consideration, I believe Linda and I were instrumental in creating a warm and embracing nuclear as well as extended family. In this sense is also included Linda's brother Albert's family, with wife Doris, and their children, Lisa, Julie, and Stacey, as well as Linda's parents, who had all relocated to Raleigh, North Carolina.

I repeat here now what I've proclaimed in the afterword of this memoir: that in a memoir lies a deep structure, a synthesis embraced by a more representative genre than merely a day-to-day episodic listing of a diary. Such a synthesis must rise to the occasion of representing the philosophy underpinning the ostensible real meaning of a life—in this case, of my life.

I therefore understand this memoir as the vision of my life, and more specifically as the vision and version of my life. In this sense, I tried to identify whatever were the basic thematic strands of my life that cut across all events: feelings, insights, epiphanies, chronologies, and conclusions that are then tied to motivations, behavior, and a worldview comprising a life—that which makes the person, the person. For me it needs to include both my optimism and cynicism.

Thus, this memoir is my characteristic and personal logline defining what I'm always motivated to do; that is, *to bring good news.* Hence, it could be that these three themes—*home, anonymity,* and *contribution*—combined, I believe, had the effect of keeping my ultimate motive of *to bring good news* as a viable lifetime pursuit. In this sense, a memoir, this memoir, is probably the poetry of one's life—my life—wrapped and embraced in its philosophy. Along with this, I think writing this memoir was in some oblique way an attempt to reassert my optimism and moderate my cynicism. And so as my son Harry said: "Life is the best writer."

P.S. After reviewing what I define as my various careers of: ball playing and Claremont Parkway (along with Richie) and my neighborhood friends; my Yiddish tip-of-the-spear performance career (including the shula and Kinderland experience); my girls and women so-called career; my career of having all those great pals; my dance career; my college career (with Arty); graduate school and doctoral career; my clinical practice career; my career of making contributions in the clinical and scientific literature—that is, my career as a writer (especially of books); and finally my career as a fantasized Pimpernel retribution artist who rights all wrongs—leads me to ask myself what I consider to be (at least for me) a startling though expected probable question. The question is:

Which career, with respect to my deepest sense of self as the one relating to, was the most pleasurable?

I believe the answer will be surprising.

- You see, ball playing in my early years was incomparable. I loved it especially because it was also Richie and me doing it together and with the same skill and attitude about it. Yet we were still kids, and the moderating force was that we were still under supervision.
- Girls and women were definitely without compare, and it was a swinging time. Yet that too required a lot of interpersonal considerations and responsibility.
- All my pals (I'm only noting male friends here) were great to have, but after some time even that comes up against people pursuing their lives, so that some of it becomes event related for the time you were in those many foxholes with each—though the sentiment obtains forever. As noted, my lifelong pals are Richie and Arty, Stanley, Bernie, Hank B., Hank H., Alex, Jerry, Adrian, Bob, and Abe. And now I need to add Leon G., who is an intellectual and who was also a great basketball player. He's an astute observer of sociopolitical phenomena. Almost finally, Dr. Richard H. is a highly intelligent physician with specialty in oncology/hematology. We often meet for lunch. Our offices are across the street from one another. We first saw one another on a visiting day at Brown University, where two of his children and two of mine were students. Then of course there is Dr. Anthony (Tony) Burry, my great collaborator on six books. And finally, there is Dr. Robert (Bob) Marshall and Dr. Arnold W. Rachman, my psychoanalytic friends and colleagues. We meet for dinner the first Thursday of every month. Finally there are Mr. Nathan Kamen, Dr. Robert Plutchik, and Ms. Edith Segal—three of the most influential people of my life. Edith is the renowned progressive poet and dance choreography/teacher. At Camp Kinder-

land, social dancing after the concert each Saturday night would be the thing, and Edith would seek me out because she loved dancing the last dance of the evening (a waltz) with me.

- My college career is inextricably tied with Arty and was freedom at last from any supervision whatsoever, and we had a fabulous time. Man oh man, studying at night at my great table/desk, loving my classes, having beers at Ryan's, and Arty and me climbing that fence every morning. But there was studying and tests and papers to write—and a lot of it.

- Graduate school with master's degrees and a doctoral degree was a lot of work and required a focus on doing it while not being distracted by other sirens that I gladly kept hearing.

- The postdoctoral work was exhilarating, and yet there too, work, and work, and work, and supervision, and supervision, and supervision, and the serious responsibility of seeing patients.

- My clinical private practice and hospital work was similarly enormously interesting and I learned an awful lot. I also believe I contributed a lot. And in my practice, I've had patients from all walks of life: from Pulitzer Prize winners to CEOs of Fortune 500 companies; from Hollywood stars to diplomats; from doctors, lawyers, and Indian chiefs to the average person struggling with a variety of life's dilemmas—all the way to those with entangled psychopathological issues. Yet, there too, in all of it, I needed to fulfill my professional responsibilities, so that it was not a situation where there was total freedom—and it was all quite serious.

- My career of contributing to the psychotherapeutic and psychoanalytic literature was important, and writing books was a privilege to do. Yet, again, it required a ton of work, although great in the sense that it always gave me tremendous focus, joy, and inspiration. Nevertheless, it also required a great deal of work. Yet having the idea for a book, researching its subject matter, contributing something new as well as synthesizing this new material with what has already been known, and then writing the book is, for me, in my solitary pursuit, simply my favorite silent place where there is nothing happening except this very special creative experience. For me it is the full texture of experience, primarily because I'm procreating something and then giving birth to it. It's probably the closest a man can get to understanding the entire birth process from conception to delivery. Then when I receive the published book, I look at it, examine it, leaf through, read some stuff in it, and caress it—just handle it. Then, one or two days later, having looked at it several times, I put it among my published oeuvre, and it's then essentially in the public domain. In this sense, I'm also conscious of my need for, or proclivity toward, anonymity, which also figures here insofar as I don't really care if no one in the world ever reads a word of what I've written, and at the same time I also don't care if everyone in the world reads every word I've written. Once the book is in the public domain, for me, it's on its own. Like it, don't like it; love it, hate it. It's okay. But for me to write a book is, as noted, an absolute privilege.

• And my Pimpernel invisibility of my alternate life kept my wariness alive and kept me worrying about those I loved so that in the end I could, in my mind and in my feelings, rescue my parents from the pogroms of my important alternate home in Yaruga. Yet such rumination didn't really correlate to living in reality and, in addition, required a kind of vigilance.

• Almost finally, there is Linda and my sons, Max, Sam, Harry, Jack—and my forever loving daughter-in-law, Erin, with my granddaughters, Esther, Sam, Mira. And of course that wins the contest. However, when I started this shebang I was six foot four, and now I'm four foot six. Ha. So that tells the story of what happens when you love all of your family and then put in the required effort to help it all work—which at the least, in reality, is really never perfect.

Here are two things that occur often and are kind of my favorites. In our apartment one of our rooms is Linda's studio; another is my library. Many times when we were both working in our respective rooms, Linda would walk across the apartment to my library while holding a canvas in her hands and would ask me what I thought of it, and did I think it was a finished painting. I would tell her exactly how I felt about it. Or I would walk into her studio because I couldn't think of a word I needed and because she was such a wordsmith, I knew she would get it in a second. So even before I described the word, usually and in almost that second, Linda would tell me the word. Or, either of us would ask the other about how much time we might need before we could both go to dinner in a nice, quiet restaurant with soft jazz playing.

The usual answer from each of us was: "About twenty minutes." These are of the most beautiful moments. It also reminds me of how Arty and I would ask one another the same question and then go to the college bar and shoot the breeze for some time into the wee hours.

But then about Linda: I like to hear her talk; I love to look at her; I like looking at her paintings; I love her poems; I like the way she walks; I love her mind; I like, I love, I like, I love.

- The Yiddish thing was also great but it required a corresponding great deal of effort to achieve—the kind of effort that meant learning a mountain of material and then rendering it all at hundreds and hundreds of performances. And I saw it as a great responsibility also containing the wisdom that nothing worth doing is ever easy. The joy of it was in working it all out and in the performing of it. I knew how to do it in a way that moved people. And the kind of material I did was of the utmost importance. Clearly, this experience of my anointed position with respect to the continuity of progressive Yiddish life in America remains of essence in the marrow of my bones. And so does the ending of Shulshtayn's "sacred mountain of shoes" poem in which he espouses the connection between injustice and the necessary persistent pursuit of justice.

> **Oon hert, oon hert ver s'flegt nit veln derhern**
> (*And listen, and hear, you who would not ever listen*)
> **Oonzer gayn doorkh toitn-shveln.** (*To our march through the threshold of death.*)
> **Itzt hert shtut ois shtut ayn—** (*Now listen—from country to country.*)
> **Meer gayn—toiter upheelkh foon a lebn** (*We're marching with the echo of our lives,*)
> **Meer veln kaynmull aykh kine roo nisht gebn** (*And we will never give you any rest.*)
> **Oon gayn, oon gayn, oon gayn.** (*And march, and march, and march!*)

Of course with this Yiddish poem and all the others, and my entire history of Yiddish theater performance, such activity is quite high on my hierarchical list of profound experiences.

- But then finally there is—dancing. Just dance the night away. No work to it at all. No demands—either explicit or implicit. Just swing. Just, good lord, give me a great dance partner. That's all I ask for. Listen to the music and naturally feel that beat in every fiber of your body. You, and the music, and the beat, are irrepressibly united. There is no teaching and no learning. It's just extemporaneous "knowing" movement to the beat and the music that you and your partner both sense the same way, and both do perfectly, effortlessly, and with the form this American culture calls for. And it's cool. Yes sir—it is cool! And there's no worry.

In my case, each and every great partner I've danced with, or with whom I've won contests, feels my every nuanced lilt, so that we can move anywhere and any way that the instantaneous message by the beat informs us to do. Then we effortlessly anticipate our very next move almost even before we both know it. Thus, the exhilarating truth is that I myself do not know what the next extemporaneous dance move will be. Yet, with a great dance partner we naturally know how to do it together flawlessly—and guess what? No rehearsals! No rehearsals! Not on the dance floor and also not in the psychotherapy treatment room.

So that's what great partners in dance feel, even if it's the first time you've ever danced together. As for rehearsals, as much as I found them intolerable, nevertheless there might be an additional factor that caused me to avoid almost anything requiring rehearsals—especially for anything concerning the inhabiting of a character role: it could be that in such a context I start to feel a bit inert, that is, in inhabiting a character role for as long as the stage play requires.

Linda and me dancing at our wedding party at Tavern on the Green in Central Park, New York City, April 1972.

But along with these reasons for not pursuing an acting career, I must also add that I was in a hurry to support my family (at the beginning, especially my parents), and to seriously consider, as I've noted earlier, that an acting career might have been too risky. I knew that I was not interested in "iffy." Therefore my final and certain decision was to pursue something more certain, but with the opportunity to also satisfy my creative impulses as well as supplying myself with the sense of *home, anonymity,* and *contribution* (productivity)—also with a dash of considerable probable success.

Thus, I opted for what I considered to be greater simplicity (although not at all simple)—that is, enacting continual and various dramas existentially and with improvisational art, and as I've pointed out, necessarily also with a scientific underpinning. And this meant ultimately a private practice in the science and art of psychoanalysis. Of this I was certain. Yet, when I see a scene beautifully acted, it is great art and I love it. Also in an acting career, great pal-ships are nourished, as you're both in that foxhole. To top it off, I do think I would have been pretty good at it, and I've kept my toe in by writing a half dozen screenplays, and now I'm an executive producer of a couple of feature films: *Who Framed Tommy Callahan*, written and directed by my son Harry Kellerman.

Yet in the long run, it is dancing that is pure delectation in the absence of any and all commitments, and in your bones you implicitly understand the culture of the dance. That's the character role which I relish—and at most it lasts about three or four or more minutes each time. That's the best news. It's all spontaneous; not planned or rehearsed. It's pure exaltation, improvisation, excitation, and freedom. You're simply in your *own* character, and, therefore, it's:

— TO BRING GOOD NEWS —
ONLY TO ME!

Yet, writing books is undoubtedly also very similar, in finding and keeping the rhythm of the book in step, and then dancing to it. It could turn out to be a swing dance, a waltz, a mambo, pachanga, cha-cha, rumba, or even a paso doble. Might even be a Ukrainian two-step, or how about the Salty Dog Rag?

Afterword I

The Bringer of Good News

The Yiddish poet and novelist I. E. Ronch published a poem in the Yiddish newspaper entitled "Der Sholkhmouness Trayger," meaning the bringer of good news, or the carrier of good tidings, or the one who gives comfort. Under the title of the poem he wrote:

Mine leebn Henry Kellerman geveedmet.
(*To my dear Henry Kellerman dedicated.*)

Here are portions of the poem that I believe gives the gist of it.

Ven eekh vel darfn letstn kheszbn gebn
   (*When I will need to report the last pluses and minuses of my life,*)
Foon fooln shyr minehm, foon mine lebn,
   (*Of the sum total of my contribution during that time,*)
Vell eekh zeekh nit bareemen oon nit zugn (*I won't boast and I won't say*)
Az 'khub vee Ahtlas unzer velt getrugn. (*That like Atlas I held up the world.*)

Azah bin eekh geblibn oifn lebn (*Such is how I remained throughout my life*)
Dee frayd foon efenen a teer oon gebn
   (*With the joy of opening a door and giving,*)
Oon oifdekn dee tatz mit gutteh zakhn (*And opening the pot with good things*)
Oon zen vee oign glantsn, bakkn lakhn.
   (*And seeing how eyes are glowing and cheeks are laughing.*)

Es hut dee noit gelernt mikh dem saykhl (*Experience gave me the sense of it all,*)
S'iz tiehrehr foon gold dem mentchn's shmaykhl.

(*The person's smile is worth more than gold.*)

Doo gay a gang oon trug a gutteh pisurah

(*The important thing is to bring good news*)

Dem shvakhn brengstu moot—oon zeekh gevoorah.

(*To the weaker person you give strength—and it's gratifying.*)

Oon shtultz dine enfer iz far rikhter, kleger:

(*And proud is your answer to those who accuse or criticize—because you can say:*)

Eekh bin geven a sholkhmouness trayger. (*I was a bringer of good news.*)

Afterword II

Original Preface (First Draft)

In thinking about writing a memoir and then in reading and reviewing several of them (especially the almost seven hundred pages of Rousseau's *Confessions* published in 1782, as well as the memoir by Eugene Goodheart entitled *Confessions of a Secular Jew* (the first edition published in 2001), which in 2020 I read for the second time over a ten- or twelve-year span, it occurs to me that understanding the internal structure of a memoir is not a simple matter.

In thinking further about the formulation of a memoir, it also occurred to me that it would be important to understand the putative or perhaps implicit difference between the form of a memoir (if there is such a thing as an organic form) and that of biography, autobiography—even diary. It would also be important to understand the intention and discernment of issues such as chronology and conceptualizations of an event-versus-process difference; that is, that the process of one's life is not the same as the sum of given events. In fact, the sum of given events (of an event-driven reportage) is, in essence, basically a diary form of such reportage.

To consider that a memoir should not be designed as an event-related step-by-step chronology is the simple thought I had, which made it instantly clear to me that a serious attempt at the prospect of creating a memoir could or even should never be guided by such an obvious initial principle as the one governing a diarist-like event-related chronology.

The Eugene Goodheart memoir (2001) was important to me because of a number of personal issues. First, he and I have known one another since we were children, although he is about seven years older. Gene's parents and my parents were best of friends, and certain crucial events of my life parallel those of his. Further, and profoundly important, is that in certain respects his development as an adult as it reflects his early experiences was also quite interesting to me, mainly because of how different were our experiences—despite all of our congruencies.

I emerged from my immersion in trying to understand memoir from other forms of reportage (or paradigms of self-disclosure), and reached a so-called horizon point where in my search I could see that in memoir lies a deep structure, a synthesis that would in all likelihood be akin to a genre that is other than biography, or autobiography, or diary—or even other than memoir!

In this sense, *where* the genre of one's memoir exists is important because if the genre attempts to locate you or even tries to define who you are, one should be aware as to the correlation of how you define who you are with that of perhaps the memoir's natural genre or, more simply, to which genre a memoir, in essence, really belongs.

Therefore, my question and my first task of beginning to think of, and then to write, this memoir, concerned the task of identifying this ostensible biographical or autobiographical recounting, or diarist notion (or ostensible memoir) that would need to be embraced by a reflective and more representative genre—one that perhaps is the secret intrinsic mother of any memoir—of all memoirs.

Thus, what I considered the daunting task of taking on such a project was to assume that there exists, as noted, a deep structure of memoir that doesn't quite meet the eye. As a psychologist/psychoanalyst/author, my attempt to understand such "deep structure" was first to assume this deep structure as one connected to insight and even something that needed a precise new synthesis concerning an understanding of what this mysterious genre might be that doesn't exactly nor immediately meet the eye. Therefore, and further, perhaps even if intuited, this newer proposed genre basically needed to be decoded, not simply identified. After contemplating it all for a while, one day it suddenly hit me. Philosophy! That must be it—or *perhaps* must be it. Further, in this sense of what the true nature of a memoir might be, the underpinning of any memoir or the something underlying the template of *any* memoir likely contains a philosophical underpinning—the thing that makes sense of it all. This self-defined insight hit me like lightning and, in addition, had for me the unmistakable ring of truth. In fact, the very definition of philosophy reflects that it is generally speaking a vision of life; that is, in addition to involving love, reason, and logic, philosophy is in a central way concerned with wisdom. Philosophy is derived from the Greek translated as *philo* (love) and *sophos* (wisdom). It is therefore understood generally as the vision of life and more specifically as the wisdom (vision and version) of one's life.

Therefore, in order to organize one's thinking regarding construction of a memoir, I believe the memoirist must try to identify whatever are the basic thematic strands of the memoirist's life that cut across all events: feelings, insights, epiphanies, chronologies, and conclusions. And then, whatever are these two or three major latitudes and longitudes of one's life (one's basic thematic strands) need to be conflated into what then appears as the memoirist's motivations, behavior, and world view comprising that person's life—that which makes the person, the person.

Thus, the basic issue becomes one of a contrast between agreeing that a memoir is a body of work in which randomness—yes—*presumably* plays an important part of one's life, *or*, that one's life is *more* governed by two or three principles that chart almost everything in one's life—thereby reducing the issue of randomness almost to a point of irrelevance.

I begin this memoir, therefore, with this philosophical template in mind. I believe this underpinning contains three basic themes of my life that together are components of what might be considered the components of the synthesis—dare I say—of my life, so that when combined, they account for the greatest variance in the circumference of my life. Since the relative amount of variance is a statistical concept that broadly reflects the amount of space such a template reflects or occupies in one's life, I believe these three following thematic components are the major thematic strands that largely reflect and even in a majority of situations explain the motivations, decisions, and effects of the experiences of my life—eschewing the assumed importance of randomness. These three components may be identified as:

1. *Home*:
>In my case, the issue of *home* essentially means, How do I feel about home? And where is home? That is, I believe "home" can be felt in various arenas of one's life and that, for me, "home" also relates to most arenas *not at all* feeling like what home should feel like. Along with this, I need to consider the possibility that for me, the conventional definition of *home* might be a place I've never been. Or, perhaps, in contrast, in an alternate reality—an unconscious one—an imagined one, in which I, yes, had then felt I had actually been.

2. *Anonymity*:

In my life, a deep need seems to have been the achievement of *anonymity*—despite a contrary history of recognition that I've gotten—even, shall I say, recognition I've gotten that could be defined in terms of celebrity. Nevertheless, there you have it: I'm frequently eschewing the limelight; even when I wear a suit, my tie is just about monochromatic, always matching the color of the suit rather than it contrasting with the suit. Possible reasons for this shall be proposed.

3. *Contribution*:

For me, achievement in life is not what life is about—especially if the achievement is simply meaning upward mobility in life or material success. For me, achievement and success must be accompanied by the value of contribution. Therefore, success and achievement as goals would be met only if such goals also hopefully contribute something, shall we say, to the greater good.

It seems to me that these three components regarding how they combine and therefore how they seem to account for, may I say, who I am, also become synthesized into a philosophical heading as my characteristic and personal logline defining what I'm always motivated to do; that is, what I'm always motivated to do is—*to bring good news*. Hence, it could be that these three thematic strands: *home, anonymity, contribution*, combine to keep my ultimate motive of *to bring good news* as a viable lifetime pursuit. In this sense, a memoir is probably the poetry of one's life wrapped in its philosophy, and as my son Harry said, "Life is the best writer."

And here I must mention Ms. Florence Howe. Florence was the founder of the Feminist Press, and an important contributor to the women's studies movement. She was also the professor of my freshman college English in 1955. On the first day of class she assigned a paper on some activity we all experienced that previous summer. I based my paper on visiting Philadelphia (the City of Brotherly Love), where the Liberty Bell is located.

There, in Philly, I took a walk through the poverty-stricken Black area. I had the sense that in a city of brotherly love, there should be brotherly love. Yet here, there was none—so far as governmental concern. So, I wrote about the abysmal conditions of the people living there (all Black Americans). When Professor

Howe (whose name was then Cohen) handed the papers back to us, she asked Mr. Kellerman to stand (which of course I did). She then exclaimed that mine was the best paper by a freshman that she had ever received. My first grade in college then was an A+.

It reminds me that Harry's comment regarding life as the best writer is something to seriously consider.

A Note About the Text

In 2023, Henry Kellerman suffered an accident that left him unable to write or articulate, but just months before the accident, he succeeded in finalizing his memoir. This is his life story, exactly as he told it. Today he has regular physical, occupational, and speech therapy, and hopes to make a full recovery.

Yiddish Literary Material by Poets and Authors Included in the Memoir

Pgs. 6, 8, 18, 57, 156, 218, 234–235, 293: "**Ikh Hub Gezen a Barg**" (*I Saw a Mountain*) by Moishe Shulshtayn

Pg. 21: "**Ikh Bin ah Eed**" (*I Am a Jew*) by Itsik Feffer

Pg. 39, 40: "**Hynt Bin Ikh Zibn Your Alt**" (*Today I'm Seven Years Old*) by Nathan Kamen

Pg. 42: "**Foon Land tsoo Land**" (*From Land to Land*) by Yuri Suhl

Pg. 49: Warsaw Ghetto Commemoration Poem: "**In Varshever Ghetto Is Itzt Khoidish Nissan**" (*In the Warsaw Ghetto Is Now the Month of Nissan*) by Binem Heller

Pg. 50–51: "**Faygalakh**" (*Birdies*) by Sorah Barkan

Pg. 58: "**Zug Nit Kaynmul**" (*Never Say Never*) by Hirsh Glick

Pg. 68: "**Mizmer Sheer L'Eedish**" (*The Story of Yiddish*) by Ber Green

Pg. 80: "**Am Isroel Khie**" (*The Jewish People Live*) by Yuri Suhl

Pg. 101: "**Dus Gluz**" (*The Glass*) by S. Halkin

Pg. 118: "**Leed**" (*Poem*) by Rutka Veksler

Pg. 134: "**Ahn Oitzer**" (*A Treasure*) by Sorah Fell Yellin

Pg. 141, 142: "**Gedenk**" (*Remember*) by Ber Green

Pg. 160: "**Zing, Zing, Paul Robeson**" (*Sing, Sing, Paul Robeson*) by Z. Vineper

Pg. 166: "**America**" by I. E. Ronch

Pg. 185–187: "**Shmooleek**" by Dora Teitelbaum

Pg. 188, 189–190: "**Dus Leed foon ahn Elnt Kind**" (*The Story of a Lonely Child*) by Anonymous

Pg. 206: "**Shtul oon Eyezn**" (*Steel and Iron*) by Aaron Kurtz

Pg. 209–210: "**Shtim foon Sholem**" (*Voice of Peace*) by Khana Safran

Pg. 212: "**Aybik**" (*Forever*) by H. Layvik

Pg. 213: "**Ah Hoikher Boim, ah Shayner Boim, ah Shtarker Boim**" (*A Tall Tree, a Beautiful Tree, a Strong Tree*) by Shika Dreez

Pg. 226–227: "**Hoib Oif Dieneh Oign Uh Folk**" (*Be Conscious My People*) by I. Buvshahver

Pg. 242: "**Dee Finif Vus Zynen Avek**" (*The Five Who Went Away*) by Yuri Suhl

Pg. 251–252: "**Moisheleh's Kholem**" (*Little Moishie's Dream*) by Yuri Suhl

Pg. 272: "**Dee Myseh foon Purim**" (*The Story of Purim*) by Martin Birenboim

Pg. 286–287: "**Dee Historisheh Pecklakh**" (*The Historical Packages*) by Morris Rozenfeld

Pg. 297–298: "**Der Sholkhmouness Trayger**" (*The Bringer of Good Tidings*) by I. E. Ronch

Yiddish Writers and Poets Represented in the Memoir

Anon
Sorah Barkan
Martin Birenboim
I. Bovshavar
Shika Dreez
Itsik Feffer
Hirsh Glick
Ber Green
S. Halkin
Binem Heller
Nathan Kamen
Aaron Kurtz
H. Layvik
I. E. Ronch
Morris Rozenfeld
Khana Safran
Moishe Shulshtayn
Yuri Suhl
Dora Teitelbaum
Rutka Veksler
Z. Vineper
Sorah Fell Yellin

Bibliography

Books, Clinical and Scientific Papers, and Films Referred to in the Memoir

Bollas, C. (1987). *The shadow of the object.* New York: Columbia University Press.

Brookhiser, R. (2006). *What would the founders do?* New York: Basic Books.

Chambers, W. (1952). *Witness.* Washington, D.C.: Regnery Publishing.

Chomsky, N. (2005). Three factors in language design. *Linguistic Inquiry, 36*(1), 1–22.

Cohen, A. I. (1982). *Confrontation analysis: Theory and practice.* New York: Grune & Stratton.

Coppola, F. (Director.) (1957). Eugene O'Neill's *The rope* [Play]. Little Theater, Hofstra College, Hempstead, New York.

Coppola, F. (Writer & director.) (1966). *You're a big boy now* [Film]. Seven Arts Productions.

Coppola, F. (Director.) (1972). *The godfather* [Film]. Paramount Pictures.

Coppola, F. (Cowriter & director.) (1982). *One from the heart* [Film]. Columbia Pictures.

Darling, M., & Huber, J. E. (2011). Changes to articulatory kinematics in response to loudness cues in individuals with Parkinson's disease. *Journal of Speech, Language, and Hearing Research, 54*(5), 1247–1259.

Dreifus, C. (Jan. 19, 1999). A mathematician a play in the fields of space-time: A conversation with Sir Roger Penrose. *The New York Times.*

Dostoyevsky, F. (Originally published 1866). *Crime and punishment.* New York: Vintage, 1993.

Faulkner, W. (1951). *Requiem for a nun.* New York: Random House.

Forsyth, F. (1971). *The day of the Jackal.* New York: Viking Press.

Freud, S. (1900–1953). The interpretation of dreams. In J. Strachey (Ed. & Trans.), *The Standard edition of the complete psychological works of Sigmund Freud* (Vols. 4–5). London: Hogarth Press.

Freud, S. (1926–1959). Inhibitions, symptoms, and anxiety. In J. Strachey (Ed. & Trans.), *The Standard edition of the complete psychological works of Sigmund Freud* (Vol. 20). London: Hogarth Press.

Goodheart, E. (2001). *Confessions of a secular Jew: A memoir.* New York: Overlook Press.

Greenberg, H. (1964). *I never promised you a rose garden.* New York: Holt, Rinehart, Wilson.

Hackman, G. (1971). *The French connection* [Film]. Screenplay by E. Tidyman, Directed by William Friedkin. 20th Century Fox.

Kellerman, H. *12-volume archive of performance contribution of Yiddish literature and stage plays.* Dorot Division, New York Public Library, New York City.

Kellerman, H. *12-volume archive of performance contribution of Yiddish literature and stage plays.* Yiddish Book Center, Amherst, MA.

Kellerman, H. *12-volume archive of performance contribution of Yiddish literature and stage plays.* YIVO Institute for Jewish Research, New York City.

Kellerman, H. (1966). *The emotional behavior of dolphins,* Tursiops Truncatus*: Implications for psychoanalysis.* New York: International Mental Health Research Newsletter.

Kellerman, H. (1987). *The nightmare: Psychological and biological foundations.* New York: Columbia University Press.

Kellerman, H. (2005a). *Haggadah: A Passover seder for the rest of us.* New York: Lulu Press.

Kellerman, H. (2005b). *Shackled, beaten, and starved: The untold story of one of the most shameful scandals in American psychiatric history (the Raphael Osheroff story)* (with Raphael Osheroff, M.D.). (Unpublished manuscript).

Kellerman, H. (2008). *The psychoanalysis of symptoms.* New York: Springer Science.

Kellerman, H. (2009). *Dictionary of psychopathology.* New York: Columbia University Press.

Kellerman, H. (2009). *Greedy, cowardly, and weak: Hollywood's Jewish stereotypes.* New Jersey: Barricade Books.

Kellerman, H. (2009). *Love is not enough: What it takes to make it work.* Santa Barbara, CA.: ABC/CLIO—Praeger.

Kellerman, H. (2011). *Hollywood movies on the couch: A psychoanalyst examines 15 famous films.* New Jersey: Barricade Books.

Kellerman, H. (2011). *A consilience of natural and social sciences: A memoir of original contributions.* New York: ORI/Academic Press.

Kellerman, H. (2012). *Personality: How it forms.* New York: American Mental Health Foundation Books.

Kellerman, H. (2012). *The making of ghosts: A novel.* New Jersey: Barricade Books.

Kellerman, H. (2013). *Discovery of God: A psychoevolutionary perspective.* New York: Springer Science.

Kellerman, H. (2014). *Psychoanalysis of evil: Perspectives on destructive behavior.* New York: Springer Science.

Kellerman, H. (2015). *Anatomy of delusion.* New York: American Mental Health Foundation Books.

Kellerman, H. (2016). *There's no handle on my door: Stories of patients in mental hospitals.* New York: American Mental Health Foundation Books.

Kellerman, H. (2018). *Psychotherapeutic traction: Uncovering the patient's power-theme and basic-wish.* New York: American Mental Health Foundation Books.

Kellerman, H. (2020). *Curing psychological symptoms.* New York: Lantern Publishing & Media.

Kellerman, H. (2021). *The origin of language.* New York: American Mental Health Foundation Books.

Kellerman, H. (2021). *The 7 keys to: Your unconscious mind.* (Awaiting publication).

Kellerman, H. (2021). *To bring good news: A memoir.* (Awaiting publication).

Kellerman, H. (2021). *Injustice of the predatory world: A book of essays* (Awaiting publication).

Kellerman, H. (2021). *Acting-out and sin: Psychoanalytic and theological perspectives.* (Awaiting publication).

Kellerman, H. (2022). *On the nature of nature.* New York: ORI/Academic Press.

Kellerman, H., & Plutchik, R. (1968). Emotion-trait interrelations and the measurement of personality. *Psychological Reports* (23), 1107–1114.

Kellerman, Harry (Writer, producer, & director). (2021). *Who framed Tommy Callahan* [Film].

Kellerman, J. (2010). New York Clips: Images of New York City. Private business of leasing images of New York City. President, Jack Kellerman.

Kellerman, M. (2014). *On the incorrect left philosophy that strength is bad and passivity is good.* Interview by Christa Whitney on the Wexler Oral project of the Yiddish Book Center, Amherst, MA.

Kellerman, M. (2014). *Yiddish is transcendent.* Interview by Christa Whitney on the Wexler Oral Project of the Yiddish Book Center.

Kellerman, M. (2020). *Race and class is inextricably linked in America.* First Take/ TV. ESPN.

Kellerman, M. Appeared in Sylvester Stallone's *Rocky* movies.

Kellerman, M., & Kellerman, S. (1994). *Young man rumble.* Record of a rap song written by Sam Kellerman and performed by Max and Sam. Produced by Ruffhouse Records of Sony Records.

Kellerman, S. (1988). *Cove of the ghoul.* Original screenplay by Sam Kellerman.

Kellerman, S. (1995). *Infinity King of All Everything Man.* Original screenplay by Sam Kellerman.

Kellerman, S. (1997). *Ha, ha, stick em.* Original screenplay by Sam Kellerman.

Kellerman, S. (2000). *Conversations with Zayda.* Book of interviews with paternal grandfather.

Kellerman, S. (2001). *Troilus and Cressida.* By William Shakespeare. Adapted and directed by Sam Kellerman. Performed at the fountain area of Washington Square Park, New York City.

Kellerman, S. (2002). *Shakespeare's Henry IV: The Percy Rebellion.* Adapted and directed by Sam Kellerman. New York City: The Producers Club.

Kellerman, S. (2002). *The man who hated Shakespeare:* Written and directed by Sam Kellerman (Based on the true story of Robert Greene). Bardolatry Theatre. New York, N.Y.: Producers Club.

Kramer, A. Translator of the Yiddish poem "Shmooleek." Aaron Kramer was a noted translator of Yiddish poetry and prose.

Laban, R. (1956). *Principles of dance movement notation.* London: MacDonald and Evans.

Lazarus, E. (1883). The new colossus. Published in the *New York Times* (1903). On a plaque at the Statue of Liberty, Liberty Island, New York, N.Y.

Lucas, G. (Writer & director). (1977). *Star wars* [Film]. Lucasfilm and 20th Century Fox.

Luther, M. (1533). *On the Jews and their lies.* Wittenburg.

Machover, K. (1949). *Personality projection in the drawing of the human figure: A method of personality investigation.* Springfield: Charles C. Thomas.

Mann, T. (1949). *Dr. Faustus.* London: Secher and Warburg.

Martyn, D. W. (2007). *Beyond deserving: Children, parents, and responsibility revisited.* Grand Rapids, Michigan: William B. Eerdmans Publishing Co.

McCourt, F. (1996). *Angela's ashes.* New York: Scribner.

Medal of Honor Ceremony (2014). Seen on YouTube. Presented by President Barack Obama and inspired by Mitchell Libman.

Orczy, E. (1905). *The scarlet pimpernel.* London: Folio Society. Published also by Simon & Schuster, 2004.

Osheroff, R. (1989). *The patient's right to effective treatment.* San Francisco: American Psychiatric Association.

Parish, M. (1984). *Boogie-down Bronx.* By Man Parish, featuring Freeze Force. Hip-hop genre. Published by Sugarscoop, Inc.

Plutchik, R. (1962). *Emotions: Facts, theories and a new model.* New York: Random House.

Plutchik, R. (1980). *Emotion: A psychoevolutionary synthesis.* New York: Harper & Row.

Plutchik, R., & Kellerman, H. (1974). *The emotions profile index.* Los Angeles: Western Psychological Services.

Plutchik, R., & Kellerman, H. (Eds.). (1980). *Emotions: Theory, practice, and experience. Vol 1: Theories of emotion.* New York: Academic Press.

Plutchik, R., & Kellerman, H. (Eds.). (1983). *Emotions: Theory, practice, and experience. Vol. 2: Emotions in early development.* New York: Academic Press.

Plutchik, R., & Kellerman, H. (Eds.). (1986). *Emotions: Theory, practice, and experience. Vol. 3: Biological foundations of emotion.* New York: Academic Press.

Plutchik, R., & Kellerman, H. (Eds.). (1989). *Emotions: theory, practice, and experience. Vol. 4: The measurement of emotion.* New York: Academic Press.

Plutchik, R., & Kellerman, H. (Eds.). (1990). *Emotions: Theory, practice, and experience. Vol. 5: Emotion, psychotherapy, and psychopathology.* New York: Academic Press.

Protocols of the elders of Zion (1903). *Znamya* (St. Petersburg, Russia).

Ronch, I. E. (n.d.). Hent (Hands) [Yiddish poem]. Valuing the work of a working man—reflecting toiling. Unknown publisher. In Henry Kellerman's permanent collection of Yiddish performance archive, New York Public Library, Dorot Division.

Rorschach, H. (1924). *Psychodiagnostics: A diagnostic test based on perception.* Berne, Switzerland. (New York: Grune & Stratton, 1942).

Rousseau, J. J. (1782). *The confessions.* Printed privately for the members of the Aldus Society, London, 1903.

Safer, J. (2002). *The normal one: Life with a difficult or damaged sibling*. New York: Bantam Dell.

Sapir, S., Spielman, J. L., Ramig, L. O., Story, B. H., & Fox, C. (2007). Effects of intensive voice treatment (the Lee Silverman voice treatment [LSVT]) on vowel articulation in dysarthric individuals with idiopathic Parkinson's disease: Acoustic and perceptual findings. *Journal of Speech, Language, and Hearing Research, 50,* 899–912.

Shinahora, U., & Shinahora, N. (2013). *Cutie and the boxer.* Documentary film. Directed by Zachary Heinserling. Produced by Zachary Heinserling and Lydia Dean. The Weinstein Company.

Shorter, E. (1997). *A history of psychiatry: From the era of the asylum to the age of Prozac.* New York: John Wiley & Sons.

Sinatra, F. (1944). Nancy [Song]. Music by Jimmy Van Heusen, Lyric by Phil Silvers and Jimmy Burke. Produced by Columbia Records.

Soltau, T. (Writer). (2023). *Searching for Tom Mulloy* [Film].

Steffens, L. (1931). *The autobiography of Lincoln Steffens.* New York: Harcourt Brace.

Tanenhaus, S. (1997). *Whittaker Chambers.* New York: Modern Library.

Terenzio, S. (Ed.). (1992). *The collected writings of Robert Motherwell.* New York: Oxford University Press.

Tas, T. (2023, April 16). Open mic: How poetry and performance combined to become a new genre. *The New York Times Book Review,* 13.

Turkel, L. M. (2014). *My animal alphabet: Paintings and poems.* New York: Mind Mend Publishing Co.

Vineper, Z. (n.d.). Zing, zing, Paul Robeson [Poem]. In Henry Kellerman's permanent Yiddish performance collection, New York Public Library, Dorot Division.

Watson, J., & Crick, C. (1968). *The double helix.* New York: Touchstone.

Weinberg, S. (1999). *Comment on religion.* Washington, D.C.: American Association for the Advancement of Science.

Wilkerson, I. (2020). *Caste: The origins of our discontents.* New York: Random House.

Zwerdling, A. (2017). *The rise of the memoir.* Oxford, United Kingdom: Oxford University Press.

Zylbercweig, Z. (Ed.). (1969). *Lexicon of Yiddish Theatre, Vol. 6.* Mexico: The Hebrew Actors Union of America, 5885–5886, 5871–5872.

Other Papers I've Published

Relating emotions and traits in the measurement of maladjustment. *Proceedings of the 73rd Annual Convention of the American Psychological Association*, 1965, 229–230.

The emotional behavior of dolphins, Tursiops Truncatus: Implications for psychoanalysis. *International Mental Health Research Newsletter*, 1966, VIII, No. *1*, 107.

New York State Psychological Association Newsletter. Division of Clinical Psychology.
> Series of Editorials:
> July 1970: "The language of the 60's"
> Jan. 1971: "The new therapies"
> Nov. 1971: "The private practice conundrum"
> March 1972: "The efficacy of clinical psychologistsas community consultants"
> Oct. 1972: "Status seekers"
> March 1974: "Is suicide a civil right?"

Relating suicidal potential to flight into health states. *Transnational Mental Health Research Newsletter*, 1976. XVIII, No. *2*, 15–16.

Hate. In B. B. Wolman (Ed.), *International encyclopedia of neurology, psychiatry, psychoanalysis, and psychology.* New York: Van Nostrand Reinhold Co., 1977.

Shostrom's mate selection model, the Pair Attraction Inventory and the Emotions Profile Index. *Journal of Psychology,* 1977, *95*: 37–43.

A structural model of emotion and personality: psychoanalytic and sociobiological implications. In R. Plutchik and H. Kellerman (Eds.), *Emotion: theory, research, and experience. Vol. 1, Theories of emotion.* New York: Academic Press, 1980.

The deep structures of group cohesion. In H. Kellerman (Ed.), *Group cohesion: theoretical and clinical perspectives.* New York: Grune & Stratton, 1981.

An epigenetic theory of emotion in early development. In R. Plutchik and H. Kellerman (Eds.), *Emotion: theory, research, and experience. Vol. 2, Emotions in early development.* New York: Academic Press, 1983.

A structural model of ego-defenses and emotions. In C. Izard (Ed.), *Emotion, psychopathology, and behavior.* New York: Plenum Press, 1978. Multiple authorship.

Nightmares and the structure of personality. I. Psychoanalytic dream theory, and an introduction to a theory of nightmares. In H. Kellerman (Ed.), *The* nightmare: Psychological and biological foundations. New York: Columbia University Press, 1987.

Nightmares and the structure of personality. II. The basic nightmare themes and their relation to personality. In H. Kellerman (Ed.), *The nightmare: Psychological and biological foundations*. New York: Columbia University Press, 1987.

Nightmares and the structure of personality. III. The intrapsychic function of defense mechanisms. In H. Kellerman, (Ed.), *The nightmare: Psychological and biological foundations*. New York: Columbia University Press, 1987.

Nightmares and the structure of personality. IV. Cognitive and psychosomatic structures. In H. Kellerman (Ed.), *The nightmare: Psychological and biological foundations*. New York: Columbia University Press, 1987.

Projective measures of emotion. In R. Plutchik and H. Kellerman (Eds.), *Emotion: theory, research, and experience. Vol. 4, The measurement of emotion*. New York: Academic Press, 1989.

Emotion and the organization of primary process. In R. Plutchik and H. Kellerman (Eds.), *Emotion: theory, research, and experience. Vol. 5, Emotion, psychopathology, and psychotherapy*. New York: Academic Press, 1990.

Anger: A love story. (2013). In S. Koepp and N. Fine (Eds.), *The science of you: The factors that shape your personality*. Time-Home Entertainment. Pg. 60–63.

Presentations I've Made at Professional Conferences

The relationship of M and FM to long- and short-term planning. Delivered at the American Psychological Association Meeting, Philadelphia, PA, Sept. 1963.

Differential diagnosis in children. Delivered at the Orange County Psychological Association, Goshen, New York, June 1964.

Emotion measures of personality. Delivered at the Postgraduate Center for Mental Health Research Department, New York City, Feb. 1965.

Dolphin Communication Patterns. Delivered at the Postgraduate Center for Mental Health, New York City, Nov. 1965.

Social behavior of dolphins. Delivered at the City College of the City University of New York City, May 1966.

The use of personality-emotion models in clinical research. Delivered at the Psychiatric Institute, Columbia University, New York City, June 1966.

An emotion category system and its implications for research. Delivered at the American Psychological Association, New York City, Sept. 1966.

Discussion and critique of Leopold Bellak's paper: Ego function patterns in schizophrenia. Delivered at the Professional Association Meeting, Postgraduate Center for Mental Health, New York City, Nov. 1966.

Studies in the analysis of behavior: An ethological approach. Delivered at Upsala College, New Jersey, March 1967.

The infrastructure of groups. Delivered at the Orange-Rockland Psychological Association, Middletown, New York, May 1969.

Group process. Delivered at Yeshiva University, New York City, Feb. 1970.

The Multi-factor Analytic Theory of Emotion. Delivered at John Jay College, New York City, March 1970.

Introductory speaker and senior conference coordinator. National Conference on New Developments in psychotherapy. Delivered for Interaction Dynamics, Inc., New York City, May 1970.

Emotion and personality elements of a therapy group. Delivered at the American Psychological Association Meeting, Chicago, IL, Sept. 1971.

The new therapies. Delivered at the New York Psychological Association Meeting, New York City, May 1971.

Daydreaming. Interview radio program, WMCA, New York City, March 1972.

A career in psychology. Delivered at the New York Psychological Association Meeting, Lake Placid, New York, April 1972.

Discussant in symposium on research problems in encounter groups and group psychotherapy. American Society of Group Psychotherapy and Psychodrama, New York City, April 1972.

Psychology internship training. Delivered at the New York Psychological Association Meeting, New York City, April 1973.

Human figure drawing analysis. Delivered at Bellevue Hospital conference, New York City, 1976.

The possibility of introducing Yiddish in the language department of New York City public schools. Presented at national conference on the state of Yiddish as a viable language, New York City, 1976.

The sociobiology and physics of group psychotherapy structure. Delivered at the Association of Science, Psychotherapy, and Ethics, Wagner College, Staten Island, New York, Nov. 1976.

Professional training in psychology. Delivered at the New School for Social Research, New York City, March 1977.

The psychology of suicide. Delivered at the Training Institute for Mental Health Practitioners, New York City, April 1977.

Emotion and the structure of language. Delivered at conference on language and the unconscious, Postgraduate Center for Mental Health Conference Series, New York City, Oct. 1977.

A model of personality structure. Delivered at Albert Einstein College of Medicine, Bronx, New York, May 1979.

The deep structure of groups. Delivered at the Postgraduate Center for Mental Health, New York City, Feb. 1980.

Group culture and group process. Delivered at Bellevue Hospital Center, New York City, March 1980.

Summation speaker. New York Cancer Society, Cancer conference on the psychosocial aspects of cancer, New York City, April 1982.

The conceptualization of psychotherapy treatment. Delivered at the Postgraduate Center for Mental Health, New York City, Feb. 1984.

Decoding symptoms. Delivered at the Center for Modern Psychoanalytic Studies, New York City, Jan. 1997.

Chairperson: Symposium – Writing the book: the pivotal motive. Delivered at the Postgraduate Center for Mental Health, Library Department, New York City, Feb. 1999.

Decoding psychological symptoms. Delivered at the Psychoanalytic Society of the Postgraduate Center for Mental Health, Stockbridge, MA, March 2001.

Keynote speaker: Woody Allen: Psychoanalysis of *Annie Hall*, and *Husbands and Wives*. Tracing Allen's view of relationships: Symposium. The Psychoanalytic Society of Postgraduate Center, East Hampton, New York, Feb. 2003.

Psychology of sports: Symposium. A template for baseball. Delivered at the Psychoanalysis and Sports Colloquium, New York City, April 2005.

The four terms of the symptom-code equation. Delivered at the Freud Reading Group, New York City, March 2006.

Hollywood's Jewish stereotypes. Delivered at the 92nd St. Y., New York City, 2009.

Invited to discuss my book, *Personality: How It Forms*, on the Diane Rehm National Public Radio (NPR) Program, October 18, 2012, Washington, D.C.

Psychoanalysis of evil: A treatise on the relation of evil to delusion and symptom formation. Delivered at the Postgraduate Psychoanalytic Society, New York City, Jan. 2015.

The Psychology of Stereotypes: Jewish stereotypes in Hollywood movies and a review of a performance-archive of Yiddish theater. Delivered at a temple presentation, Saratoga Springs, New York, August 2015.

Discussion of my book Greedy, Cowardly, and Weak: Hollywood's Jewish Stereotypes. National Radio, March 2015.

List of My Books

Group Psychotherapy and Personality: Intersecting Structures, 1979 (reissued with the subtitle A Theoretical Model, 2015)

Sleep Disorders: Insomnia and Narcolepsy, 1981

Haggadah: A Passover Seder for the Rest of Us, 2005

The Psychoanalysis of Symptoms, 2008

Dictionary of Psychopathology, 2009

Love Is Not Enough: What It Takes to Make It Work, 2009

Greedy, Cowardly, and Weak: Hollywood's Jewish Stereotypes, 2009

Hollywood Movies on the Couch: A Psychoanalyst Examines 15 Famous Films, 2011

A Consilience of Natural and Social Sciences: A Memoir of Original Contributions, 2011

Personality: How It Forms, 2012 (translated into Korean, 2017)

The Discovery of God: A Psychoevolutionary Perspective, 2013

Psychoanalysis of Evil: Perspectives on Destructive Behavior, 2014

Anatomy of Delusion, 2015

There's No Handle on My Door: Stories of Patients in Mental Hospitals, 2016

Psychotherapeutic Traction: Uncovering the Patient's Power-Theme and Basic-Wish, 2018

Curing Psychological Symptoms, 2020 (translated into Romanian, 2008, Japanese, 2011, and Bulgarian, 2021; originally published as The 4 Steps to Peace of Mind: The Simple Effective Way to Cure Our Emotional Symptoms, 2007)

The Unconscious Domain, 2020

The Origin of Language, 2021

On the Nature of Nature (in press)

Acting-Out and Sin: Psychoanalytic and Theological Perspectives

The 7 Keys to: Your Unconscious Mind (represented for publication)

Injustice of the Predatory World: A Book of Essays (in press)

Covid—A Love Story: On the Psychology of the Virus (in press)

The Psychoanalytic Codes: Encryption and Decryption (in press)
The Psychology of Diagnosis: What Your Diagnosis Is Saying to You (in press)
Shackled, Beaten, and Starved: The Untold Story of One of the Most Shameful Scandals in American Psychiatric History (The Raphael Osheroff Story) (with Raphael Osheroff, M.D.) (represented for publication)
To Bring Good News: A Memoir (in press)

The Ghost Trilogy
The Making of Ghosts: A Novel, 2012
Ghosts of Dreams: A Novel, 2015
The Ghost: A Novel, 2018

Coauthored Books (with Anthony Burry, Ph.D.)
Psychopathology and Differential Diagnosis: A Primer
    Vol. 1. *History of Psychopathology*, 1988
    Vol. 2. *Diagnostic Primer*, 1989
Handbook of Psychodiagnostic Testing: Analysis of Personality in the Psychological Report
    1st edition, 1981; 2nd edition, 1991;
    3rd edition, 1997; 4th edition, 2007;
    Japanese edition, 2011

Edited Books
Group Cohesion: Theoretical and Clinical Perspectives, 1981
The Nightmare: Psychological and Biological Foundations, 1987

Coedited Books (with Robert Plutchik, Ph.D.)
Emotion: Theory, Research, and Experience
    Vol. 1. *Theories of Emotion*, 1980
    Vol. 2. *Emotions in Early Development*, 1983
    Vol. 3. *Biological Foundations of Emotion*, 1986
    Vol. 4. *The Measurement of Emotion*, 1989
    Vol. 5. *Emotion, Psychopathology, and Psychotherapy*, 1990
The Emotions Profile Index: Manual and Test, 1974

List of Publishers

ABC–CLIO
Academic Press
Allyn & Bacon
American Mental Health Foundation Books
Barricade Books
Brunner Mazel
Columbia University Press
Grune & Stratton
Lulu
ORI/Academic Press
Praeger Publishing
Prometheus Books
Rowman & Littlefield
Springer Science
Western Psychological Services

List of My Twelve-Volume Yiddish Performance Archive

Vol. 1. Reviews (1945–1951)

Vol. 2. Reviews (1952–1961)

Vol. 3. Reviews (1962–1965), with ongoing significantly fewer performances.

Vol. 4. Advertisements of events

Vol. 5. Letters of appreciation

Vol. 6. Letters of appreciation

Vol. 7. Letters of appreciation

Vol. 8. Scripts/narrations of shows

Vol. 9. Scripts/narrations of shows

Vol. 10. Scripts/narrations of shows

Vol. 11. Inscriptions to me by authors of books whose material I performed.

Vol. 12. Biographical material (certificates, awards, photos, music, parents).

Photos for the Memoir

Pg. 11: Mom and Dad

Pg. 16: Smiling photo of me as a young child

Pg. 23: The four boys—Max, Sam, Harry, Jack

Pg. 27: Mom, Dad, and me

Pg. 30: Frankie, Joey, Willy, me, and Richie; Richie and me

Pg. 33: House in Yaruga

Pg. 42: Nathan Kamen

Pg. 43: Me at seventeen and older

Pg. 44: New York Times and Herald Tribune notices of 1955

Pg. 45: Town Hall playbill of 1955

Pg. 46: Brooklyn Academy of Music playbill of 1962

Pg. 47: Maurice Schwartz and me onstage

Pg. 48: Second Avenue Theatre playbill with Schwartz of 1949

Pg. 56: United Jewish Appeal for Hagganah playbill of 1948

Pg. 63: Sonnenbruch Family playbill—Barbizon Plaza Theatre

Pg. 84: Bubba and me

Pg. 93: Arty and me

Pg. 94: Photo of the six of us (me, Linda, Max, Sam, Harry, Jack)

Pg. 106: Plutchik and me

Pg. 110: "Contribution of Dr. Henry Kellerman" newspaper article, 1980

Pg. 111: Newspaper article titled "Henry," 1951

Pg. 116: Bernie B. and Hank B.

Pg. 124: Alex and me

Pg. 127: Adrian A. and me

Pg. 161: Paul Robeson with me at the microphone

Pg. 168: Jerry Y. and me

Pg. 201: Linda and me

Pg. 211: Granddaughters (Esther, Sam, Mira) along with son Max and daughter-in-law Erin

Pg. 278: Swimming with dolphins

Pg. 284: Family photo of Mr. Goldstein and Gaffy (cats). Gaffy's full name was GAFAR (acronym for Golden Acres Farm and Ranch).

Pg. 294: Me dancing with Linda

To Dear Friends Not Yet Referenced

Berrell
Carol
Deeana
Dottie G.
Egans
Foxes
Gilberts
Lillian
Margaret R.
Migdalia
Violet
Zeena

References to Mentors

In all I've had a total of fifteen publishers listed in this last part of the book. I especially extend my most, highest, best, greatest, super-duper appreciation to publishers and executive editors: Sharon Panulla, Evander Lomke, Carole Stuart, Don Peavy, Sr., and Inna Rozentsvit.

To my scientific, psychoanalytic, and personal touchstones: Lucille Blum, Ph.D., Max Geller, Ph.D., Deborah Hample, M.A., Harold Leopold, M.D., Emanuel K. Schwartz, Ph.D., D.Sc., Eleanor Wimble, MSW, and Edith Segal—my lifelong gratitude, and with special mention to: Robert Plutchik, Ph.D., and Nathan Kamen.

And to top it off, as in my dedication in this book, to my ever-loving parents, Samuel (Sol) and Esther Kellerman.

L'Chaim

www.ingramcontent.com/pod-product-compliance
Lightning Source LLC
Chambersburg PA
CBHW020242010526
44107CB00039B/1468/J